At Home in the World

JENNIFER WELSH

At Home
in the World

*Canada's Global Vision
for the 21st Century*

HARPER
PERENNIAL

HARPER ⬤ PERENNIAL

At Home in the World
© 2004 by Jennifer Welsh.
P.S. section © HarperCollins Publishers Ltd 2005
All rights reserved.

Published by Harper*Perennial,* an imprint of
HarperCollins Publishers Ltd

First published in hardcover by HarperCollins
  Publishers Ltd: 2004
This trade paperback edition: 2005

HarperCollins books may be purchased for educational, business, or sales promotional use through
our Special Markets Department.

HarperCollins Publishers Ltd
2 Bloor Street East, 20th Floor
Toronto, Ontario, Canada
M4W 1A8

www.harpercollins.ca

Library and Archives Canada Cataloguing in
Publication

Welsh, Jennifer, 1965–
At home in the world : Canada's global vision for the
21st century / Jennifer Welsh.

Includes index.
ISBN-13: 978-0-00-639451-8
ISBN-10: 0-00-639451-5

1. Canada – Foreign relations – 1945–
2. Canada – Relations – United States.
3. United States – Relations – Canada.
I. Title.

FC635.W44 2005   327.71'009'0511
C2005-901800-3

RRD 9 8 7 6 5 4 3 2 1

Printed and bound in the United States
Set in Garamond 3

Contents

*For my parents, Gerry and Ellie Welsh,
who gave me life not once — but twice*

Preface

URING my student days, sitting in one of Oxford's dimly lit and drafty libraries, I came across a particular passage from philosopher and parliamentarian Edmund Burke. Writing in the late eighteenth century, Burke described a nation as an "idea of continuity." Nations, he believed, are the product of choice—not just of one day or of one set of people, but "a deliberate election of ages and generations."[1] When I now think of Canada, I carry this idea of continuity with me. Our country is ultimately founded on one massive partnership, between those who are long dead, those who are living, and those who are yet to be born. The generations that preceded us have left us with valuable lessons and practical tools for confronting today's challenges.

At Home

My own roots offer one perspective on how the partnership called Canada emerged and on the foundations it is built upon. The rough outlines of my heritage are straightforward: a Métis father, whose parents came from the Qu'Appelle Valley and whose grandfather was one of the last buffalo hunters on the Saskatchewan plains,[2] and a mother of German-speaking Romanian stock, whose parents immigrated to the prairies just before the First World War. As a kid, I enjoyed joking with those who would ask, "I know you come from Canada, but where do you *really* come from?" "Here," I would reply. "No, but where did

1

your parents come from?" they persisted—as though every Canadian had to originate from somewhere else. "Here," I answered again, and again. Alas, at some point here means *here*.

Thanks to my oldest sister, a documentary filmmaker, I have come to learn much more about my father's Métis lineage and about the original coming together of European and Aboriginal peoples in North America. Our story of the big encounter begins with a Hudson's Bay Company man, George Taylor, who lived in Berwick-upon-Tweed on the English-Scottish border. George travelled to Canada on one of the Company's big ocean-going sailing ships. Once he reached Hudson Bay, he became employed as a sloopmaster, responsible for keeping the ship's log on smaller trading vessels that went up and down the coast. One of the more interesting logs he kept tells the story of his trip on the *Discovery*, which set off one summer up the west coast of Hudson Bay to look for the Northwest Passage. George began the trip as the first mate, but he ended up taking charge of the expedition. The original captain, disappointed at his failure to find the passage, went mad aboard the ship; George had to tie him up and take over steering to get the vessel home.

Like the explorer Samuel Hearne, Taylor carved his name on the rocks of Sloop's Cove, across the river from what is now Churchill, Manitoba. His name can still be seen today. When he wasn't travelling with the Company, he took an active part in the life of the fur-trade settlement at York Factory.

Most of us are familiar with the stories of conquest and assimilation of North American Aboriginals by the Europeans. But early fur-trade life in the eighteenth century, of which George Taylor was a part, was more collaborative. Communities like York Factory could survive and prosper only by combining Aboriginal and European customs and technology. The Cree, for example, provided furs and country provisions to help the fur traders make it through the long and harsh winters. In return, the Europeans introduced guns, knives, axes, kettles, beads, and brandy into Aboriginal society. According to Canadian historian Sylvia Van Kirk, this mutual dependency between Aboriginal peoples and Europeans had a cultural as well as an economic dimension. In other words, it wasn't just commodities that were being exchanged.[3]

The rugged Europeans with their fur hats were not womanless frontiersmen, but participants in a unique New World institution: the *marriage à la façon du pays.* Intermarriage between European men and Native women became one of the key social features of the fur trade's progress across the country. And the relationships that formed between these men and women were more complex than meets the eye. As my sister explains it, "In offering their women as wives for the newcomers, the Cree were making a remarkable gesture of friendship and goodwill, one that drew the white men into the heart of Aboriginal society in a way that nothing else could and established bonds of kinship, understanding, and trust that formed the very foundation of the fur trade."[4] So-called country wives were not mere objects of sexual pleasure, but played key socio-economic roles: preparing and preserving food made from buffalo, fish, and geese; making moccasins, leather garments, and snowshoes for the trappers and traders; washing and chopping firewood for the cabins; dressing furs; and interpreting and teaching languages. The invaluable skills of Native women both allowed traders to survive in the wilderness and increased the productivity of fur-trade operations.

Some of these alliances between Europeans and Aboriginals developed into lasting and devoted unions. George Taylor and his Native wife, Jane, had eight children together. One of their daughters, named Margaret (my great-great-great-grandmother), was born in 1805 at York Factory. She ultimately became the "country wife" of Governor George Simpson, ruler of Rupert's Land and one of the most important figures of the nineteenth-century fur trade. It was Margaret, in fact, who accompanied Simpson on his historic cross-continental

3

canoe and snowshoe journey from Hudson Bay all the way to the Pacific in 1828.

These Métis, or "mixed-blood," offspring went on to play an essential role in commercializing both the fur trade, through their invention of the York boat, and the buffalo hunt, with their invention of the Red River cart. They participated actively in trading-post life as trappers, guides, interpreters, canoe paddlers and boat operators, and couriers of the very first postal services. In all this, they provided a bridge between the subsistence economy of the Aboriginal world and the market system of the European one.[5]

By the third decade of the nineteenth century, the relationship between Aboriginal and European communities began to change drastically. The fur traders no longer relied on Indian or Métis women to teach them the skills needed to brave the winter landscape. They brought their European spouses to the New World, severed their ties with their country wives, and settled in for good. The result was a rapid decline in status for Native women, the deepening of racial prejudice, and the closing of ranks within Aboriginal and European-settler societies.

And what became of Margaret? Despite bearing Simpson two sons, she was "turned off"—the phrase used in those days—to one of the governor's Métis canoe paddlers, Amable Hogue. He and Margaret eventually made their way down to a riverfront lot on the Assiniboine River, which today is in the middle of downtown Winnipeg. Margaret died there in 1885, just after Louis Riel's hanging in my hometown of Regina. By then, Rupert's Land had become part of a new country called Canada, and, as we know from our history books, the fate of Aboriginal communities became increasingly perilous.

This story has taught me much more than the names and dates of my ancestors. It has also given me a vivid rendition of what our country springs from—not just the business dealings of the great men of the fur trade, as Peter C. Newman and Donald Creighton tell us, or a historic contract between the French and the English, as the federalists proclaim, but a partnership between diverse societies that conquered the challenges our climate and geography presented. During the early decades of the fur trade, Van Kirk explains, "white and Indian met on the most equitable footing that has ever characterized the meeting of 'civilized' and 'primitive' people."[6] Yes, it was a partnership of necessity, and it was marred by injustice and acts of violence. But when compared with other colonial situations—such as those that Burke wrote about—life in the early fur-trade communities offered real opportunities for exchange and collaboration.

This vision of Canada's beginnings is one that I have always held dear, and I have found myself explaining and promoting it to others around the world. Canada is a nation not imposed, but built painstakingly from the ground up. And it is one that I and every other Canadian have a duty to keep building.

In the World

As a child growing up on the Canadian prairies, my gaze was always cast outward, to things that were different and far away. I was the only one in our family of six kids to learn French, and I was a keen admirer of the cosmopolitan prime minister Pierre Trudeau—both novelties in the Saskatchewan of the 1970s. In high school my favourite subject was social studies. I gravitated to world events such as the nuclear arms race, the Camp David accord, the famine in Ethiopia, and the Iranian hostage crisis.

A member of the post–baby boomer cohort, I was also among the first generation of teenagers to experience the Information Revolution and the onset of globalization. Unlike teens who had come before me, I learned quickly how to gather, organize, and transmit information, from everywhere and to everywhere. I developed a new set of global tastes—whether the exotic international foods that stocked the shelves at Safeway (such as tacos and kiwis), for the new global news network CNN, or for the hot new Sony Walkmans that everyone at school had clipped to their blue jeans. My school chums carried surnames such as Ramgotra and Ngo—a consequence of the wave of immigration that hit North America after 1970.

The impact of technology and globalization was profound for my generation. Whereas in the past, touching and feeling the global community had meant joining the diplomatic service or a humanitarian organization, I could access the international without leaving the comfort of my own home. I no longer had to imagine what the outside world looked like. I had seen it, and I wanted to be a part of it.

It was once I hit university, however, that my love affair with things global really took off. After sitting through a second-year political science class in international relations at the University of Saskatchewan, I knew this was the subject that would make all the pain of my undergraduate education worthwhile. At graduation, when many of my friends were going to law school or entering the workforce, I was lucky enough to receive a scholarship to attend Oxford University to do a master's degree in international relations. Getting on the plane at the Regina airport, I had a profound sense that my life was undergoing a fundamental change. I was right.

Once I arrived in Oxford, I became part of a global student body that constantly exchanged experiences and dreams. In my house of twenty rooms, there were students from Zambia, India, Hungary, China, and Pakistan, who not only taught me how to cook new dishes, but also gave me an insider's view on the political and economic transformations occurring in those countries. Like most students at that time, I also began to travel and to experience these places first hand. One of my favourite Oxford professors liked to refer to students like me as the "international jet-setting whiz-kids." Even though many of the creaky old planes I rode in could hardly be called jets, I did manage to rack up a few frequent-flyer miles. From the Grand Bazaar in Turkey to the pyramids at Giza to the castle in Prague, I tramped around with my backpack and wrote postcards to my family back in Saskatchewan. The world I had seen on television was even more intoxicating close up.

After a few years as a passive observer, I started to share in the global events that were making headlines. I went to Berlin in November 1989 to interview jubilant West Germans chipping away at the wall and reluctant East Germans trickling through the concrete openings to buy Western televisions and stereos. I spent a summer in Czechoslovakia teaching politics and international affairs to young academics and public servants from the former Communist bloc who were preparing themselves to take up leadership roles in their new democracies. A few years later, I joined an international management consulting firm and the ranks of a global business class. After a while, all the hotels and airport lounges started to look the same and crossing state borders became as easy as catching a bus. No matter what country I went to, the offices of the company I worked for looked and operated the same way. All consultants were trained to speak the same language—a language of bar charts, graphs, and other financial data that were used to advise corporate decision makers around the world.

Today, as a professor of international relations, I have made a career out of studying and commenting on global issues. But underlying all of my experiences there has been a nagging question: where do I *really* belong? Floating around the global arena may be exciting, but it is also difficult to reconcile with a sense of roots. World citizenship is a nice concept in theory, but it doesn't factor in the human need to feel connected to a real, as opposed to a virtual, community. Real communities provide a multitude of supports; they also demand participation and commitment. As I've grown older, I've realized that it's crucial to have a stake in something. And for me, that something is Canada.

Having a stake in Canada means three things: understanding its roots, appreciating what it is—both in sickness and in health—and striving to make it work better. This book is my effort to put my stake in the ground.

Introduction

> In this post 9/11 world, we all have to figure
> out what our roles are. Things are not as sim-
> ple as they once were—for the U.S. and for
> other countries.
>
> *U.S. ambassador to Canada Paul Cellucci*
> *April 17, 2003*

J UST AS my ancestors lived in a New World, so do you and I. The
goal of this book is to help Canada chart its way in this uncertain
terrain and to develop a new sense of purpose for our relations with
the world beyond our borders.

While every generation likes to claim it is on the cusp of great
change, there is no doubt that we are living through a transformational
moment in world affairs. The original impetus for this book was the
events of September 11, 2001, and the various reactions and events that
have followed. The initial shock and bewilderment have subsided, and
the dust has begun to settle. We have lived through the first battles of
the "war on terror," but they have strained old friendships and opened
up new problems and divisions. All across the globe, the actors on the
international stage—whether countries, international organizations,
companies, or civil society groups—are settling into their new roles for

the twenty-first century. The script for this New World is full of uncertainty, which for many brings uneasiness, but it is also full of possibility. What lines will Canada write for itself, and how will it play them out?

Where Were You?

It's a game we all like to play. Remembering where we were, what we were doing, and even what we were wearing on the day that the shuttle *Challenger* exploded, the Berlin Wall fell, or O.J. Simpson was chased in his white van down the Los Angeles freeway. But nothing quite compares to the memories of that clear, warm morning of September 11, 2001, when nineteen hijackers made their way through airport security, with penknives tucked into their carry-ons.

I was in Oxford in front of my computer doing e-mail when a colleague of mine barged in to tell me about the attacks. I immediately logged on to CNN, but found that on that day the Internet would fail us. It was not only jammed with users, which made most Web sites inaccessible, but also incapable of showing—in full size and colour— the horrifying image of those jetliners crashing into the World Trade Center. I rushed out to find a television in the common room of one of Oxford's colleges, and joined a hastily gathered crowd of students and faculty. Few words were spoken; eyes were glued to the TV screen and the unforgettable spectacle of the second tower coming down, almost like a waterfall. I scrambled to find out about friends who worked in or near the financial district in New York and was relieved to learn that no one I knew personally was killed in the terrorist attacks.

Very quickly, my horror and concern turned to questioning: Would another attack soon follow? How quickly would the U.S. respond? Would missiles start flying from North America toward the Middle East? What would happen to Arab minorities in Western states? On September 10, I had attended an academic conference in Canterbury, during which we calmly debated topics such as the future of the European Union and U.S.-Russian relations; I wondered how much of our agenda would still be relevant in the world after 9/11.

Above all, I wondered how Canada would react. Sitting in Oxford, it was difficult to get information from the other side of the Atlantic. Phone lines were jammed. E-mail was unreliable. But from what I could gather, the immediate Canadian response was nothing short of heroic. In an amazing feat of co-ordination, our air-traffic controllers managed to divert over 250 airplanes (with more than 40,000 passengers) from U.S. airspace to land on Canadian soil.[1] Canadian officials faced the possibility that terrorists remained on some of these flights but accepted this risk to our own territory and population without hesitation. Our communities opened their arms to bewildered and frightened travellers who couldn't get back home. We dispatched hundreds of firefighters and emergency workers to assist in the rescue efforts in Washington and New York. Our own national day of mourning saw 100,000 people gather at Parliament Hill to support the United States in its time of trial.

In official and political terms, however, the response was underwhelming. In fact, a report written two weeks after 9/11 criticized Canadian authorities for being confused, slow, and uncoordinated in their initial response to the crisis. An overall lack of leadership meant "no one had a picture of the national response within the government of Canada."[2] Former prime minister Chrétien laid low for the first two days, concerned to strike the right balance between supporting the U.S. and maintaining Canadian foreign policy independence.[3] Chrétien had always been cautious about his relationship with the United States, anxious not to repeat the Mulroney-era coziness. In a moment when statesmanship and decisiveness were required, our key political leaders were found wanting.

This low profile by the Canadian government was in striking contrast to the inspirational leadership of British prime minister Tony

Blair, whose first comments on September 11 calmed the fears of the British people and left no doubt as to what course Britain would follow. An inside source in the British government described to me the first emergency meeting of Blair's cabinet and key advisers. The prime minister entered the room and immediately stated, "This is an attack on all of us. That is the line we are taking." He then issued a series of orders, including one to British foreign secretary Jack Straw to fly to Brussels and lobby his NATO colleagues to invoke the collective defence clause of the North Atlantic Treaty.* The meeting lasted no more than five minutes. Afterward, Blair walked out of the room into an immediate press scrum, where he delivered—without notes—one of the most impassioned speeches heard during the September 11 crisis. The British prime minister had blasted out of the starting block, carrying the torch for the democratic West against its new enemy.

Another speech, this time by U.S. president George W. Bush, sparked a second example of lacklustre Canadian performance. The world had been waiting for Bush to address his nation—and the wider world—about the goals and progress of the coalition against terrorism. The atmosphere in Congress that night of September 20 was electrifying. In addition to the who's who of the American political class, foreign dignitaries were sitting in the balconies, hanging on the U.S. president's every word. In his rabble-rousing oration, Bush outlined his plan to capture the network of terrorists that had carried out the 9/11 atrocities and to protect the United States from future attacks. He also thanked fifteen countries that had joined with the United States in its new war against terror. Surprisingly, Canada was not one of them.

Call it an accident—after all, the president has been known to bumble his words and slide off message. My response was "So what?" We quietly did our part, and would no doubt continue to participate both

---

* Article 5 of NATO's founding document states that an armed attack on one member of the alliance shall be considered as an attack against all.

politically and militarily in the coalition. For its part, the Chrétien government explained that Bush's list of countries had been chosen for political reasons: to demonstrate that support for the U.S. was widespread and to persuade those strategically important countries to join the U.S.-led coalition. The fact that Canada was not mentioned was therefore understandable and nothing to pay particular attention to. As Foreign Affairs Minister John Manley put it the following day, "I don't think Canadians did it to get thanked . . . They did it because it's what you do in situations like that."[4]

But the reaction of the Canadian media and general public was not so cool-headed. What became known as "the snub" steamrolled into a national conversation carried on by all Canadian publications and radio call-in shows. Reactions ranged from accusing President Bush of the sin of omission to worrying about whether Prime Minister Chrétien's response to the terror attacks had been too lukewarm for American tastes. The *Toronto Sun* and the *National Post* were the most negative in their interpretations, with the former carrying an editorial entitled "Canada gets Bush-whacked"[5] and the latter arguing that Bush's failure to thank Canada was a reflection of the White House's concerns about our loose immigration laws and insufficient military resources.[6] This suggestion—that somehow this was all *our* fault—provided a legitimate platform for a broader critique of Canadian government policies. Opposition MPs from the Canadian Alliance and the Progressive Conservatives raised concerns about whether Canada was becoming a staging ground for terrorists, through its lax border controls and its tax deduction schemes for questionable "non-profit organizations." It was open season on the Canadian way.

I was deeply embarrassed by the reaction of the Canadian media. It was a raw and unattractive display of our national inferiority complex. How could we turn an international crisis, an impending war, into an opportunity to navel-gaze and wring our hands over our lack of influence with Washington? How small of Canada, I thought. We had made the mistake that all psychologists warn against. We had made it all about us.

The War on Terror

Once the initial impact of the terrorist attacks had been absorbed, the United States moved to the offensive and launched its so-called war on terror. We have heard it said many times since 9/11 that the enemy in this campaign is unlike any we have seen before and therefore requires new strategies and tactics. But while the "war on terror" is being waged on many fronts, including new legislation to control financial transactions and the movement of people, its military component has been the most visible. In the first two battles in the war on terror, Afghanistan and Iraq, the United States dazzled the world with its military prowess. Yet these battlefield victories have not made Americans invulnerable to terrorism. Nor have they improved the standing of the U.S. in the Islamic world. In fact, as reflected in public opinion research conducted by the Pew Research Center in March 2004, anti-Americanism is on the rise all across the globe, from Southeast Asia to North Africa to Western Europe.[7]

The opening salvos in the war on terror have also posed serious challenges and dilemmas for America's allies, particularly Canada. So far, the record is not encouraging.

Let's begin with the decision-making process that led to the dispatch of our troops as part of the U.S. combat mission in Afghanistan in late 2001. Soon after September 11, the Canadian government indicated its desire to take an active part in the Afghan campaign, above and beyond sending ships and transport planes. Given Canada's high-profile role in past peacekeeping efforts, the mission seemed a natural fit for Canada and a golden opportunity to gain exposure and high marks for collaborative international behaviour.

But by early January 2002, Canada's participation looked decidedly different. Rather than taking part in the British-led international stabilization force in a peacekeeping capacity, Canada opted for a direct combat role. The intricate politics of international peacekeeping had taken hold, and the Europeans had managed to grab the lead role in the stabilization mission. Canada was offered a bit part (a smaller military unit and 200 civil engineers) rather than a significant peacekeeping presence. But we were also promised first dibs on the leadership of the stabilization force after the British left in three to six months.[8] The Canadian government saw only limited opportunity for profile in this scenario and was anxious to get our military into the action right away. Consequently, the decision was made to send 750 Canadian soldiers to join the U.S. operation in Kandahar, reporting to the American 101st Airborne Division.[9]

The evening television news story revealed the real motivation behind Canada's decision: the desire to gain political credit with the United States and to counter both foreign and domestic criticism of Canada's military. Two press conferences were shown in immediate succession. The first was with then Canadian defence minister Art Eggleton, glowing about Washington's gratitude to Canada for responding to the U.S. request for troops. "The Americans asked the Canadian forces—and only the Canadian forces—to operate alongside their troops," the minister boasted. The second was with the chair of the U.S. Joint Chiefs of Staff, General Richard Myers, thanking Canada for offering up its soldiers to participate in the U.S. mission: "I think they will meld in very nicely and the offer is much appreciated."[10] From a military point of view, the United States clearly didn't need Canadian help; it was us, not them, that did the asking. To me, it looked as if Canada was virtually dying to get involved.

Our battalion from the Edmonton-based Princess Patricia's Light Infantry was directed to do everything from tracking down terrorist cells and Taliban fighters to removing land mines and protecting humanitarian relief efforts. What wasn't fully appreciated, however, was the implication of this decision: the impact on Canada's reputation as peacekeeper, the problems that would arise when Canadian soldiers captured Taliban fighters and had to hand them over to the U.S. forces (with no guarantee of how they would be treated), and, of course, the challenges of co-ordinating our activities with the U.S. military—challenges that were made painfully apparent by the death of four members of the Canadian military in a friendly-fire incident in April 2002.

16

If we fast-forward the story to the U.S.-led war on Iraq in March 2003, we see similar signs of ambiguity. The now famous Security Council Resolution 1441, which promised "serious consequences" if Saddam Hussein did not comply with weapons inspections, at first seemed to offer a clear way forward and to reflect a new-found sense of purpose among council members. The resolution was passed unanimously on November 8, 2002, after eight weeks of intense negotiations. Countries such as Canada, traditional backers of the UN approach to collective security, breathed a sigh of relief: we did not have to choose between supporting the United States and supporting multilateralism. In reality, however, Resolution 1441 hid deep differences between Security Council members over the future role of the weapons inspectors and allowed for varying interpretations as to whether UN member states could use "all necessary means" (UN-speak for "war") to uphold the resolution's provisions. While the U.S. interpreted the text of 1441 as backing the use of force, all other council members (save Britain) insisted that no such blank cheque had been given. According to Canadian international lawyer Michael Byers, the potential for dispute over interpretation was not an accident: the resolution contained intentional ambiguities that enabled prominent states such as Russia, France, the U.S., and Britain to agree to disagree.[11] The facade of unity was a ticking time bomb.

Meanwhile, the Canadian public—along with the publics of many

European states—stated its opposition to a war not endorsed by the United Nations. In an Ipsos-Reid poll taken in January 2003, 62 per cent of respondents claimed that Canada should provide assistance for military action only with UN authorization, while only 15 per cent of Canadians declared that the government should support the U.S. if it decided to take military action on its own.[12] Canada thus articulated what would become its mantra during the build-up to hostilities: we would support war if sanctioned by the United Nations; if there was no such sanction—well, that was a hypothetical question not worth entertaining. In fact, Prime Minister Chrétien berated his newly minted defence minister, John McCallum, for daring to respond to that scenario and suggest Canada might reconsider its opposition to fighting in Iraq without UN authorization.[13]

Our ambiguous position became increasingly untenable when the United States began dispatching troops to the Middle East in preparation for military action against Saddam Hussein. As winter turned to spring, both the Iraqi desert and diplomatic activity began to heat up. Fear mounted that the "World War I effect" would take over: having prepared for war and mobilized the armed forces, it would become impossible to turn around. The cracks in the previous consensus over Resolution 1441 began to show. Everyone expected another chance to debate the necessity and wisdom of war should Saddam prove implacable. For the U.S., it was only a matter of time before countries would be forced, in George Bush's words, "to show their cards."

Despite this call from Washington to pick sides, Canada played its traditional part as "honest broker" and "helpful fixer," by attempting to forge a compromise within the Security Council. The premise of the idea—more time for Saddam to disarm—had been abruptly dismissed by the Bush administration as unhelpful procrastination. In the words of U.S. State Department spokesman Richard Boucher, "Setting another date farther into the future only delays . . . a decision we should all be prepared to make and to face up to facts that we should all be able to see."[14] Undeterred by the lack of U.S. enthusiasm, our ambassador to the UN during the Iraq crisis, Paul Heinbecker, floated a series of proposals that he hoped might appeal to both sides of the debate: more time for inspections, a fixed date for their termination, benchmarks for Iraqi compliance, and a commitment to use force in the event of non-compliance. But Heinbecker soon learned that you cannot forge a solution if there is no genuine will to compromise. It was now two minutes to midnight.

With the Canadian-sponsored compromise in tatters and a U.S. attack on Baghdad all but certain, it was time to choose. Our government continued to hold its hand close to its chest—so close, in fact, that many in the U.S. were caught off guard when we finally articulated our position. On March 17, Chrétien stood up in the House of Commons to announce, "If military action proceeds without a new resolution of the Security Council, Canada will not participate." By insisting on this condition, we were effectively standing aside.

Canada then found itself in an extremely awkward position—one that called upon our diplomats to practise their very best verbal gymnastics. What about Canada's participation in Operation Apollo, the ongoing multinational naval patrol designed to intercept fleeing al-Qaeda and Taliban members? Yes, three of our warships were in the Persian Gulf, escorting vessels through the Strait of Hormuz and reporting to U.S. vice-admiral Timothy Keating. And, yes, we did have a small group of Canadian Forces members (thirty-one, to be exact) involved in an exchange program with U.S. troops massed along the Iraqi border. But—and this was a big "but"—this presence was restricted to the war on terrorism and did not extend to the campaign against the regime of Saddam Hussein. In effect, Canadian military personnel, marked with the maple leaf, would be fighting alongside U.S. military personnel in a war that the Canadian government had refused to join. For all the talk of standing aside, Canada was indirectly providing more support for the U.S. in Iraq than most of the members of the "coalition of the willing," including Australia.

A number of delicate questions naturally followed. For example, would Canadian exchange soldiers be permitted to take part in aggressive actions against "Iraqi combatants," or could they fire their weapons only in self-defence? What would Canada do if one of its ships intercepted a member of Saddam's regime fleeing Iraq? Long pause. Well, we wouldn't turn them over to the Americans, since that would suggest we were on their side. Clear as mud, right? As our national wordmaster Rex Murphy put it, reading the prime minister on the Iraq question "required the skills of a séance master and the deductive power of a Sherlock Holmes."[15]

The Courage to Choose

These examples from the post–September 11 landscape illustrate three disturbing truths about Canada. The first is our leaders' lack of confidence and their hesitancy to take a firm stand on key issues of the day. Always anxious to test out public opinion and the reaction of the United States, Canada too often looks indecisive on the world stage. When will we develop the courage to get out in front? Even an event as momentous as September 11 only spurred us to obsess about our identity and lack of appreciation by the United States. On the one hand, we want to criticize the U.S. and distance ourselves from American society, which we routinely condemn as boorish, lacking in "real" culture, materialistic, and prone to violence. Yet, on the other hand, we are thrown into a crisis when the U.S. does not acknowledge us or our efforts, or expresses displeasure at a stand we have taken. When will we finally grow up?

The second problem is that Canada's leaders have lost the capacity, or desire, to explain their policy positions and the effects of those positions to allies and the wider public. Let me hasten to add that I am not endorsing the Bush-like approach of good versus evil: "You are either with us or against us." For many of us, the stance of the Chrétien government over the war in Iraq was not the problem; rather, the problem was how that stance was justified, articulated, and carried out. There was an alternative. Rather than leaving President Bush to learn about the Canadian position on the evening news, our government could have approached U.S. officials days prior to the bombing and expressed our sincere regret that—in this instance—we could not support our traditional ally. The Chrétien government could have explained, to both Washington and the Canadian public, *why* Canada was rejecting the case for war. As I will argue later, putting all of our eggs into the UN basket isn't sufficient. We also need to articulate Canada's values and goals: a rule-governed international system, a viable strategy for dealing with weapons of mass destruction, and security for the people of the Middle East. Instead, the dominant voices in Ottawa were those such as Carolyn Parrish and Herb Dhaliwal, who used one of the greatest diplomatic crises of the post–Cold War period as an opportunity to showcase their anti-American credentials.

Canada can and must do better than this. As an independent country with a unique history and national character, we have interests and views distinct from those of the United States. But they must be pursued with confidence, through a clear articulation of our interests, reasoned arguments about why we dissent, and a compelling alternative that we seek through diplomatic means. My perspective is clearly influenced by my presence in Britain during the war in Iraq, where I witnessed the dramatic leadership of Prime Minister Tony Blair. Not only did Blair make a stark and unpopular choice (which I personally disagreed with), he also took pains to defend that choice repeatedly and eloquently in the British parliament, where the debates among MPs were some of the most animated of the past century. The prime minister also took his case to the British people. In an hour-long program on the BBC in February 2003, Blair argued his position in front of a hostile room of British voters. As I watched it, I asked myself, "Could Jean Chrétien (or, indeed, George W. Bush) pull off such a performance?" I think we all know the answer.

The final truth is that Canada is unstrategic about its role—both within North America and in the wider world. As a country, we have enormous strengths and abilities to draw on. Rather than using them to guide our priorities, as we might have done in the case of peace-keeping in Afghanistan, we attempt to play a variety of roles at once. As any good strategist knows, choice and focus are the keys to success. It is as true for nations as it is for organizations or individuals.

A New Identity Crisis

A 2003 cover story in the Canadian edition of *Time* magazine asked a provocative question: "Would anyone notice if Canada disappeared?" The article asserted that Canada's influence in the world is shrinking fast, that we are living off dividends from past investments that will soon be depleted. The central claim of this book is that this first decade of the twenty-first century will be a crucial one for the future of our country. While the twentieth century, as Wilfrid Laurier once pro-claimed, belonged to Canada, our success in the next one is by no means assured. We find ourselves at a significant crossroads. Either we make the choices that will allow us to thrive on the North American continent and contribute actively in creating a better world, or we will cease to exist—in anything but name—as a sovereign country. Sovereignty is not a symbol or badge that we wear. It is something that must be exercised every day by those who project Canada's values and pursue Canada's interests in the wider world, and by all of us, in our individual decisions about how we live and what we value.

Canadians, it seems, are always engaging in this process of self-reflection. For decades we lived under the shadow of a seemingly unending national unity crisis, which compelled us to think about why we exist and what defines us as a people. At last, Canadians are feeling confident—almost bullish. Surely after surviving the referendum and slaying the crippling deficit we can now sit back and relax?

Unfortunately not. In fact, there is no better time to be having a national conversation about Canada's global vision for the twenty-first century. First, there is the noise in the atmosphere about Canada's decline in the world community and its lack of distinct personality on the international stage. Whether it is the *Time* magazine article or the visible symbol of crashing Sea King helicopters, there is a sense that our country is not doing what it once did. Indeed, voices from outside Canada are lamenting our country's fading reputation as a constructive member of the international community. "Canada," warns one friendly observer, "will continue to be irrelevant unless there is a political will to change. Today it adopts high moral standards from a safe distance."[16] Second, we are experiencing a profound shake-up in the global architecture that has managed peace and security for half a century. Institutions such as the United Nations are being called into question, and new rules and arrangements are being created before our very eyes. Finally, after ten years of leadership by Jean Chrétien, there is new captain at the helm of government. And with that fresh blood has come a review of Canada's foreign and defence policy. Our twenty-first prime minister, Paul Martin, has called for a new "politics of achievement" in Canada—one that will lead to a place of influence and pride for our country in the world.[17] But underneath Martin's government is an even broader turnover in leadership. A new Information Age generation—one that is ethnically diverse and raised on a diet of globalization—is taking on leadership positions in all sectors of society. Members of this generation, whose names and faces are only starting to hit the national radar screen, will take us forward into the twenty-first century. I provide some examples of who they are, what values they hold, how they view the choices facing Canada at this crossroads, and what kind of nation they might pass on to future generations.

Choice and *contribution* are two themes that run throughout the follow-ing pages. For too long, we have heard Western leaders tell their popula-tions that they "have no choice." Unstoppable economic or political trends have tied their hands and made unpopular policies inevitable. Shrugging their shoulders, Canadian politicians point to actors outside our borders, such as the International Monetary Fund, midwestern U.S. farmers, or New York investment bankers, as forcing their hand. But in politics choice is always possible—if not always in ends (*what* we do) then in means (*how* we do it). When looking ahead to the future of North America, Canada faces not inevitable absorption by the U.S., but difficult choices about how we want our society to operate in the north-ern part of this continent. In plotting that future, we must be proactive rather than reactive. That means identifying the challenges that face all three countries on the continent—Canada, Mexico, and the United States—and coming to the table with ideas and strategies for addressing them. We must also choose carefully the issues over which we are will-ing to do battle with an ever-more-powerful United States.

Contribution is the theme that dominates Canada's relationship with the wider world. During the last decade, we have rested on our laurels and on our reputation for good international citizenship. "While Canada slept,"[18] our military has deteriorated rapidly, our thought leadership on key issues like the environment has evaporated, and our international aid budget has dwindled. To play a meaningful role in international affairs, Canadians must do more than just participate. We must genuinely con-tribute—leadership, ideas, money, and people—to creating a working world. As former deputy prime minister John Manley is rumoured to have said, Canada cannot continue to "run to the bathroom when it comes time to pay the bill." But this too requires a framework of choice. If we want to make the most of our resources, we cannot continue to be all things to all people or to be part of every international club. A focused agenda that strives for real impact will allow Canada to fight back against those who prematurely forecast our demise from the international stage.

Challenging the Mythology

This book is organized around two myths that Canadians hold about themselves and their place in the world. Both, I would argue, have become increasingly untenable in a post–September 11 world and are impeding our ability to craft a compelling vision for the twenty-first century. Until we see ourselves more clearly, and honestly assess our strengths and weaknesses, we cannot hope to assume our new continental and global responsibilities.

The first myth is "Canada as America's best friend." There is no doubting the depth and breadth of the Canadian-American relationship. It is one that is vital to Canadian prosperity and security, and it requires constant and skilful management. But in the current context, trying to be the *best* friend of America (notice where I put my emphasis) will at best invite disappointment and at worst lead to the wrong policy choices for Canadians. The reality is that no country is the best friend of America today; instead, the White House is forming short-term coalitions to address specific challenges. In some cases, we will not be part of the team—either because we don't possess the right capabilities or because we don't agree with the desired goal. More importantly, the United States itself is undergoing monumental change and is internally divided on a whole host of political, economic, and social issues. It is therefore still uncertain what course it will chart for itself. Some of the transformation brought about during the George W. Bush era is permanent: Americans have been deeply scarred by the 9/11 experience. But other shifts in policy may "correct" themselves during a second Bush term. The stand-off in the U.S. Senate over the confirmation of George W. Bush's controversial nominee for Ambassador to the United Nations, John Bolton, has shown that there are different views in Washington over how the United States should wield its power in the global arena.

Rather than trying to be liked or appreciated by the current Bush administration, Canada must strive to build what seems to have eluded us for so long: a confident and mature relationship with the United States. I believe this is what Canadians of my generation want—not knee-jerk anti-Americanism or fundamentalist continentalism, but rather an ability to appreciate what is vibrant and exciting about our southern neighbour and to cherish the unique experience that we have built north of the 49th parallel. That relationship will need to be built on mutual respect and the pursuit of common interests. But it must also recognize and build upon common values where they do exist, rather than decrying any hint of shared purpose as an act of treason against Canada.

The agenda for that relationship is not a mystery. As I will show, it includes a forward-looking strategy for the management of our joint assets (such as the border and energy supplies), further economic co-operation where it does not compromise the public interest, and new forms of collaboration to address threats to our continent. Moving ahead in these domains does not require, as some have argued, a new "grand bargain" with the U.S., linking all areas of co-operation into one mega-framework. The better approach for Canadians is one that builds upon the myriad of treaties and informal arrangements that already exist between our two countries, and that proactively seeks creative solutions to new problems on the horizon. Above all, in pursuing this agenda Canada must let go of the "fear factor": fear of being shut out of the U.S. market, fear of economic retaliation, and fear of being forgotten by Washington. Instead, we must approach the United States with confidence, and with a clear vision of how we want to share this continent.

The second myth that I challenge is "Canada as a middle power." This Pearsonian mantra, which has defined our foreign policy for fifty years, is increasingly problematic in a world where the United States stands as the sole superpower and where the potential of other countries—such as China, Brazil, and India—is rapidly increasing. What are we in the middle of? Furthermore, I will argue that being a middle power has focused us on process rather than on substance. It is all about forging consensus and building coalitions—but to what end? In this post-9/11 world, countries increasingly need to have a view on where they stand and what values they hold most dear.

Once we let go of the middle-power vocation, a variety of new global roles become possible. Some have argued that Canada should realign its foreign policy in a regional direction and focus on the Canada-U.S. relationship as the best way of furthering Canada's interests internationally. Others would like to see us follow the lead of Norway, which has in recent years staked out a niche position as a peace negotiator, or Australia, which has worked energetically to ally itself closely with the Bush administration. As another alternative, former foreign affairs minister Lloyd Axworthy has called upon Canada to leverage its "soft power" resources and pursue a liberal internationalist agenda focused on human rights and the rule of law.

I believe that Canada must be more than a regional player. Choosing the continent and leaving behind our global responsibilities flies in the face of our geography, our history, our national identity, and our interests. But we must also move beyond the stereotype of ourselves as peacemakers and peacekeepers. Changes both at home and abroad require us to think differently—and in more expansive terms—about how "we" act internationally. In the final chapter, I introduce the notion of Canada as a Model Citizen. Canada can model in two senses: first, it must strive to show others what a liberal democracy might look like in the post–September 11 era; second, it must work side by side with others in less stable parts of the world, demonstrating how they might create the foundations for healthier societies. Rather than seeking to transplant our model into other countries, we can seek to help others help themselves. The idea of citizenship refers to Canada's place in a world community and to the kinds of rights and duties that status entails. But it also suggests activism: model citizens continually strive to make the commons more just. They are comfortable in public spaces, working alongside others who are different. Model Citizens also pull their weight, which in the context of the world community will sometimes necessitate a willingness to sacrifice Canadian citizens for a greater good.

Why Canada Still Matters

Some may say that focusing on the future of a national community, like Canada, is a backward-looking approach. We live in an era of globalization, where nation-states no longer have the capacity or power to make a difference. In our postmodern, post industrial world, it is technology, global markets, and transnational networks that make the wheels go around. National attachments are passé—only for those who have yet to taste the benefits of cosmopolitanism. 27

I think this prognosis is exaggerated, for two main reasons. First, near the end of the 1990s, the prophets of globalization began to recognize that national governments still had the ability to control their participation in a globalized world. Some, such as China, proved that the forces of economic and political liberalism were not unstoppable, and that state controls on free movement—of people and ideas—still had plenty of bite. Even Western industrialized states have proven able to choose which versions of capitalism and democracy best suit their citizenry. While the United States opts for unbridled free-market liberalism, European powerhouses like Germany choose a path with greater state regulation and a broader social safety net. In short, capitalism has proven to be a many-flavoured thing.

Second, in the aftermath of 9/11, sovereign states are reclaiming some of their former jurisdiction and increasing their governing power to affect the daily lives of their citizens. Airline passenger lists are screened by immigration officials, private e-mail is routinely monitored by intelligence services, and hidden cameras watch drivers run red lights at intersections—all in the name of "national security." This growth in the power of national governments doesn't mean that international co-operation stops or that global institutions no longer matter. What it does mean is that sovereign states are still the most important building blocks of international order and the main providers of prosperity, justice, and protection for their citizens. In this, Canada is no exception.

Not long after September 11, Canadian historian Michael Bliss painted a bleak picture of the prospects for our country. Within the North American continent, we confront unrivalled U.S. hegemony, an increasingly powerful Mexico, and a complex set of issues around continental integration. In the wider world, Canada faces new security threats and a growing list of global problems that demand co-operation and better international governance. These realities combine to make our continental and global positions less assured, and our identity and prosperity more vulnerable. In Bliss's view, Canadians lack "what it takes" to manage these challenges. Younger Canadians of my generation, he argues, should reduce our expectations and resign ourselves to a "national half-life," sliding further into the arms of a more affluent and dynamic United States.[19]

I profoundly disagree. I am holding out for a different plot to our national story. I see a renewed and confident Canada that skilfully manages its relationship with the United States but that also contributes constructively to the resolution of global problems. Yet I also see a Canada that is much more than the corporate entity represented by our flag or our government. We need to update the old image of international relations as a game played by centralized states. In reality, the game is much more disaggregated,[20] and Canadian "foreign policy" is being made by a whole host of individual Canadians, in their roles as businesspeople, professionals, scholars, advocates, and artists. Many of us are already at home in the world—it is our politicians and civil servants who need to catch up to that reality. This book calls for a new vision to guide Canadians in the twenty-first century, one that is rooted in our history and that draws on and develops our collective strengths. I believe that the next generation of leaders, from all sectors of society, has the passions, skills, and ideas to craft a new script for Canada. Let's get on with the job.

CHAPTER ONE

America's Best Friend?

O N THE MORNING of September 11, 2001, Saul Benjamin was rushing to the United Airlines counter, hoping to make a connection that would take him to visit his sister in California. An executive with an e-learning company in Denver, Saul had just completed a restful vacation in Switzerland, and his luggage was slowly making its way from one side of the airport to the other. The United Airlines staff member behind the counter told him that while he would just manage to make it onto UA Flight 175 to Los Angeles, his baggage likely wouldn't. Saul paused for a moment and thought about what was inside his suitcase. Given he had been travelling for quite a while, there was a variety of things he needed in it. He therefore made the decision to wait and catch the next flight.

We all know what happened to Flight 175. It had a routine climb out of Logan Airport, but at 8:42 a.m. things began to go wrong. The plane veered from its course over northern New Jersey and briefly continued south before making a U-turn to the north toward New York City. At 9:03 a.m., packed up with 24,000 gallons of jet fuel, it crashed into the second tower of the World Trade Center, killing not only its fifty-six passengers and nine crew members, but countless others who were inside or near the tower.

30 But what happened to Saul? With his luggage safely on board, he was settling into his flight when he felt a sudden jolt. He looked out the window and saw that the plane's wing had dipped. Were they all about to go down? The captain immediately came on the audio system

to explain to frightened passengers that "an incident had occurred in the United States" and that the plane was being diverted to Canada. "I thought a nuclear war had started," Saul remembers. "The captain was obviously cautious about telling the real story—even though he clearly knew what happened—for fear that passengers would panic. He also had to contend with the possibility that there might be hijackers on our own flight."

During the course of that fateful day, the passengers aboard Saul's flight, UA 929, along with those on thirty-seven other planes, landed at Gander Airport in Newfoundland and were instantly embraced by the local population. In the words of one chronicler, "If the terrorists had hoped their attacks would reveal the weaknesses in western society, the events in Gander proved its strength."[1] Since Gander couldn't accommodate all of the unexpected visitors, those on Saul's flight were transported to the tiny town of Gambo on the Kittiwake Coast. With a population of 2,339, Gambo is the proud birthplace of Joey Smallwood, the larger-than-life figure who led Newfoundland into Confederation. But on September 11, and for the five days that followed, Gambo would have something else to take pride in, as it played host to more than a thousand stranded passengers from around the world. For the remainder of that week, the citizens of the town disrupted their lives and came out to help—whether it was making meals, filling prescriptions, setting up Internet connections, or opening up their homes so that passengers could shower. The generosity, compassion, and good humour of Gambo residents have left a lasting impression on the passengers of Flight 929, who have established a Web site (http://www.ua929.org) to facilitate continued communication and to reminisce about evenings spent at the Trailway Pub.

For Saul, the events of 9/11 were a vivid illustration of the warmth and friendliness of Canadians—and particularly Newfoundlanders. "The people of Gambo literally gave me the clothes off of their backs," he recalls. "The fellow who lent me his was a bit shorter than

I was, so I walked around with flood-pants for most of the week." But for those from Gambo, these overtures demonstrated nothing uniquely Canadian. As one resident put it, "We only tried to be good neighbours, just as we know they would have done had the circumstances been reversed."[2]

For more than two hundred years, Canada and the United States, as "good neighbours," have shared the longest and most peaceful border on our planet—the 49th parallel, 8,891 kilometres long. While our political systems have important differences in *form*, they agree on many aspects of *substance*: a commitment to individual freedom, democracy, and the peaceful resolution of disputes.

Over the past century, Canada and the U.S. have also developed the biggest bilateral trading relationship in the world. Today, our economic interdependence with our American neighbours is a reality we cannot ignore, especially since so many jobs and livelihoods depend upon it. I'll let the facts speak for themselves. Eighty-one per cent of all Canadian trade in goods and services currently goes to the United States,[3] a figure that represents 38 per cent of Canada's gross domestic product (GDP). Indeed, for many manufacturers in Canada today, the U.S. market is more important than the domestic one. While the percentage of U.S. exports going to Canada is much smaller, at 19 per cent, for thirty-nine of the fifty U.S. states Canada is their largest export market. The value of trade in goods and services that crosses the 49th parallel every day is now CDN$1.9 billion. Each day, more than half a million people and 45,000 trucks cross our common border.[4]

But the closeness of the Canada-U.S. partnership is deeper than these statistics reveal. Over several generations, the Canadian and U.S. populations have intermingled, through migration and immigration, through everyday cross-border travel, and through the exchange of ideas. In the words of former prime minister Jean Chrétien, Canada-U.S. ties are "found in the relations between our two national governments, our states and provinces, our cities, our institutions of learning, our businesses, our hospitals. Above all, in our people, who work together, marry one another, go to one another's schools and universities, play in the same sports leagues, and even sometimes live in one country and work in the other."[5] The citizens of English-speaking Canada, unlike those of any other country, can travel to and work in the United States without being noticed as "different."

But similar does not mean identical. In fact, one of Canada's key strengths on September 11 was precisely its separateness. This allowed it to be a safe haven for airplanes and passengers.

33

Canada's historical development tells a very different story than the one that is told in the United States. In his well-known work on Canada-U.S. relations, *Continental Divide*, Seymour Martin Lipset recounts the decision of British Empire Loyalists to reject the Americans' revolutionary experiment and set up a counter-revolutionary alternative in the northern part of the continent.[6] Ever since that time, Canadians have emphasized different values, set different priorities, and used different means to bring about our goals. To put it simply, we have made different choices.

Those choices have led to a particular conception of who we are. Canadians have learned to distinguish carefully between our *relationship* with the United States—the kind of ties we have—and our *identity*—whether we want our country to become more like the United States. In survey after survey, a strong majority of Canadians insist that our identity is distinct from the American one, and that we have more in common with Canadians from other provinces than with Americans in nearby states.[7] Moreover, even after the signing of the Canada-U.S. Free Trade Agreement (FTA) and the subsequent North American Free Trade Agreement (NAFTA), 50 per cent of Canadians claimed that we should be doing more to develop that distinct identity, particularly in our approach to social policy.[8] Thus, for example, while Canadians believe that they enjoy roughly similar wages to their American neigh-bours, 73 per cent believe that we enjoy a higher quality of life and 66 per cent believe that we are doing a better job than the U.S. at pro-viding "equal opportunity for all."[9] As Michael Adams's fascinating study *Fire and Ice* has shown, the evolution of the views of Canadians and Americans has confounded the predictions of those who believe that economic co-operation between these two peoples of North Amer-ica will lead inevitably to a convergence of social and cultural values.[10] Rather than coming together, the feelings and beliefs of Canadians and Americans are becoming more and more distinct.

At any given moment, if we take a snapshot of the two countries, we can see these different values and priorities at work. Take, for example, March 2003. While the U.S. was sending the world's largest military to the Persian Gulf, Canada was trying to broker a deal within the Security Council that would avoid war. While the Bush administra-tion was mounting up a $450 billion deficit and (paradoxically) implementing a massive tax cut, the Liberal government was basking in the glow of a surplus budget and establishing new priorities for government spending. Canadian distinctiveness is also the theme that our political leaders and diplomats take with them abroad and that they try to operationalize in our foreign and trade policy. The Cana-dian challenge has been to walk the fine line between warm friendship with and cool detachment from the United States. In fact, the struggle to define the Canada-U.S. relationship has, in itself, become an impor-tant part of the Canadian identity.

The period since the terrorist attacks on New York and Washington has challenged this balancing act as never before. While the initial reaction to 9/11 in Canada was one of sympathy and solidarity, a series of issues has surfaced (and, in some cases, resurfaced) that put a strain on our most important foreign relationship. Furthermore, September 11 removed any lingering doubt about the status of the United States as the world's sole superpower. Canada is no longer just "sleeping beside an elephant," as Pierre Trudeau famously quipped. We are living next to the hub of a new kind of empire. This brute fact has significant implications for Canada's place in the new world order. First and foremost, it is forcing us to rethink whether we are, or want to be, "America's best friend."

We Are All Americans Now

While the remarks of our prime minister following the World Trade Center attacks were less poetic than those of British prime minister Tony Blair, they contained an important and little-noticed phrase that, until then, no Canadian leader had dared to express. Americans, Chrétien proclaimed, were *family*. This notion of blood ties recast the Canada-U.S. relationship and took it a big step beyond where it had traditionally been—one of close friends and neighbours. It suggested something permanent and unshakeable. But it also suggested that our ties are deeply *private* ones—people-to-people transactions beyond the glare of diplomats or media. Within families, after all, we rarely declare our love and support. They are assumed and felt, rather than stated. Therefore, though the newspapers cried out after Bush's failure to thank Canada during his address in Congress, there was another possible interpretation: George Bush himself later declared that our country was not mentioned in his address because Canada was taken for granted. It was family.

The theme of family also dominated the Canadian public's initial reaction to September 11. Not known for their bold displays of anything, let alone friendship toward the United States, ordinary Canadians went to extraordinary lengths to demonstrate their solidarity. In this moment of trial, our traditional worries about Canadian identity and autonomy seemed to have been set aside. Conferences I attended in late 2001 and early 2002 began to speak of a common North American identity and a new *domestic* policy of continentalism. In this moment, we dropped the traditional chip on our shoulder and stood shoulder to shoulder with the United States.

But the honeymoon was short-lived. *Maclean's* magazine's 2001 end-of-year poll showed that Canadians had not been drawn any closer into the orbit of the United States as a result of the terrorist attacks on North American soil. As pollster Allan Gregg put it, "September 11 may have caused Canadians to change their assessment of the world they live in, but it has not changed them as people . . . While we may empathize more as a result of the common threat, we are no more likely to want to be U.S. citizens or feel that we have become any more American in recent years." Though our ties with the U.S. were recognized as extremely important, our sense of differentiation continued. The poll found that Canadians were twice as likely to describe their relationship with the U.S. as "friends but not particularly close" (47 per cent) than they were to describe it as "the best of friends" (23 per cent).[11] By the time of the first anniversary of September 11, surveys would show that Canadians no longer believed the terrorist attacks would have a lasting impact on their lives.[12]

Even more significant than changes in public opinion was the appearance of a number of thorny issues that alienated the Liberal government from the Republican administration in Washington. Some of these had predated 9/11: the failure of the Bush administration to support the Kyoto Treaty on climate change, its opposition to the creation of an International Criminal Court, and its plans for a national missile defence scheme. To these contentious issues were added a number of examples of "anti-social" behaviour by the Bush government: the U.S. treatment of al-Qaeda detainees at Camp X-Ray in Cuba and refusal to accord them rights under the Geneva Conventions; U.S. protectionist measures against European steel and Canadian lumber; and threats by the U.S. to veto the extension of the UN peacekeeping mission in Bosnia, due to concerns over the potential vulnerability of U.S. soldiers to the new provisions of the International Criminal Court.

Most worrying of all, however, was the new "Bush Doctrine" of pre-emptive defence, which proclaimed the U.S. intention to seek out and counteract potential threats to American security at their source, before they could damage the U.S. homeland or U.S. interests. Bush's 2002 National Security Strategy, on which this new doctrine was based, contained three important shifts.[13] First, it suggested that the United States was moving away from traditional justifications for the use of force, based on self-defence and imminent threat as enshrined in the UN Charter, toward a willingness to judge for itself when security problems justified military action. But the National Security Strategy was not all about hard power, as commentators have suggested. It also brought ideology firmly back into the discourse of U.S. foreign policy, after a brief respite in the 1990s, by clearly articulating *American* demo-cratic principles and *American* standards of appropriate behaviour for members of a global community. Using these ideological criteria, the United States would differentiate between allies and enemies. Finally, with the new Bush Doctrine and its potent mix of democratic ideal-ism and pre-emptive power, international relations got personal. The rhetoric of U.S. foreign policy became dominated by the demoniza-tion of individual leaders. One of the most prominent, of course, was Saddam Hussein.

On the question of Iraq, there were growing fears in Canada and Europe that the U.S. would disregard the misgivings of its allies and the collective decision-making procedures of the United Nations. Concerns were raised about the Bush administration's intention to pursue a reckless Middle East adventure that would lead to more, rather than less, stability and security. While the Western allies of the United States were firmly behind Bush in his war on terror, most (except for Britain) were openly skeptical about the alleged immi-nence of the Iraqi threat and the supposed link between Saddam

Hussein and al-Qaeda (a skepticism that has been borne out by post-war revelations about inaccuracies in intelligence). In fact, many in Canada and Europe worried more about how the U.S. would handle the problem of Iraq than they worried about the threat from Iraq itself. In her open letter to the United States, Canada's Margaret Atwood captured the unease that was gripping Washington's allies: "When the Jolly Green Giant goes on the rampage, many lesser plants and animals get trampled underfoot. . . . If you proceed much further down the slippery slope, people will stop admiring the good things about you."[14]

The Big Disappointment

There are defining moments in all friendships, when loyalty is tested and emotions run high. For Canada and the U.S., there have been many of these high-water marks over the past century—Canadian disappointment over U.S. neutrality in the early years of the Second World War; American disappointment with Canada's failure to support the U.S. attempt to "draw the line" against communism in Vietnam; the notoriously strained relations between Pierre Trudeau and Ronald Reagan.

Canada's decision to stand aside in the U.S.-led attack against Saddam Hussein's regime in Iraq will go down in history as another such moment. What the Bush administration wanted and needed was obvious: with the lean Canadian military already stretched and plans afoot to send more Canadian peacekeepers to join the stabilization force in Afghanistan, there was never any question of a strong *military* contribution from Canada. Instead, the U.S. was seeking to legitimize its use of force by demonstrating that other states were standing behind it. As Jean Chrétien said himself in a speech to the Chicago Council on Foreign Relations, "The price of being the world's only superpower is that [the United States'] motives are sometimes questioned by others.

Great strength is not always perceived by others as benign. Not everyone around the world is prepared to take the word of the United States on faith."[15] What the U.S. needed from us was *political* support. And we didn't give it to them.

This foreign policy decision was perfectly defensible. I was personally opposed to the use of military force in March 2003 and argued that case both in Canada and in Europe. But the *way* in which Canada articulated and pursued this policy was deeply flawed.

Aside from the awkward questions about what our frigates and soldiers were doing in the Persian Gulf, there was the deeper issue of where we would stand once the war was underway. Though disapproving of the U.S. invasion, our prime minister declared in the House of Commons that he wished the U.S. military well and expressed the hope that it would accomplish its mission "as quickly as possible with the fewest casualties." This reflected the sentiment of Canadians themselves, who began to get cold feet about their government's decision not to take part in the war. A poll taken by Ipsos-Reid between March 25 and 27, 2003, showed that almost half of respondents agreed that Canada had turned its back on the United States and that "it is now time for us to come aboard and offer our military support." But a few days later, after Foreign Affairs Minister Bill Graham indicated that Canada would welcome the fall of Saddam Hussein, the prime minister rushed in to insist that our government did not support the goal of regime change. Following this apparent clarification, a motion was tabled in Parliament declaring support for a U.S. victory.

Taken together, all three of Chrétien's statements added up to a coherent—if nuanced—position, even if those in the media and opposition benches delighted in portraying it as confused and hypocritical. Point #1: While Canada was committed to assisting the United States in its war against terrorism, it did not support the unilateral use of force by the U.S. to address Saddam's alleged possession of weapons of mass destruction and defiance of UN resolutions; the position of the Canadian government was that the threat had not been proven imminent, that diplomacy had not been fully exhausted, and that the action lacked the international support necessary to give it legitimacy. Point #2: Nonetheless, once the decision to use force had been made, Canada wished for speed in bringing hostilities to an end—both for civilians and for the soldiers of its key allies, the United States and the United Kingdom. Point #3: Canada remains willing to intervene militarily in the sovereign jurisdiction of another state in situations of (a) self-defence, as outlined in Article 51 of the UN Charter; (b) a collective peace-enforcement mission authorized by the UN; and (c) extreme humanitarian emergency or gross violations of human rights. However, it believes the use of force to overturn a regime or government without a justifiable cause (that is, one of the three conditions listed above) is both illegal and immoral.

Two factors made this policy difficult, if not impossible, to pursue. The first is the general climate of "good vs. evil" that has marked international politics in the post-9/11 period. Ever since the collapse of the twin towers, George W. Bush has called upon countries to demonstrate what he calls "moral clarity." Be among "freedom-loving peoples," Bush proclaims, or be among the terrorists. Nuance, hesitation, and awkward questions are difficult to accommodate. The second factor relates to the execution of Canada's position by the Chrétien government. While the three positions listed above conceivably worked as a package, they were rarely—if ever—presented as such. Nor were Canadians told what interests and values were really at stake in Iraq, or in the process of deliberation occurring within the United Nations. Ottawa erroneously made multilateral co-operation the end, rather than the means, of Canada's position. Most of all, our government did not communicate an alternative strategy for addressing threats to international peace and security, beyond giving weapons inspectors more time or letting the "UN process" run its course. As a result, our politicians often looked like deer caught in the headlights, as each new development presented another opportunity to publicly disagree with the United States. Safety tip: When disappointing a friend, try not to make things worse.

In spite of these clumsy tactics, the direction of our policy remained reasonably clear: on this occasion, we had chosen not to support the military action of our closest ally. The real problem was that we didn't fully understand, or seem willing to live with, the implications of that choice. The comments made by Paul Cellucci, former U.S. ambassador to Canada, offered an opportunity to test Canadian resolve. Some sectors of Canadian society buckled under the pressure and were quick to distance themselves from the official government position.

The ambassador's now famous remarks were made on March 25, 2003, in a breakfast speech to the Economic Club of Toronto—in retrospect, a very shrewd choice of audience. "There is disappointment in Washington," the ambassador said, "that Canada is not supporting us fully." That was the first blow. The coffee cups stopped clinking as all eyes fastened on the ambassador. Cellucci went on: "There is no security threat to Canada that the United States would not be ready, willing and able to help with. There would be no debate. There would be no hesitation. We would be there for Canada—part of our family." That was the second blow. The corporate executives present began squirming in their seats. But it was the next comment that really sent heartbeats racing. While the long-term relationship between the U.S. and Canada would endure, the ambassador speculated, "there may be short-term strains here." When asked what those might be, Cellucci replied, "You'll have to wait and see."

There were many ways to respond to the U.S. ambassador's not-so-diplomatic words. The first was to say "we have been here before." Terse words have been exchanged in the past, but the U.S.-Canada relationship has weathered these storms. Some of our more distinguished historians and political scientists, such as Queen's University

41

professor Kim Nossal, made exactly this point: "History shows that Canadians understand that our interests in the global order are enhanced when we are listened to in Washington . . . However bad things are right now, a 'correction' will occur."[16]

The second, more defensive response was to gently remind the Americans that we had indeed "been there" for them. Canadians had done their part at Ground Zero. We had joined, with as much force as we could muster, the war on terror. Seven of our soldiers died in Afghanistan— four of them due to U.S. friendly fire, no less—in the name of that war. On the question of Iraq, however, Canada was not yet convinced of the rationale for war—particularly the alleged link between Saddam Hussein and al-Qaeda—and preferred a multilateral solution to the disarmament of Iraq. As *Globe and Mail* columnist Jeffrey Simpson put it in his open letter to Paul Cellucci, "With respect, Saddam Hussein, odious as he was, posed no direct threat to the United States."[17]

A third, more virulent response came from those who resented the ambassador's meddling. The day of the Cellucci speech, Prime Minister Chrétien presided over an unruly meeting of his caucus, during which some Liberal MPs called for a formal protest against the U.S. diplomat.[18] Journalist Lawrence Martin, known for his strong Canadian nationalism, also had strong words for the ambassador: "In the Cellucci world, any time America marches off to war, Canada is supposed to follow in lock-step . . . Had he tried out his thesis on Mr. Trudeau or Mr. Pearson, they would have politely told him to go jump in a lake. The one near Toronto."[19]

But it was the response from the other side of the political spectrum—the Canadian Alliance and some members of the business elite—that caught the biggest media headlines. The initial reaction of those present at the March 25 breakfast was to confirm whether Cellucci's comments really reflected the official view of the Bush presidency. Perhaps the ambassador was just speaking off the cuff? This hope was quickly dashed when Cellucci confirmed to reporters that he had spoken to his superiors in Washington before giving the speech. The line had been vetted by no less than National Security Adviser Condoleezza Rice.

Hope turned to fear. Canadians awoke the day after Cellucci's speech to the spectre of an American economic backlash. "Business groups warn of big Canada-U.S. rift," the front page of the *Globe and Mail's* business section proclaimed. The range of economic ills we were likely to face ranged from chaos at the border to consumer boycotts to trade sanctions to the decline of our aerospace industry. No doubt about it: Canadians were going to pay a price for daring to diverge from the U.S. line. Were we really so keen on foreign policy independence after all? Thomas d'Aquino, head of the Canadian Council of Chief Executives (CCCE), summed up the mood of those in the business community who worried about economic fallout: "Is a negative impact on $2 billion a day of business . . . important? Damn right it's important." Ambassador Cellucci had generated just the response he had intended.

More evidence was added to the critics' case when the White House announced that the planned visit of George W. Bush to Canada (scheduled for May 5, 2003) was to be postponed until "sometime later in the year." Apparently, the president was too busy with issues such as the reconstruction of Iraq to pay a state visit to Ottawa. Not too busy, however, to invite Australian prime minister John Howard, who had supported the U.S.-led war in Iraq, to Crawford, Texas. An invitation to ride horses and barbeque steaks on the Bush ranch has become *the* symbol of being in the president's good books. (So far, no senior Canadian figure has been extended this hand of friendship.) The U.S. president's remarks about the Australian leader seemed pointed directly at those allies who had not backed the use of force against Iraq. "Things get tough when you make tough decisions," Bush said. But Howard had "stood his ground when he needed to stand his ground because he understands the difference between right and wrong."[20]

43

So, what kind of price is being paid by Canada for its war stance? Despite the dire warnings of some journalists and business leaders, the macroeconomic impact has been relatively small. As predicted, the Bush administration carried through on its promise to reward those who joined the coalition with lucrative contracts to rebuild Iraq—and to shut out firms from those countries, such as Canada, that had stood aside. In addition, a series of micro-effects rippled across the U.S. in the weeks following the Canadian decision not to take part in the coalition: Canadian snowbirds were heckled in restaurants in Florida; some small- and medium-sized businesses decided to buy their inputs from non-Canadian suppliers; a small number of U.S. consumers protested against Canadian maple syrup and beer. These ramifications have undoubtedly been unsettling for some Canadians. But we need to put them in perspective.

The reality is that endorsing U.S. foreign policy will not necessarily translate into significant economic benefits. Our support for the U.S. war in Afghanistan did not bring resolution, for example, to our hottest trade disputes, such as wheat or softwood lumber.[21] Similarly, taking a principled stand against Washington is unlikely to damage the deep and entrenched economic ties between our two countries. Legal obligations (such as those codified in both the FTA and NAFTA) and basic economic self-interest make retaliation an unwise course for the U.S. government to pursue.

Soon after Ambassador Cellucci's expression of disappointment, Cellucci made two important—but less noted—announcements that demonstrate my point. First, on March 29, 2003, he called for a merger of the Canadian and U.S. energy markets, acknowledging the vital importance of oil and gas imports from Canada (which represented 94 per cent of U.S. gas imports in 2002). With political unrest in both the Middle East and Venezuela, and in light of the difficulties the Bush administration faces in trying to drill for oil in the wildlife refuges of Alaska, the demand for Canadian energy is expected to intensify in the years ahead. Indeed, Vice-President Dick Cheney, an oil and gas man himself, reported in 2001 that Canada was "America's largest overall energy trading partner."[22] In spite of the war of words over Iraq, the American government realizes that Canadian trade—particularly in energy—is a strategic necessity and a key ingredient in sustaining the current (high) levels of American consumption.

Second, despite predictions to the contrary,[23] Ambassador Cellucci announced on April 16, 2003, that Canadians would be exempt from new U.S. laws requiring all people entering or leaving the United States to register with customs officials. This legislation—a product of the post-9/11 efforts to strengthen "homeland defence"—had been seen by officials in Ottawa as a potential nightmare for cross-border trade in services (that is, for the countless lawyers, consultants, bankers, and entertainment and media professionals who go back and forth across the 49th parallel). But after an intense lobbying effort by Ottawa to ensure the continued free movement of people and commerce between the U.S. and Canada, the Bush administration was convinced to exclude Canadian citizens from its new entry-exit controls. During his announcement, Cellucci identified the border as one of the issues on which the U.S.-Canada relationship was making the greatest strides, despite strains over the issue of Iraq.

This was the lesson learned by the hundred-odd Canadian business leaders who participated in the CCCE's "fence-mending" pilgrimage to Washington in early April 2003. Going into the meeting, many executives expressed fear about the dire economic consequences that would befall Canada as a result of its war stance. At the end of the two-day meeting, however, most had been convinced that the issues had been overblown.[24] Ironically, it was former U.S. defence adviser Richard Perle, one of the key architects of the Bush administration's policy against Iraq, who had some of the most soothing words for Canadian CEOs: "Our economies are intertwined, and even if people wanted to be punitive—and I don't know anyone who does—when

45

you have an economic relationship like that existing between us, it's like setting off a munition within your own lethal radius."[25] The partnership that exists between the U.S. and Canada is bigger than any single government, whether in Ottawa or in Washington, and longer-lasting than any single event. Why did Canadians need Mr. Perle to convince them of that?

This is not to suggest that there is no impact from the "big disappointment" of 2003. But that impact is subtler than the cancellation of a state visit or a massive trade sanction. It is less about dollars and cents and more about our standing in American eyes. In terms of the general public, the evidence shows that our government's stand on Iraq has had a tangible effect on Canada's image in the United States. Research conducted as part of the Pew Global Attitudes Project shows that while Canada had been viewed "very favourably" by 48 per cent of Americans surveyed in the summer of 2002, that number had dropped to 25 per cent in May 2003. In addition, the number of Americans who gave Canada an unfavourable rating increased from 4 per cent in 2002 to 24 per cent in 2003.[26]

At the level of government officials, the "big disappointment" translated into the lack of any meaningful voice in Washington on issues *outside* the core of our bilateral relationship—issues of peace and security. One of the key ways Canada can pursue its broader international agenda of creating a world that is more prosperous, secure, and just is by influencing the world's only superpower, which happens to live next door. When the relationship is damaged, trust is broken: the avenue for influence becomes much narrower. Speaking just ahead of the G8 summit meeting in France in May 2003, Condoleezza Rice claimed that differences with Canada had put bilateral relations through a difficult period, and that healing the rift would "take some time."[27] The personal relationship between Chrétien and Bush was one of the frostiest between a Canadian prime minister and American president in fifty years; as a result, Canada's access to the inner circle of decision-making

46

in Washington was extremely limited. As former Canadian ambassador to the U.S. Allan Gotlieb puts it, "Access is, after all, the sine qua non of exercising influence in Washington. No access, no influence."[28]

In reality, this decline in influence began before September 11th. As U.S. journalist Stephen Handelman has observed, while Canada and the United States have never been so interdependent, and while people-to-people contacts are on the rise, Canada is figuring less and less in the U.S. government's world view.[29] A combination of global developments and policy decisions by the Canadian government has contributed to this paradox. But it is also due to a realignment of political power in the United States away from the Northeast and toward the Southwest, and to the rise of a new political generation in the United States—one that is less interested in and less aware of Canada than its predecessors. This is what made the defeat of Democratic candidate John Kerry so troubling to many Canadians. He represented the last vestiges of a political class, rooted in the Northeast, that has "family resemblances" to our own brand of liberalism. But those family resemblances are quickly disappearing. In the words of Chris Sands, a senior associate at Washington's Center for Strategic and International Studies, "There is no bias against Canada in the current U.S. leadership, but there is also no residue of an image of Canadians, either. It is not clear that the new political elite, based in the U.S. Southwest, has any particular affinity for Canadians."[30]

Canada will have to re-establish its right to participate in the reorientation of American foreign policy that is currently underway. So it should, and so it can. As in any friendship, rifts can be healed.

47

Our American Partners

In the public debate about the deterioration in Canada-U.S. relations during the course of 2002–2003, some Canadians have been too quick to lay the blame at the feet of the United States. In order to move forward, I believe we must readjust our thinking about our neighbours to the south. This involves two important shifts. First, we need to relinquish the myth that we are "America's best friend." This is partly an issue of fact, and partly an issue of principle. Let me explain.

Immediately after 9/11, the countries of the Western world went out of their way to establish their pro-American credentials. Heads of state flocked to Ground Zero. Strong condemnations of terrorism and proclamations supporting freedom and democracy could be heard from all corners of the globe. But joining with the U.S. in the war on terror is one thing—endorsing all their actions on the international stage is another. There are those in Canada, such as Conservative Party leader Stephen Harper and writer and journalist Richard Gwyn, who argue that Canada can no longer walk its historic tightrope—refraining from making a conscious choice between the United States and the institutions and rules that make up international society. In this new century, they argue, "middle ways" are passé. Standing apart from the U.S. and proclaiming the virtues of multilateralism has become an expensive luxury from which Canadians must henceforth abstain.[31] We must declare, once and for all, our allegiance to the United States and view every foreign policy decision through the lens of how it will affect the U.S.-Canada relationship.

But what does it mean today to be "America's best friend"? In a post–September 11 world, in which the U.S. feels under siege, its greatest priority is to secure the American people and the American way of life. The al-Qaeda attacks, in the words of Condoleezza Rice, "crystallized America's vulnerability" and put the idea of threat—even more than power—at the forefront of the Bush administration's foreign policy. The strategies to secure America are new; they are in many ways departing from the traditional alliances that defined our world in the past. They also involve reaching out to new "friends" around the world, who share the same assessment of the threat and who have particular assets at a particularly opportune moment. Thus, while in

March 2004 50 per cent of Canadians claimed that the United States was Canada's "best friend," only 20 per cent of respondents from the U.S. paid Canada the same compliment.[32] Today, the U.S. is working through ad hoc coalitions—of the willing and of the capable—rather than through long-term partnerships. And, in Defence Secretary Donald Rumsfeld's words, "the mission determines the coalition," rather than the other way around.[33]

One example of this trend is the co-operation between the U.S. and two relatively minor European states, Romania and Poland. Given its strategically important location close to the Middle East and Central Asia and its willingness to provide the U.S. with new bases, Romania has quickly become one of Washington's "new friends" and has been rewarded with U.S. support for its entry into NATO. Similarly, Poland's commitment of troops to the war against Iraq was rewarded with a zone of occupation in northern Iraq once military hostilities ended. In contrast, some of the U.S.'s longest-standing supporters throughout the Cold War, such as Germany, were left outside the tent and certainly off the list of countries whose businesses would receive lucrative contracts to rebuild Iraq. The U.S. is also in the process of reducing the more than 60,000 U.S. soldiers in Germany.

Rejecting the mantra of America's *best* friend is not to deny the very real links that exist between the U.S. and Canada. As I argued above, our economic interdependence is substantial and growing. But it does mean that Canada should stop trying to claim, or to prove, that it is "America's best friend." The very idea is outdated, suggests John Herd Thompson, head of Duke University's Canadian Studies program: "There isn't any special relationship between the United States and anybody, much less Canada. American policy toward Canada pretty much conforms with American policy towards other countries. It serves what the U.S. perceives is in its national interests at any particular time."[34]

This new world order is one in which the United States is cherry-picking its allies, according to specific issues and challenges. And

49

what does the U.S. need from others to further its security agenda? Intelligence. Airports. In some cases, land mass. Most of all, moral and political cover. Many states can and will offer these things. Canada will not always be among them. We must also remember that our status will largely be a function of "what we have done for the U.S. lately." When asked in June 2003 who was their best friend, the American public overwhelmingly chose Britain,[35] due to the substantial diplomatic and military commitment shown by Prime Minister Blair during the campaign to unseat Saddam Hussein. Will this continue to be the case? It depends. New "coalitions of the willing" may change this assessment.

50

Canadian Exceptionalism

There is one other habit Canadians must shrug off as they reorient their relationship with the United States. For lack of a better name, let's call it "Canadian exceptionalism": the tendency to assume the worst about the U.S. and the best about Canada. In fact, as commentator Doug Saunders has astutely noted, Canadians have acquired many of the habits we once liked to criticize our American cousins for having—including flag-waving patriotism.[36] Just as we should be skeptical of "servile" pro-Americans, reflected in the statements of members of the now defunct Canadian Alliance, so we should push back against the "puerile"[37] anti-Americanism of those such as former Canadian National Party leader Mel Hurtig.

In his book *The Vanishing Country*, Hurtig sets up a one-sided picture of the United States as a country of racial violence, money-hungry lawyers, dirty cities, and bad beer. The tale even involves a rewriting of history, where the opening of the American West is characterized by a "gunslinger mentality" and the opening of Western Canada is depicted as "peaceful and orderly."[38] (Try asking some of my Métis ancestors who took part in the Riel Rebellion.) Similarly, Hurtig's narrative about U.S. foreign policy revolves around the most controversial episodes that critics of the United States love to trot out, such as the war in Vietnam and the overthrow of Salvador Allende's democratically elected government in Chile, conveniently forgetting the pivotal role played by the United States in reconstructing Europe after World War II, creating international institutions such as the World Bank, and, after the Cold War, helping to rebuild the new democracies of Eastern Europe.

Let's take another example, the much-heralded diversity of Canadian society. We pride ourselves on being a multicultural country, and so we are. But the *face* of America—in ethnic terms—is no less heterogeneous. In today's United States, nearly one third of young adults are black, Asian, or Hispanic.[39] Furthermore, while Canada pursues an official policy of bilingualism *on paper*, many parts of the United States (particularly in the Southwest) are *in practice* much more bilingual, given the presence there of almost 40 million Hispanics. There is a massive demographic shift occurring in the U.S. that is different in character from, but no less impressive than, the one occurring in our country. We urgently need to understand its implications.

Canadians constantly, and rightly, complain about Americans' lack of knowledge about our country. But I would argue that we don't know the U.S. as well as we *think* we do. Do we know, for example, that millions of Americans tuned in to foreign broadcasts (such as those of the BBC and CBC) during the aftermath of 9/11, because they wanted a non-American perspective? Do we know that it is American civil liberties activists who have led the charge in challenging the Bush administration's detention of prisoners at Guantanamo Bay? To maintain a productive relationship with the United States, we must see and understand the *whole* story—the good and the bad. We must also be aware of the skeletons in our own closet, both domestically (such as the treatment of our Aboriginal peoples) and internationally (such as the crimes committed by our peacekeepers in Somalia).

Our neighbour is an extremely complex country, with many weaknesses we might not wish to emulate, but also with many strengths. The task for Canadian policy-makers is to continually invest in "knowing" the United States, so that they can pursue our best interests without relinquishing control over how we organize our society. Why not, for example, establish *in Canada* the best research institute in the world to study the United States? Old-style nationalists would scream at such a proposal. But why? We have academic centres to study China, Latin America, and the Middle East. Is it not equally important to research long-term economic, political, and social phenomena in the United States? Studying does not automatically mean endorsing. It means *understanding*. And understanding the United States must be one of Canada's key skills.

I believe we are at a point in Canada's history where we can confidently make these kinds of investments. In Lipset's famous framework, Canada is set up as the antithesis to the United States. Because we were established as a "counter-revolutionary" country, it was inevitable that we would define ourselves in a negative sense. We are *not* Americans. But this framework is becoming increasingly outdated. A series of changes, including globalization, immigration, and our own political and economic progress, has made it possible for a new generation of Canadians to be fiercely proud of their country but also favourably disposed (or at least neutral) toward the United States. Similarly, we have shown that we can be both pro–free trade and pro–social justice, pro-Canada and pro-globalization. This way of thinking, as Michael Adams has suggested, is in many ways revolutionary. In fact, it might be Canada, rather than the United States, that is the real revolutionary beacon for the twenty-first century.

The Rogue Superpower?

As we reformulate our continental and global policies for the twenty-first century, we can use one of two images to depict the United States. The first, "America as rogue superpower," is frequently employed by those on the left (both in Canada and abroad) and on the surface appears particularly well suited to the extremities of the Bush administration. This image of is made up of three main claims: (1) that the U.S. has a simplistic view of the world, dividing it into good and evil, black and white, rather than recognizing the complex interplay of social and political forces; (2) that the United States prefers to act unilaterally, rather than through multilateral institutions, and willingly disregards international law; and (3) that the U.S. is prepared to resort to force more quickly than it should and is impatient with diplomacy. For many, America's behaviour during the Iraq crisis conformed to this picture. In my view, the story is more mixed.

There is a second image of the U.S. that captures more accurately the nature and behaviour of the world's only superpower: "America as problem solver." This view paints a picture of a superpower that seeks short-term solutions, rather than one that is willing to engage—for the long haul—in processes that build lasting peace and security.

Because of its history and geography, the U.S. has always been skeptical of long-term engagement outside its borders. There are, of course, exceptions to this, such as the stationing of troops in Europe during the Cold War. But the U.S. by and large seeks finality: to eliminate threats, to install the right institutions, and to get out as quickly as it can. This is why the reconstruction phase of the Iraq conflict has tested U.S. patience and resolve. Canadians—and, I would argue, Europeans—recognize that creating good governance is an extremely complex business: the problem isn't solved just by removing the bad guy and staging an election. Both Canada and the European Union are

53

themselves works in progress, and this is also how we see other regions of the world.

An example that highlights this tension is the mild row that emerged between the U.S. and Britain over the long-term presence of American forces in Afghanistan. From December 2001 onward, the British were keen to obtain a strong stabilization force to rebuild Afghanistan after the Taliban had been overthrown. The U.S., however, showed very little interest, claiming that "nation-building" was not something that it was in the business of doing. Its troops would be dedicated to rooting out al-Qaeda, not to creating secure conditions for the Afghan people. Today, it is those very people who are feeling the effects of America's unfinished business. And it is 1,500 Canadian peacekeepers, sent to Afghanistan in May 2003, who led the process of stabilization.

The challenge for countries such as Canada is to turn America's fondness for short-term fixes into a new and sustained commitment to build the necessary architecture for peace and security in the twenty-first century. It is a role that the United States has played before, most notably after 1945, and one that will best allow it to preserve its power and to project its values in the coming century. Indeed, there is already evidence emerging that the vision behind Bush's "hard-right turn" in U.S. foreign policy is under attack and that Washington is open to giving up some freedom of action in return for political support and burden-sharing from key allies.[40] But we won't re-engage the U.S. by continually criticizing the Bush administration for its abandonment of multilateralism. I would go even one step further and argue that the common Canadian (and European) practice of harping about U.S. unilateralism is an unhelpful distraction. The fact of the matter is that the United States is not interested in the dichotomy between multilateralism and unilateralism. It is interested in results, and where those results can be achieved through collaborative means it is perfectly willing to pursue them. This maxim would have been just as true if John Kerry had been elected in November 2004.

What has surprised me about the Bush administration is not its preference for so-called unilateralism—which many of us expected—but rather its willingness to work through the United Nations at all after 9/11. You could argue, quite ironically, that the Bush administration has invested more time in the UN than any administration of the past twenty years. When did Madeleine Albright dedicate three hours before the UN Security Council arguing for intervention in Kosovo? Her successor, Colin Powell, did so over Iraq. It is also worth noting that in the four cases in which the United States has used force against terrorism—once by Ronald Reagan, twice by Bill Clinton, and once by George W. Bush—only the last bothered to take his case (against Afghanistan) to the United Nations.

Moreover, the Bush administration is hardly revolutionary in its skepticism about international institutions. In fact, American ambivalence about submitting to rules made "outside America" is rooted in two particular features of its democracy. The first is its revolutionary tradition and fight for independence from colonial rule. The mantra of "no taxation without representation," shouted by the American revolutionaries, has translated into a widespread belief that laws and rules must be a direct reflection of the will of Americans. In the U.S. view, not just sovereignty but also democracy is compromised when decision-making is taken beyond the nation-state. The U.S. Senate's rejection of the League of Nations in 1920, for example, was less about America's new-found great power status and more about fears that collective security would compromise its sovereign right to decide when to go to war. The Republican Party's current opposition to the International Criminal Court is therefore part of a longer tradition of U.S. opposition to indirect representation. The Democrats, even had they been elected, would have had difficulty getting Congress to change its mind.

The second explanation lies in America's federal trajectory. The U.S. polity today is, relative to countries such as Canada or Germany, a highly centralized federal state. The long road to this unity has conditioned Washington's attitude to any whiff of an external check on its decisions. As a consequence of fighting—and winning—a long battle with the states of the union for ultimate authority, U.S. federal administrations are leery of entering into power-sharing arrangements with anyone. For evidence, just compare the structure of NAFTA with that of the European Union. The latter is made up of a complex and dense set of institutions that regulate the flow of goods, people, and capital across the borders of its member states. The structure of the EU is supported by a powerful commission whose sole function is to pursue community-wide interests and to develop policy initiatives that will affect all members equally. The EU also contains a parliament of elected representatives from each of the member states, but also a robust court of human rights that can hear cases from individual citizens across the Union. NAFTA, by contrast, remains largely a treaty: there are no centralized institutions to co-ordinate policy-making and only rudimentary mechanisms to resolve disputes. The drafters of NAFTA—and particularly those from the United States—explicitly avoided any formal institutionalization of the continent along the lines of Europe, leaving North America without a body that could sit above or beyond individual nation-states.

I don't want to press this point too far and gloss over the Bush administration's real disillusionment with multilateralism and the UN. What I do want to suggest is that America's allies, including Canada, must engage with the United States on the terrain of results. If there is a genuine multilateral way to address a problem, then we should clearly lay out what that is. If there isn't, then we should be willing to support U.S. actions that we view as being in the best interests of international peace and security. Or we should stand aside with principle and conviction when we disagree—as Germany did over the use of force against Saddam Hussein. What we cannot do is continue to use multilateral forums as tools for reining in the United States.

This new results-based focus doesn't mean always agreeing with the United States on what the best results are; here, our own interests and values may lead to a different perspective. But it does require us to change our language and approach to dealing with our American partner. This is true not only on the world stage, but also, as I show in the next chapter, in the slippery area of continental integration.

CHAPTER TWO

Sharing the Continent

G RAHAM FLACK spent most of the day on September 10, 2001, mulling over two new job opportunities. As a civil servant within Ottawa's prestigious Privy Council Office (PCO), thirty-three-year-old Flack had spent six years working in the trenches of Canada's national unity crisis—most recently laying the groundwork for the Chrétien government's signature piece of legislation, the Clarity Act. After devoting long hours to keeping Canada together, Graham was ready for, in his words, a "lighter assignment" that would allow him to spend more time with his partner and two young children. The following morning, after watching the hijacked planes wreak havoc in New York and Washington, Flack felt that the two offers he was considering would no longer cut it. What he didn't foresee was that he would be catapulted into the heart of the Canadian government's response to the 9/11 attacks.

Overnight, Washington's talk of "open borders" and of the free flow of commerce and people was transformed into a more ominous discourse about security perimeters and homeland defence.[1] Flack was asked by Deputy Secretary to the Cabinet Robert Fonberg to build a Borders Task Force, with a mandate to support Deputy Prime Minister John Manley in the development of a new Canada-U.S. approach to the management of the 49th parallel. The task force began on an apprehensive note. "The conventional wisdom was that the best we could accomplish was damage control," Flack recalls. "Key stakeholders believed the objective was to get as close as possible to the situation that had existed on September 10—and to limit the negative impact of the attacks on Canadian jobs and businesses." But what began in a climate of fear and caution evolved into a policy triumph for Canada. What Flack and his team quickly realized was that U.S. officials had no clear vision of what a post-9/11 border might look like and were therefore receptive to innovative and bold ideas. Canadian civil servants, led by Manley, used the "political oxygen" provided by the terrorist crisis to draft an ambitious new proposal for the Canada-U.S. border—one that viewed economic prosperity and security as reinforcing rather than competing objectives. Proposals that had been tabled in Ottawa well before 9/11 were packaged together in a comprehensive "smart border" strategy to keep high-risk cargo and people out but to make the free flow of low-risk cargo and people even easier than on September 10. As Flack recalls, "There was a huge potential for countries like the U.S. and Canada to turn inward after 9/11, and to let fear dominate our public policy-making. But this would have been a huge gift to the terrorists. Instead, we showed the world how to build a twenty-first-century border."

59

The deeper lesson for Flack was about the influence that Canada can have at pivotal moments: "Even at an hour when the U.S. was at its most vulnerable and consumed with its security, its officials were open to fresh ideas from up north." Flack remembers a meeting between John Manley and his U.S. counterpart, Director of Homeland Security Tom Ridge, in early December 2001, just before the two men signed the Smart Border Declaration. "Ridge came to Ottawa with a huge entourage, and we expected the Americans to table significant changes to our draft of the declaration. To our surprise, the draft went through virtually unchanged." It was Canadian ideas and Canadian language that formed the basis for Washington's first major policy initiative on homeland security after 9/11. For Flack, the implications of this incident are clear: "As a country, Canada needs to stop being so timid. We should seize opportunities to be ambitious and help to shape the future agenda of Canada-U.S. relations."

In this chapter, I lay out some of the key continental issues that will confront Canadian policy-makers like Flack in the decades ahead. To date, the debate that Canadians see and hear in the media about our future in North America has been extremely polarized. On one side are those who oppose further co-operation with the United States, for fear of being swallowed by the American colussus. On the other side are the strong continentalists who risk compromising the very essence of Canada's unique social, political, and economic experiment. The reality is that Canada *does* have an important regional destiny in this new century. The challenge is to define that destiny in a way that is consistent with Canadian interests as well as Canadian values. Furthermore, we need to pursue that regional agenda proactively; too often in the past Canada has been reactive to developments in and overtures by the United States—usually out of fear of being shut out of the U.S. market. My vision for the future of the North American continent envisages a confident Canada that knows what it wants and that puts its talent and energy behind getting it. In other words, it's not a question of *whether* we will shape the continent we share with Mexico and the U.S.—but of *how*.

A North American Community

In late 2000, newly elected Mexican president Vicente Fox put forward a series of proposals to transform NAFTA into a fully fledged common market modelled on the European Union. U.S. president George W. Bush, fresh from his own (narrower) electoral victory, expressed his openness to the idea. Bush's eagerness reflected both personal and electoral realities: his home state of Texas has many natural links with the U.S.'s southern neighbour, and the large Hispanic population in the southern part of the U.S. is an important constituency for the Republican Party at election time. At a meeting at Fox's ranch in Guanajuato in February 2001, the two presidents issued a joint com-muniqué—aptly named the Guanajuato Proposal—pledging to "con-solidate a North American economic community whose benefits . . . extend to the most vulnerable social groups in our countries."[2]

It was a bold vision, and one that spurred frenetic activity in the North American policy world. Conferences sprang up in all three countries on the future of North America. Meetings were held. Research was conducted. Studies and books were published. And then, on that fateful morning in September, we received a sharp reminder that the forces of economic integration face formidable opponents.

Today, we are once again discussing the future of North America— albeit in a new context of uncertainty and of heightened fears about security. It has become clear that the spectre of "fortress America," despite the apocalyptic warnings of the business community, is less likely to materialize. Economic interests, in all three of the NAFTA countries, are simply too far advanced in the direction of openness and co-ordination. Moreover, as events such as the mad cow crisis have demonstrated, the problems facing our respective governments have become increasingly continental and cannot be solved through inde-pendent action. Consequently, at the North American summit in Waco, Texas, in March 2005, the leaders of Canada, Mexico, and the United States unveiled a new *Security and Prosperity Partnership of North America*, designed to extend co-operation in security and intelligence and to launch new forms of collaboration in the fields of energy, sci-ence and technology, and financial services.

What is still unclear, however, is what a "North American Commu-nity" will actually look like. Will it be limited to Europe's initial starting point: a customs union, where internal trade barriers to trade

61

are eliminated and a common external tariff is applied to goods and services from the outside world? Alternatively, will it adopt the model of Europe in 1992: a common market, where labour, goods, and capital move freely across borders, where standards on things like health and safety are harmonized, and where a common currency is introduced? Or will it follow Europe's dramatic steps toward political union, with shared institutions for political decision-making, common justice and immigration policy, a convention on human rights, and a common security and defence policy?

One of the strongest proponents of creating a North American community along the lines of Europe is U.S. analyst Bob Pastor. A former member of the National Security Council under President Jimmy Carter, and now a professor of international relations at American University, Pastor has been making the rounds in Washington, Ottawa, and Mexico City, promoting his plan for modernizing the U.S.-Canada-Mexico relationship.[3] In his view, NAFTA's potential has been hampered by the tendency of its signatories to revert to bad habits. In the case of Mexico and Canada, that habit is opting for single-issue, bilateral negotiations with the U.S. rather than pursuing trilateral solutions; in the case of the U.S., it's the traditional gut instinct to go it alone. Pastor argues that only by creating common institutions—with the power to constrain and change the behaviour of sovereign states—can we get away from these old patterns and move to the next phase of integration for the North American continent. He proposes the establishment of a North American Commission (akin to the European Commission in Brussels), composed of distinguished individuals from the three countries, that could set a continental agenda for those countries' respective political leaders. Once created, the commission could design and implement solutions to the most pressing North American issues, such as a common plan for transportation and infrastructure, and collective mechanisms to handle the illegal flow of people, arms, goods, and drugs across the continent's internal borders.[4]

But the analogy of Europe, no matter how enticing, is not the appropriate model for thinking about the future of North America. The main reason for this is the fundamental asymmetry of power that exists on our continent. The North American space contains three states, one of which—the United States—far outweighs the other two economically, politically, and culturally. Within NAFTA, the U.S. accounts for by far the largest share of population (69 per cent) and GDP (88 per cent). In the newly enlarged European Union, by contrast, there are twenty-five states of varying sizes. The largest power among them, a united Germany, is no match for the might of the United States. In fact, no state in modern history has ever come close to the current dominance by the United States of the international system, whether you use military, economic or political measures.[5] Furthermore, Germany takes great pains (because of its history) to limit its national ambitions and to champion European institutions. The contrast with the United States could not be more striking. In the post-9/11 context, this U.S. reluctance to share its power with other states is even more pronounced. The current Bush administration is confidently flexing America's superpower muscles and using its relative power to huge advantage in bilateral negotiations. In the U.S. view—and this is not limited to Republican Party strategists—schemes to build or strengthen institutions are a subtle ploy to try to restrain U.S. power and influence. Even former Secretary of State Colin Powell (usually a proponent of multilateral diplomacy) drew this lesson from his attempts to work through the UN in dealing with Saddam Hussein, against the advice of George W. Bush's more hawkish advisers. In particular, Powell felt betrayed by the actions of the French government, which used public meetings of the Security Council to try to isolate the United States and emphasize U.S. differences with its European allies.

Aside from power is the question of shared purpose. The driving force behind the creation of the European Community after 1945 was largely political: a desire to avoid another catastrophic war on the

63

European continent, by tying Germany to the fate of its European neighbours. It was not consumers or producers who led the charge, but visionary policy wonks, such as Jean Monnet and Robert Schuman, who recognized that Europeans would enjoy a future of prosperity only if they remained at peace with each other and committed themselves to a common project. Thus, the lofty words in the preamble to the original Treaty of Rome claim that the signatories are "determined to lay the foundations of an ever closer union among the peoples of Europe." Moreover, Monnet and Schuman's efforts were strongly encouraged—some would even argue propelled—by a U.S. goal in the early years of the Cold War to create a united Western Europe to counter the Soviet threat. In the case of North America, no comparable grand purpose exists. When placed alongside the ambitious tone of the European Union's Rome Treaty, the preamble to NAFTA looks like a contract between a new homeowner and his mortgage lender. It pledges the governments of the United States, Canada, and Mexico to "create an expanded and secure market," "reduce distortions to trade," and "enhance the competitiveness of their firms." It's missing that all-important vision thing.

In addition, there are no powerful constituencies within the United States pushing their leadership to develop a vision for North American unity. Instead, the 2004 U.S. presidential election saw NAFTA become a hotly contested issue between the candidates. Democratic candidate John Kerry, mindful of the growing chorus of voices drawing a link between free trade and the flight of jobs from the U.S., announced that if he was elected he would have ordered a 120-day review of all trade deals, including NAFTA. The impact of economic co-operation in the United States (particularly in the Midwest) is framed not in collective or community terms, but rather in the zero-sum language of U.S. job losses to Mexico. It's hardly surprising, then, that the post-Monterrey North American Initiative was intentionally designed to be incremental and piecemeal, so as to avoid the legal requirement of congressional approval of any new treaty entered into by the U.S. government.

Finally, there is the issue of shared identity. While Europe's process of integration began with a largely technical agenda—the creation of a coal and steel community—it gradually came to include a notion of European citizenship. This expanded agenda was driven by the European Commission's realization that building Europe had to be about much more than the construction of a common market. In other words, the integration project had become too firmly rooted in economics—that is, a "businessman's Europe"—and needed to take greater account of the "people's Europe."[6] The by-products of this realization were the development of a common European passport and the political right to vote in and stand for local elections. The architects of Europe had come to see that European citizenship would be largely meaningless unless the peoples of Europe felt part of a community.

So what makes that collective, or community, possible? According to some, the hallmarks of a community are simply member interaction and a degree of interdependence that makes those members aware of common interests.[7] With this interpretation, it is easy to conceive of Canada, Mexico, and the United States in communal terms. Well before the ratification of NAFTA, the three countries of North America were engaged in significant levels of cross-border co-operation—even if the patterns of that co-operation were highly asymmetrical, with Mexican and Canadian dependence on the United States greater than U.S. dependence on its two North American neighbours.

According to the blue-ribbon task force on the future of North America (co-chaired by former Deputy Prime Minister John Manley, former Mexican finance minister Pedro Aspe, and former U.S. Governor William Weld), a continental community could be solidified as early as 2010, defined by a common external tariff and an "outer security perimeter." But the conception of community that underpins the task force is

65

telling: it is based "on the premise that each member benefits from its neighbor's success and is diminished by its problems."[8]

I would argue, however, that interaction and interdependence are necessary but insufficient conditions: a community also depends upon shared norms and purposes. Thus, the famous sociologist Max Weber distinguished between communal relationships (*Vergemeinschaftung*), which are based on a subjective feeling among parties that they belong together on the basis of shared values, and associative relationships (*Vergesellschaftung*), which are based on a rationally motivated convergence of interests. Viewed in this way, North America is more appropriately categorized as an association of three states with an overriding common interest in expanding trade and investment within the continental space.

Looking into the future, what are the prospects for a genuine community on our continent? Could a notion of North American citizenship gradually emerge? To date, there is little evidence to support this. Public opinion research conducted by Ekos reveals that although Canadians, Mexicans, and Americans support increased access to each other's markets, they remain strongly attached to their own values and institutions.[9] While national identity is declining in Europe, it is actually on the rise in North America. Despite ten years of economic integration, the peoples of North America have yet to be psychologically reoriented to think in collective terms.[10]

In my view, the very notion of "North American citizenship" is problematic. The collective framework necessary to make it meaningful simply doesn't exist. The concept of the North American citizen is attractive primarily for Mexicans, whose agenda for political and economic development depends upon Mexico's moving into the orbit of the more mature liberal democracies of the U.S. and Canada, much like the countries of the former Eastern bloc (such as Poland and Hungary) have moved inside the EU tent. But even there, "North Americanness" faces resistance: the majority of Mexicans still identify themselves as Latin American as opposed to identifying with North America.

The concept of North American identity also has some resonance for Canadians, mainly for those who desire an ally in efforts to change the policies of the superpower that sits between two smaller world players. According to former foreign affairs Minister Lloyd Axworthy, Canada needs to get away from its traditional approach of dealing with the U.S. one on one: "If you are a 180-pound halfback faced with blocking a 300-pound tackle, you'd better find some help."[11] Axworthy's model is a North American condominium, where "we explore our common heritage as North Americans" and develop new structures for continental governance.[12]

The problem, however, is that a North American identity has almost no meaning for the main player in Axworthy's condominium—the United States. It's hard enough for a Londoner to identify herself as European. Can you imagine an American in, say, Paris introducing himself as North American? True, the U.S. military has recently established a North American command structure, known as Northcom, designed to manage its defence and security interests from the Canadian Arctic to the tip of Mexico. But this is all about protecting territory, particularly the U.S. homeland, from twenty-first-century threats. It should not be read as a sudden conversion by Washington to the goal of fostering a North American community. It is extremely difficult to imagine that the political leadership or citizens of the United States—particularly a post-9/11 United States—will develop anything resembling a continental identity.

More importantly, for the peoples of a diverse society such as Canada identification with the North American continent can feel awkward and artificial. Instead, the prevailing Canadian identity is what Darrell Bricker and Edward Greenspon have called "Can-global."[13] On the one hand, Canadians consider themselves more Canadian than ever and are proud of our national accomplishments. At the same time, there has been a noticeable increase in the number of Canadians who describe themselves as "world citizens"[14] and who take pride in Canada's global activists, such as UN envoy on HIV/AIDS Stephen Lewis, anti-globalization movement champion Naomi Klein, and past president of Doctors Without Borders James Orbinski. A global identification is particularly true of young Canadians—the most ethnically diverse generation in our history—who are more likely to think in global than in continental terms.[15] This applies not only to consumption, but also to employment opportunities and participation in global civil society. While Canadians are aware of globalization's effects, both positive and negative, one thing is certain: globalization has expanded our horizons beyond our southern border.

68   In sum, North America is not Europe and is unlikely to adopt Europe's distinct brand of integration. The linear process that Europe has experienced—from free trade to customs union to common market to political union—is not the only way to achieve greater co-operation between states. In fact, if you consider the U.S. and Canada, there are aspects of all four of these stages in our current relationship. In some ways, we are already much more integrated than the states that belong to the European Union, particularily if we look at the movement of people across the 49th parallel. This suggests that we need a different framework for thinking about the ties that are being created on our continent and the direction in which they are taking us.

There is one sense, however, in which the European experience does provide valuable lessons for North America: through the European Union's conception of sovereignty. In its traditional meaning, originating in mid-seventeenth-century Europe, *sovereignty* referred to the right of a prince to determine the religion of the people within his jurisdiction rather than submit to the dictates of Christendom. At the Peace of Westphalia in 1648, which ended Europe's bloody wars of religion, the principle of sovereignty was defined internally as supremacy over all other authorities within a population, and externally as freedom from interference by outside authorities. The rights of sovereigns henceforth became the rights of sovereign states (the building blocks of today's international system) to control the people and activities within their territory.

As a result of the forces of globalization and technological innovation, the contemporary notion of sovereignty has evolved from this ideal type. In legal terms sovereignty is absolute—either you're sovereign or you're not—but in practical terms states exercise varying degrees of supremacy within and independence from without. Nowhere is this truer than in Europe, where economic and social linkages, combined with institutions such as the European Commission and the European Court of Justice, influence the domestic jurisdictions of EU member states in countless ways. Nonetheless, the ideas of independence and choice remain. The EU, no matter what the Euroskeptics might say, is not a "superstate." It is a union of sovereign states that retain wide and significant powers to shape their societies in ways that match their unique histories, geographies, cultures, and political traditions. Within the EU, sovereignty is not given up to some kind of overarching big brother, but rather pooled in ways that make policy co-ordination more efficient and effective. And it is the heads of European states who make the choices on when and where to pool.

With the events of September 11, the older notion of sovereignty as control over territory has regained some of its lost currency, particularly in the United States. In the process, the initial euphoria over President Fox's vision for a North American community has been dampened. In the rush to respond to the terrorist threat, the infrastructure of the U.S. sovereign state has been strengthened: "porous" borders have been filled in, spending on the national military has increased, and new legislation has been passed to intensify surveillance of both "foreigners" and citizens.

In this context, it is clear that the option of a new, comprehensive agreement between Canada, Mexico, and the United States is unlikely to materialize. Indeed, Canadian public opinion shows little interest and a lack of belief in the likelihood of creating any kind of North American "union."[16] And according to many of our civil servants and academics, such an agreement is not in Canada's interest. To back up this argument, commentators point to two realities. The first is economic. Despite the acceleration of trade between Canada and Mexico since NAFTA was signed, Canadian exports to Mexico today remain relatively small, at only 0.7 per cent of total exports.[17] Foreign direct investment linkages are even more limited. These statistics seem to warrant against any formal expansion of our relationship beyond what exists under NAFTA. The second factor, which gets particular emphasis in bureaucratic circles in Ottawa, is that Canada and Mexico have different priorities and therefore need different arrangements vis-à-vis the United States. While "we" are focused on the free movement of commerce across borders, "they" are concerned with getting a new deal for the millions of Mexicans living and working in the United States. Canada mustn't let its agenda with the U.S. (so the argument goes) be "contaminated" with the thorny issues in the Mexican–U.S. relationship such as drug trafficking and illegal immigration.

The obsession of our policy-makers with Washington is understandable, but it risks missing an opportunity. In short, we shouldn't be too quick to dismiss trilateralism. Canada's longer-term regional future undoubtedly requires deepening our understanding of Mexico and its likely impact on the shape and character of North America. Moreover, the unlikelihood of getting agreement on a new trilateral treaty should not prevent collaboration with Mexico where our interests and values come together. Mexico's approach to international issues under the leadership of Vicente Fox—including its new focus on human rights and its support for international institutions—makes it an obvious partner for Canada in forming coalitions on the international stage.

But even within the frontiers of North America, there is more we can and should do together. A strong majority of Canadians (72 per cent) continue to support free trade between Canada and Mexico.[18] Indeed, there may be much more *relative* potential for growth in trade with Mexico than with the United States.[19] In this regard, Canadian policymakers need to let go of the long-standing fear (frequently heard in the run-up to the signing of NAFTA) that the asymmetries between Canada, the U.S., and Mexico would somehow lead to a "race to the bottom," particularly in economic and environmental regulation and in social standards. Yes, Mexico is still a developing country, with huge inequalities in income. But Mexican society has also been transformed over the past fifteen years, both politically and economically.

Canada also has a strong interest in ensuring that the rules that govern economic co-operation under the terms of NAFTA continue to work, in light of NAFTA's role in helping to modernize the Mexican economy. NAFTA has the privileged status of being one of the only regional trade arrangements that include both developed and developing countries. Given that the developing world is likely to be the next frontier for trade agreements, the lessons learned from the NAFTA experience—in particular, whether and how such agreements can serve to enhance quality of life for those in poor countries—will be important for policy-makers all across the globe. As critics of NAFTA predicted in the early 1990s, large sections of the Mexican population have yet to see the benefits promised by the surge in Mexico's export manufacturing and the increase in foreign investment. A study released by the Carnegie Endowment for International Peace (designed to coincide with NAFTA's tenth anniversary) found that NAFTA has failed to generate substantial job growth in Mexico and has hurt hundreds of thousands of subsistence farmers. Real wages in Mexico are lower today than they were in 1994, when the agreement came into effect, and emigration has continued to escalate. Given this record, NAFTA partners need to ask themselves tough questions about how the benefits of this trade agreement have been distributed and whether there are particular initiatives that might be put in place to ensure that the "winners" of free trade are not limited to particular industries and corporations.[20] Canada could and should take the lead in exploring what changes would be required, including the option of creating a regional development fund within the NAFTA space.

Finally, Canada and Mexico have an interest in building up a body of rules (as opposed to a formal institution) that covers both the substance and the procedures of trilateral co-operation. The reason is simple: this is the best way to manage the reality of U.S. power. Despite their limitations, the

71

rules contained in NAFTA do serve to constrain the United States in its trade disputes with its neighbours. And why does the U.S. agree to such rules? Because even the most powerful state in the world cannot meet its economic objectives without meaningful collaboration with its regional partners. Increasingly, this is the case in the security realm as well. In developing these new rules, Canada will need Mexico. Whether we like to admit it or not, Mexico has two power advantages over us in dealing with the United States. First, given demographic realities, it is much more a part of U.S. domestic politics, which opens up possibilities for influence. Second, given its record of economic and political instability, Mexico is much more of a potential problem for the U.S., which makes it more able to impose real costs if co-operative arrangements cannot be created. Thus, while there are some downside risks for Canada in becoming involved in Mexico's' "problems," there may be some tangible gains in leverage with Washington. Above all, if significant change in the character of U.S.-Mexican relations is likely in the years ahead—both in the social/cultural and economic realms—then the costs to Canada of *not* embracing trilateralism could increase. We need to develop a sense of regional destiny, and get to work on the specific structures and agreements that will bring it to life.

Nonetheless, as important as Mexico has become to Canada in the last decade, the main focus of our policy-making in the short term will remain the United States. It is on the Canada-U.S. relationship that my discussion of co-operation will now turn, and on the growing list of issues that need to be jointly managed. The events of 9/11 have made some of these, such as security, even more pressing.

From Confederation to NAFTA

Long before notions like interdependence and integration entered into our vocabulary, the U.S. and Canada were compelled by common interests to collaborate. Some of this co-operation has been conscious and deliberately fostered by governments, while other aspects are the natural outgrowth of geographic proximity.[21]

The first tangible example of economic integration was the conclusion of the 1854 Reciprocity Treaty (what today we would call a free trade agreement), which stimulated exports from pre-Confederation Canada to the United States. The deal was terminated ten years later in the United States, where annexationists hoped that an end to free trade would cause such severe economic turmoil in the British colonies that it would force them to join the United States (obviously not a high-water mark for Canada-U.S. relations). Instead, the termination of the Reciprocity Treaty helped to foster a new sense of nationalism in the colonies and indirectly facilitated the creation of Canada. Nonetheless, post-Confederation governments remained committed to gaining access to the U.S. market and continued to try, unsuccessfully, to negotiate a new free trade deal. When John A. Macdonald came to power, he responded to U.S. protectionism by mimicking it. In his famous National Policy, Macdonald doubled the tariffs on manufactured goods (to over 30 per cent), encouraged foreigners to set up new manufacturing plants in Canada, and pressured western Canadians to purchase their finished products from central Canada. While the policy undoubtedly fostered industrialization and economic development in Canada, it also transformed our country into a "branch plant economy" of the U.S.[22]

The contentious 1911 Canadian election, which saw Laurier's Liberals go down to defeat over the issue of trade reciprocity, reaffirmed Canada's commitment to national development but did not lessen our reliance on American capital to fund that process. By the beginning of World War I, a quarter of all U.S. foreign investment was directed toward Canada. American investment in Canada intensified after World War II, particularly in mining and smelting, but also in manufacturing industries such as automobiles. This development was accompanied by a broader shift in Canadian trade priorities away from Britain, which experienced economic decline after 1945 and could no longer sustain high levels of imports from Canada. In the five-year period between 1946 and 1951, Canadian exports to the U.S. more than doubled, and came to represent almost 60 per cent of our total exports.[23] In 1965, with the signing of the U.S.-Canada Auto Pact, the reality of an integrated North American automobile market (the foundations of which had been laid years before by the big U.S. auto firms) was officially recognized. The signing of the FTA in 1988, despite the rancour it caused in Canada, really only codified what had already been occurring in practice: deepening integration between the Canadian and U.S. economies.

Aside from trade and investment linkages, Canada and the U.S. have a long history of co-operating on more technical issues, such as borders, water, pollution, and energy. In 1908, the International Boundary Commission was established to clarify Canadian and U.S. frontiers and to resolve any ambiguities about where the 49th parallel should be drawn. This was followed in 1909 by the Boundary Waters Treaty, which set out principles and procedures for settling disputes over the quantity and quality of the waters that straddle Canada and the United States. The treaty stipulates, for example, that the "boundary waters and waters flowing across the boundary shall not be polluted on either side to the injury of health or property on the other." The primary dispute resolution mechanism created by the treaty is the International Joint Commission, which continues to serve as an important example of how the U.S. and Canada can constructively work together on problems of joint concern. In 2002, amendments were made to the Boundary Waters Treaty to control the shipment of bulk water across the 49th parallel, partly as a result of environmental concerns about water supply in Canada.

Ironically, the field of Canada-U.S. integration that troubles ardent nationalists the most—security and defence—has the longest historical pedigree. In fact, the first modern arms control agreement to be signed between two great powers was concluded between the U.S. and

Great Britain in 1819, limiting naval armament on the Great Lakes.[24] During the First World War, U.S. pilots came to Canada to train for their missions and the U.S. navy provided anti-submarine aircraft and patrol vessels to help defend ships in the North Atlantic.[25] The collapse of the Versailles Peace Treaty and the rise of Hitler in the 1930s instigated a more significant set of agreements between the U.S. and Canada. These included the Franklin Roosevelt–Mackenzie King pledges of mutual defence in 1938 and the Ogdensburg Agreement of August 1940. The latter, which came on the heels of France's capitulation to the Nazis, reflected Washington's and Ottawa's real fears about the future security of the continent. It resulted in the establishment of the Permanent Joint Board on Defence (PJBD), designed to ensure high-level consultation between the U.S. and Canada on the defence of North America. As J.L. Granatstein reminds us, Ogdensburg also initiated two important features of contemporary Canada-U.S. relations: the efforts of the United States to gain assurances of security against an attack through Canada, and close co-operation between the two countries' militaries on the battlefield.[26]

In the early years of the Cold War, Canada and the U.S. institutionalized their defence collaboration through the North Atlantic Treaty Organization (NATO) and, more significantly, the North American Air Defence (NORAD) Treaty. NORAD, signed in 1957, was a direct response to the perceived threat of a Soviet nuclear attack on North American targets. From this point forward, Canadian airspace became a critical battleground of the Cold War and Canada was given a seat at the table in decisions about continental air defence. The NORAD treaty was supplemented in the late 1950s by a series of defence production and development sharing agreements between Washington and Ottawa, which effectively gave Canadian industry the right to bid on U.S. contracts. The net result of these agreements was an increasingly integrated defence-industrial base in North America.

Today, there are more than thirty agreements between the U.S. and

Canada on defence-related matters.[27] At a more informal level, the Canadian Forces have worked over the decades to increase what is known as "interoperability" with U.S. forces. Frigates from the Canadian navy, for example, have been seamlessly incorporated into U.S. carrier battle groups, and our naval officers are fully capable of commanding U.S. vessels. Since September 11, the institutionalization of defence co-operation between the two countries has expanded even further, with the creation of a Military Planning Group (MPG) within NORAD. This body is tasked with co-ordinating responses to potential crises that might occur in North America, including terrorist attacks and natural disasters. A particularly noteworthy feature of the MPG is the provision that if the forces of either country are required to respond to an emergency situation across the border, these forces would come under the operational control of the home country.

All of these achievements in U.S.-Canadian co-operation, whether in the economic or the security field, have depended on the willingness of both parties to treat issues as they emerge, one by one. It has traditionally been in Canada's interests to maintain this "administrative" approach to bilateral relations and to frame issues in terms of common interests rather than common doctrine or ideology. By avoiding linkage—that is, avoiding tying results in one area to success in another—Canada minimizes the danger that the full weight of U.S. power will be brought to bear on negotiations.[28] Although our ties with the U.S. are deep and complex, we lack formal or centralized institutions that bundle these relationships together. So far, this lack of formal structure has suited both of us.

What's the Big Idea?

For some, the events of 9/11 have called this administrative strategy into question. Proponents of a new "grand bargain" between Canada and the U.S. include University of Toronto economist Wendy Dobson, former Canadian ambassador to the U.S. Allan Gotlieb, and the Canadian Council of Chief Executives (CCCE). While their plans differ on smaller points, all of them argue that we can no longer rely on the piecemeal and informal approach. In their view, Canada's dependence on the U.S. economy, combined with the U.S. need to secure the North American perimeter after 9/11, presents a golden opportunity to negotiate a mega-integration treaty for the twenty-first century. The status quo, we are told, is untenable; the FTA and NAFTA have outlived their usefulness. It's time to put all elements of the Canada-U.S. relationship into one all-encompassing framework.

Two assumptions lie behind this big bang theory of integration. The first is that in a post-9/11 world, the U.S. government is obsessed with security and would allow it, in Senator Hillary Clinton's famous words, to "trump the economy." The immediate aftermath of September 11, when the border was closed, demonstrated just how vulnerable Canada is to the disruption of commercial traffic. Plant shutdowns and widespread economic losses occurred in both Canada and the United States. As Perrin Beatty, president of Canadian Manufacturers & Exporters, describes it, the Canada-U.S. border runs right through the middle of a "just-in-time" assembly line. This makes the ability of businesses to move goods and people across the border in a quick and unfettered way a key factor when deciding whether or not to invest in Canada. If the risk of disruption to that flow becomes too high, risk-averse investors might choose to invest in the United States. Canada needs to move aggressively to address U.S. concerns, so the argument goes, but also to ward off potential closures.

The second assumption is that any change in the status quo will happen only if we initiate it: the U.S. fundamentally doesn't care about Canada and is preoccupied with other policy priorities. In this post-9/11 moment, when the U.S. needs allies in its war on terror, we have a rare chance to play our cards. If we seize the day, we can define the next phase of integration in ways that serve Canadian interests. According to Gotlieb, the initiative "must be bold, it must come from Canada and be espoused at the highest level. It must be comprehensive so as to allow trade-offs and broad constituencies to come into play. It must address the U.S. agenda as well as ours. Incrementalism won't work."[29]

So what's the meat of the Big Idea? In Dobson's explanation, it all boils down to two fundamental aspects of the Canada-U.S. relationship: economic growth and physical security. If Canada can present these two elements in a compelling package, we can achieve our goal of greater economic security—guaranteed access to the U.S. market—and assuage the fears in the United States about northern-based threats to its homeland security.[30] Four elements, Dobson argues, should be part of the deal. The first is a mechanism to secure low-risk cargo and people as they cross the 49th parallel, making the free movement of goods and skilled people easier in the North American space. The second element is a secure North American natural resources infrastructure (given that Canada is the largest supplier of energy to the U.S.), to offset the possibility of supply disruptions from non–North American sources. According to the CCCE, the negotiation of a resource security pact should address not just energy, but also metals, minerals, agriculture, and forest products.[31] Third, Canada and the U.S. should promote greater economic efficiency by creating a customs union: one common tariff against goods from outside Canada and the U.S., and a harmonization of regulatory systems. The fourth and final element is the rebuilding of Canada's military and a unique Canadian contribution to the defence of North America. Plans are sketchy, however, on what the "unique" role would be.

While impressive in its scope, the Big Idea suffers from three flaws. First, it is not clear why a comprehensive and top-down framework is suddenly needed to manage the Canada-U.S. relationship. We already

have an enormous network of rules and agreements in place that effectively addresses a whole host of issues of joint concern and that continually changes to meet new challenges. The initiatives announced by
Bush, Martin, and Fox in March 2005 are only the most recent example. Therefore, the alternative to launching a "grand bargain" isn't the
status quo: the Canada-U.S. relationship is constantly moving and
adapting. More importantly, as Robert Wolfe has argued, such a comprehensive approach doesn't fit the model of power distribution in the
United States. "In single-point diplomacy," Wolfe writes, "state-to-
state relations are the responsibility of ambassadors and foreign ministers. But power is everywhere in the United States, not just in the
White House or on Capitol Hill." There is simply no centralized
arrangement that could be created to counteract this power on
Canada's behalf. We also need a dose of realism: if any centralized
institutions were to be created as part of the "grand bargain," they
would never be created on a basis of equality between the two countries. Most of the action would take place in Washington.[32]

Second, a grand bargain isn't going to help us with our *real* problem
with the U.S.—its resort to so-called trade remedies. These measures,
otherwise known as "anti-dumping" and "countervailing duties," allow
a country such as the U.S. to "remedy" what it perceives to be a trade-dis-
torting practice by another country. Goods are considered "dumped," for
example, it they are introduced into the market of another country at less
than their "normal value" in the country exporting them. Goods are considered subsidized if they have received specific government assistance in
the course of production, giving producers in the exporting country an
unfair advantage over producers in other countries. The importing country can respond to dumping and subsidization by imposing an additional
fee or tariff on the goods (as the U.S. has done, for example, on Canadian
softwood lumber). It is precisely this behaviour, frequently pursued by
the U.S., that Canada failed to curb during the free trade negotiations in
the late 1980s and that continues to haunt us in our trade disputes with

Washington. If you were to ask our minister of international trade what the thorniest issues are in the U.S.-Canada relationship, he would reply: softwood lumber, steel, and agricultural subsidies. Yet it is unclear how the so-called grand bargain will address these ongoing irritants.

The third and perhaps greatest flaw is that the proposed "grand bargain" flouts all the rules of good negotiation. Its proponents assume that there is a great deal that the U.S. currently wants from Canada that it isn't getting. But is this really true? Certainly Washington wants to prevent the possibility of terrorists crossing the border, but are there more concrete measures we can put on the bargaining table? The whole idea of such a bargain strikes me as amateurish. Imagine going to Washington with such a scheme in hand and promising that, in return for economic concessions, Canada will do its part to secure the North American space and defend its territory (for example, by improving its military capability and improving the oversight of immigrants and refugees). What do you think figures like Secretary of Defence Donald Rumsfeld might say to such a proposal? I predict that the response would be, "Why aren't you acting on security anyway? Why isn't this a priority for Canada already? You expect to get something for doing the bare minimum?"

The broader problem in all such schemes is that they are driven by fear. If we don't act on x, the U.S. will do y. It was fear that drove the free trade negotiations at the end of the 1980s—in this case, fear of being subject to growing protectionism in the United States. And it was fear that drove Canada's initiatives on the border after 9/11—fear of having the border closed to our trucks and people. While both efforts resulted in some benefits for Canada, I would argue that a fear-driven public policy will yield minimal results going forward. Proactive self-confidence should be our mantra for the future.

80
—

Let's pause and ask what really needs to be "fixed" in the Canada-U.S. relationship. Are we letting high-level theatrics cloud our assessment of how the relationship is actually working? As I will show, the economic issues that require our attention are not a mystery: they relate to facilitating the freer movement of Canada's skilled professionals, bringing different regulatory frameworks into line, and continuing to press the U.S. to adhere to global rules on trade. But there's nothing in that agenda that can't be pursued through what Graham Flack calls "aggressive incrementalism": a pragmatic approach that would define what is most important to Canadian citizens (who are also consumers, employees, and business owners) and that would approach the U.S. with viable solutions that can meet our and their interests. In other words, we shouldn't be complacent—we have to keep moving the relationship forward—but neither should we put all our eggs into one negotiating basket. As unsatisfactory as this answer may be for the grand bargainists, it is the right one for Canadians because it is the most likely to yield meaningful results.

81

I would argue that the immediate problem that needs "fixing" in Canada-U.S. relations is a political one. Positive steps in this direction were taken in the first weeks of the new Martin government—a government that claimed to place a premium on improving the tone of Ottawa's relationship with Washington. Prime Minister Martin boasted that the "vibes were very, very good" during his first meeting with President Bush at the Monterrey Summit, and went out of his way to say positive things about the U.S. president's "frank style" and "strong convictions."[33] But subsequent developments, including Canada's decision not to participate in the U.S. missile defence scheme, have made it more difficult to achieve real progress. Compliments and photo ops are one thing; movement on substantive issues is quite another. The real task is to inject the Canada-U.S. relationship with greater respect and trust.

I choose my words—*respect* and *trust*—carefully. The first is built on knowledge and understanding; it does not necessarily require agreement on every policy issue. Canadians have for too long assumed that they have a deep knowledge of the U.S., because of our proximity and our constant consumption of American culture. While we may know Americans better than do the citizens of any other country, that doesn't mean we should give ourselves an A+ grade. U.S. society has undergone substantial evolution over the past thirty years, and the social values and political priorities of the U.S. have become much more traditional and conservative than our own. While Canadians are distancing themselves from traditional authority, Americans are retrenching, looking to institutions such as the family and the church to provide stability in a rapidly changing world.[34] Similarly, there is a tug of war occurring in U.S. politics between the proponents of a conservative agenda and those such as Howard Dean or Michael Moore who see themselves as the guardians of Roosevelt's New Deal. Indeed, while Samuel Huntington's 1993 book *The Clash of Civilizations* was meant to describe the coming war between the West and the rest, one could argue that there is a clash of civilizations going on within the United States itself. Canadians need to watch as this war unfolds, and to resist the temptation to think that George W. Bush's America is *the* America for the future. At the same time, we need to assess the impact that these social and political changes have had on U.S. priorities and policy-making.

How do we gather this kind of knowledge? Some interesting changes have been implemented since 9/11. On the diplomatic front, the Canadian government has opened seven new consulates in key cities such as Houston and Phoenix, in order to facilitate expanded political and economic ties with new centres of power in the U.S. The move is a reflection of the migration of U.S. economic activity from the northeast to the southwest and an attempt to expand Canadian lobbying efforts beyond the White House.[35]

Taking on board Gotlieb's advice—that Canadian policy-makers need to examine domestic and foreign policy issues within the framework of how they affect Canada-U.S. relations[36]—Paul Martin has established a permanent cabinet committee on Canada-U.S. relations, which he personally chairs. Such a move raises the management of Canada-U.S. relations to the highest level of responsibility and power in Ottawa, and (in Martin's words) "serves as a catalysing force to organize horizontally many of the elements of Canada-U.S. policy—from defence and foreign policy, to transport and customs."[37] I have no objections to this scheme as far as it goes; co-ordination can certainly make for better policy. But it misses the root of the problem: truly understanding what priorities and interests are being pursued within the U.S., so that we can more effectively work with our continental partner to pursue our own priorities and interests. This is a job that must be fulfilled by many Canadians, not just members of cabinet. It is a role for MPs and civil servants, who must continue to build links with the many sources of power that exist in the United States. The senators who can make or break deals of vital interest to Canadians are likely to outlive George W. Bush. Do we know who they are? Do we know how to influence them? It's also a task for those who reside outside the confines of government, whether they are negotiating business agreements with their U.S. counterparts, observing U.S. society from a think tank or university, or analyzing trends in U.S. culture.

As for the second element—trust—the model should be the relationship that existed between John Manley and Tom Ridge. According to Graham Flack, the two men were quick to establish a strong personal connection, and leveraged this to overcome doubts expressed within their respective policy communities (it certainly didn't hurt that Ridge himself is from a northern state, Pennsylvania, and has first-hand experience of the cross-border flows between our two countries). Tasked with finding a solution to one of the most important

83

elements of the Canada-U.S. relationship—the maintenance of an open border—Manley and Ridge established a *joint* vision for success and insisted on *joint* briefings to monitor their progress. Thus, the Manley-Ridge process was built firmly on trust: trust in each other's intentions, and trust that each side had the capability and will to deliver on its promises. What the U.S. and Canada desperately need is more common projects like the border—more opportunities to pursue common objectives and to prove to each other that a constructive partnership is possible. Rather than overloading the bilateral agenda with contentious issues, which the media always love to spotlight, policy-makers need to propose other joint initiatives (ideally ones that are future-oriented, in areas such as education and science)[38] that can accentuate the positive dimensions of our relationship.

84

New Operating Principles

Before moving on to consider the future agenda for the two main areas of U.S.-Canada relations, prosperity and security, let me outline a few operating principles to guide our policy-makers.

First, Canadians must resist the logic that continental integration is an inevitable and unstoppable process. It isn't. The leaders of individual European states—and not some magical force—initiated the integration process after 1945 and reignited it in the mid-1980s after a decade of stagnation.[39] It has also been European politicians and civil servants who have given the EU its particular shape and focus, through an intricate and in many ways unpredictable process of bargaining.[40] More importantly, an inevitability mindset closes off options and produces bad public policy. National decision makers continue to have *real* choices in the twenty-first century. While they are undoubtedly constrained, they aren't in a straitjacket.

The second issue is about voice. It is critical that in this next phase of working with our American partners, all sectors of society—not only corporate elites—drive the debate. This view is not fuelled by any anti-corporate agenda; I believe Canadian business leaders have been and should be constructive participants in the policy process. But if they are perceived to be in command of the steering wheel, the future of North American co-operation could too easily become a businessman's project, not reflective of the real values and desires of citizens at large. This perception dogged the process of European integration throughout the 1980s and early 1990s, putting pressure on European policy-makers to establish and communicate a set of concrete benefits for the *peoples* of Europe—beyond the abstract promises of economic growth. We should take note of this experience and learn from it. Ever since President Fox's proposals were announced, it has primarily been the voices of corporate Canada, such as Bombardier CEO Paul Tellier and the CCCE's Thomas d'Aquino, that have been making the case for further economic co-operation. But when they proclaim that "Canada" will benefit from a grand bargain with the U.S., which Canada do they have in mind?[41] It is crucial to recognize that a great many Canadians (in fact, a majority) find the corporate priorities of enhanced investment opportunities difficult to relate to. Indeed, a large number of Canadians believe there are values worth upholding other than the holy grail of reduced transaction costs for business. We must find a way to debate the merits and drawbacks of schemes for the future of the Canada-U.S. relationship that takes account of these diverse voices.

Finally, as with all national strategies, Canadian policy-makers must approach the future of North America with Quebec in mind. The sovereigntists in Quebec, while deflated by Jean Charest's 2003 victory, have not thrown in the towel. Following the Bloc Québécois' strong showing in the 2004 federal election, they have new leverage in the House of Commons, and have been buoyed by the fallout from the Gomer Inquiry. The sovereigntists would like nothing better than to make Canada irrelevant. It is also true that while Quebeckers have had negative attitudes toward the Bush administration (as witnessed by their stronger opposition to the war in Iraq in 2003), they are also generally more positive than English-speaking Canadians about the United States. Polling by CROP and Environics shows that while 49 per cent of Canadians outside Quebec would like to see Canada become less like the U.S. over the next ten years, the number was only 38 per cent for the Québécois. The Canadian challenge is to proactively manage its relationship with the United States in a way that retains our unique social and political experiment north of the 49th parallel—which includes a very important "French fact."

CHAPTER THREE

A Fine Balance:
Prosperity, Security, and Sovereignty

I REMEMBER clearly the first time I held a euro. It was March 2002 and I had just arrived at the airport in Toulouse, France, about to catch a ride down to the Pyrenees to savour the last of the spring snow for skiing. As I waited for the automated teller to dispense my cash, I thought back to all of the controversy I had left behind in Britain about the "evils" of adopting the single currency. The anti-euro campaign in the U.K. had resorted to imposing images of Hitler on the new European currency—an ominous sign of what was to come if Britain caved in to the leadership of the new European Central Bank (which was run, according to euro opponents, by those nasty Germans).

When the crisp new euro bills emerged from the machine, I smiled and wondered what all the fuss was about. The new currency was beautifully designed, with images of bridges on one side and Romanesque and Gothic windows on the other. It was also in denominations much easier to comprehend—particularly easier than the thousand-lire bills I had previously used to buy gelato in Florence. Most of all, the euros represented freedom and ease: no more exchanging money or figuring out exchange rates at every border crossing. "It's just a matter of time," I thought, "before the Brits will see how great this is. They'll want to join in too."

Walking away from the ATM, I also wondered whether monetary union might one day travel from the old world to the new. Following the debates on Canada-U.S. relations after September 11, I had noticed a sharp increase in corporate and elite support for some kind of currency union with the United States. A December 2001 opinion piece in the *National Post*, by Paul Tellier (then CEO of CN Rail), summarized this position. "Sooner or later," Tellier argued, "there will be just a handful of currencies through which all global trade will be conducted—perhaps the euro, the U.S. dollar and the Chinese yuan."[1] According to Tellier, Canadian policy-makers must recognize this convergence, as well as our irreversible integration with the U.S. economy, and surrender the loonie. Otherwise, we will miss the currency boat, and our per capita wealth—now only three-quarters that of the Americans—will continue to decline.

Tellier's logic looks compelling if understood in narrow economic terms. But the problem is that Canadians understand notions like prosperity and security in much broader terms than either the continentalists or the Americans currently conceive of them. For most Canadians, the measures of well-being, safety, and success have always encompassed more than earning a million dollars, driving a big SUV, or building the world's largest and most hi-tech arsenal of military hardware. They've also included those less tangible but crucial elements that create a high quality of life: safe streets, healthy children, clean cities, solid public infrastructure, and a safety net to catch those who are hit by life's tragedies. Michael Moore's film *Bowling for Columbine* may have overplayed the blessings of Canada to score political points against his Republican opponents in the U.S., but his portrayal of our country struck a chord: it's the kind of place where you can leave your front door unlocked. While our welfare state has changed (and indeed downsized) significantly since the early post–World War II period, the basic ethos that underpinned it still resonates with Canadians: a collectivization of the key risks in society, such as disease, old age, unemployment, and child-rearing. In this chapter, I lay out an agenda for Canada-U.S. relations that will preserve and enhance this "distinct society."

Growing the Pie

Let me begin with an important observation about twenty-first century Canadians: we are a nation of free traders. Not only is our economy
highly dependent on trade with other countries (particularly the U.S.),
but the Canadian public now welcomes and encourages it. It is hard to
overstate the dramatic turnaround over the past decade in Canadian
public attitudes toward trade liberalization and an active trade
agenda.[2] In fact, I am one of those converts myself. While the majority
of Canadians opposed the free trade deal with the U.S. in 1988 and
fewer than 30 per cent of Canadians supported NAFTA during the
1993 election campaign, today the support for new trade agreements is
strong and growing. And despite the impression one might get from
the anti-globalization protests in Seattle in 1999, this support is particularly high among young Canadians.[3] Whereas in the early 1990s a
climate of fear surrounded all discussions of free trade—fear of its effect
on jobs and on Canadian culture—today Canadians see no contradiction between actively pursuing new avenues for economic growth and
retaining our unique social programs and national identity.

Given this permissive attitude toward trade liberalization, should
the next priority be to expand the network of free trade to more and
more countries? Some commentators, such as former deputy trade
minister Sylvia Ostry, have warned that the regional concentration of
Canada's trade (read, dependence on the U.S. market) is making us
vulnerable to U.S. pressure on other policy fronts. "What is needed
now," Ostry writes, "is a major analytical effort to determine what
scope exists in the Canadian economy . . . to expand trade with
regions outside North America."[4] Whereas the 1990s was all about
hitching our wagon to the U.S. juggernaut, the more recent ups and
downs in the U.S. economy give us a golden opportunity to diversify.
And if this incentive isn't enough, Canada should take note of the fact

89

that we are no longer the number one supplier of goods and services to the United States: the European Union recently surpassed Canada, and China is on track to do the same in the near future.[5] As our share of trade south of the border decreases, we should look to expand our relationship with other rising juggernauts.

Survey research indicates that a large number of Canadians are also uneasy about our reliance on the U.S. market and consistently support a move toward greater diversification of our trading relationships.[6] Economic analysis suggests they may be right. To date, Canadian producers have shown little interest in looking beyond the U.S., given the greater costs of exporting goods and services elsewhere. But the fact is that the relative gain from an increased share of the U.S. market is declining—especially if we measure benefit more broadly to include not just consumer choice and increased income, but also health, education, and social cohesion. If the world economy were moving toward larger and larger economic blocs, where national borders were less meaningful, then focusing all our trade energies on the U.S. market would be the sensible strategy for Canada. But as Canadian economist John Helliwell has demonstrated, the data on trade and globalization do not support that conclusion. Instead, small countries (like Canada) continue to operate with "thick borders." That means that further attempts to expand trade among industrialized countries will not necessarily provide large increases in income.[7] In other words, we might get more bang for our buck by looking for new trade opportunities in the developing world.

The case for diversifying trade can be made on moral as well as economic grounds. As the grinding poverty in the developing world continues, it is getting harder and harder for those of us in the so-called First World to deny the hypocrisy that underpins today's global trading system. While we call on poor countries to modernize and liberalize, we effectively prevent them from exporting the goods and services that can bring them higher incomes. The developed world does this in two ways: first, through formal tariffs that keep goods from the Third World out; and second, by so heavily subsidizing First World producers (particularly in the agricultural sector) that we push prices down and make it impossible for developing countries to compete. Today, the world's richest countries spend more than US$300-billion a year on subsidies—six times what they spend on foreign aid. Although the European Union remains the biggest culprit, Canada's hands are not completely clean; our wheat and dairy subsidies hurt farmers all over the world.[8] If we are serious about making poverty reduction a focus of Canadian foreign policy (an issue I'll come back to later), then efforts to liberalize trade with developing nations should be a key policy objective.

All this being said, two points should be kept in mind. First, the best way for Canada to pursue trade and investment diversification is through multilateral mechanisms, particularly the World Trade Organization (WTO). In other words, free *world* trade must be the ultimate goal. Though we've been preaching the merits of multilateralism to our U.S. neighbours—and criticizing the U.S. for bypassing collective solutions—we haven't been consistently practising multilateralism ourselves. Instead of focusing on the current WTO round of negotiations, which has the potential for deep and lasting results, Canada has been chasing a series of bilateral free trade agreements (with the EU and with countries such as Singapore, Australia, and New Zealand) that would have much more modest economic gains.

According to John Hancock, a rising Canadian star who is currently a senior counsellor at the WTO in Geneva, the Canadian government's pursuit of bilateralism undermines our ability to criticize the U.S. for its aggressive trade strategy—a strategy that can only marginalize Canada in the longer term and weaken the multilateral system. Bilateral trade deals made some sense for Canada when there was little prospect of getting a new round of global trade talks off the ground. But why, in the current international climate, should Canada encourage the carving up of the world into exclusive trade blocs? In the years following the Second World War, Canadian trade diplomats instinctively understood that Canada, as a small economy, needed access to the world's markets if we were to prosper, and needed rules to manage its economic relations, not least with the economic colossus to the south. As a result, those diplomats became some of the most highly skilled practitioners of multilateral tradecraft in the institutions created after 1945.[9]

But for Hancock, the WTO framework they established not only meshes with Canadian interests, it also represents an ideal of internationalism. Shortly before the famous Battle of Seattle in 1999, he wrote a speech for Renato Ruggiero (then the director general of the World Trade Organization) claiming that the WTO was "writing the constitution for a single global economy." This phrase ignited a firestorm among non-governmental organizations and gradually appeared on anti-globalization Web sites and posters around the world. But as Hancock asks, "What's so bad about a single world economy? Didn't we once imagine, in the words of John Lennon, the world living 'as one'? When did internationalism—a utopia for the post-1945 generation—become globalization—a nightmare for young idealists today?" For all its flaws, the WTO remains a highly successful international organization. Yet, paradoxically, the order it promotes is as fragile as it is vital. In Hancock's words, "Those who like it, don't like it that much, while those who dislike it, hate it." Yet Canada was one of the principal architects of today's global trading system. We should be proud of that creation and keep building upon it.

My second point is that even if the relative benefit of pursuing more trade with the U.S. is less than it would be with other countries, we must continue to nurture that relationship and ensure that no other country has better market access than we do. In short, we have to keep playing good defence. Though we are doing extremely well in our trade with the U.S., we can and should do better. Let's stop thinking small in terms of our economic potential. Excellence, not mediocrity, must be the Canadian mantra. I believe that two priorities should drive our economic agenda with the United States in the next decade: enhancing access to the U.S. market and prudently managing our energy resources.

TRADE AND INVESTMENT

As I argued in the last chapter, many in Canada's policy elite have been too quick to press the panic button about Canada-U.S. relations, and too ready to assume that continentalism is our country's own manifest destiny. John Hancock uses the following analogy: "Like someone with vertigo, Canada's fear of falling into the U.S. seems to have created a subliminal desire to jump." But the case for a big bang approach to integration (that is, a new comprehensive treaty) fails to convince. Where are the big problems that justify such radical steps? Adopting instead the model of aggressive incrementalism, Canadian policy-makers should focus on reducing outstanding barriers to trade with the U.S., particularly in services, and on improving the prospects for investment in our best industries and companies. In effect, these measures would get us 90 per cent of the way toward a customs union, traditionally defined, without engaging in a high-profile—and potentially costly—grand bargain.

Let's deal with the most visible issue first. While Canada's level of trade with the U.S. has never been higher, we continue to be subject to anti-dumping and countervailing measures. The most prominent example of these "trade remedies" are the duties that Washington has levied against Canadian softwood lumber in retaliation for two alleged sins: charging low stumpage fees to forestry companies that log on Crown lands (which the U.S. interprets as an unfair subsidy) and allowing Canadian producers to sell their lumber in the U.S. at below-market prices.* These U.S. duties have wreaked havoc in the Canadian lumber industry, leading to increased costs for companies, a decline in exports, and significant job losses.

Many of the grand bargainists believe that an all-encompassing pact that combines economic growth and security could do away with these "protectionist sorties" by the U.S. and establish a more stable trade relationship.[10] But it is unrealistic to think that the U.S. government (where trade is a constitutional prerogative of Congress) will give up its sovereign right to apply these measures against its trading partners. In 2002, Congress granted President Bush the authority to enter into trade negotiations on its behalf (otherwise known as "trade promotion authority," or "fast-track authority"), thereby giving up its right to oppose individual items and suggest amendments. But while this authority means that Congress can only vote for or against a negotiated agreement, the president is still required to consult Congress, and the wider public, during the negotiations. As we have seen, those politicians who represent states with declining low-income sectors (such as agriculture or forestry) can use the consultation mechanism to oppose trade liberalization. Their overriding goal is to manage large-scale economic adjustments in ways that protect American workers and shift the burden to foreigners. Furthermore, because of traditional American suspicions about submitting to anything resembling supranationalism, it is unlikely that any new institution could be established to resolve trade disputes. Because of these two factors, Canadian officials

94

---

* Part of the problem is that Canada and the U.S. are speaking at cross-purposes. When Canadians talk about subsidy codes, they want rules that would still allow subsidizing within certain parameters (such as the subsidy code that already exists within the WTO). By contrast, when the U.S. speaks about subsidy codes, it essentially wants Canada to stop any form of subsidizing. Therefore, any one-on-one negotiation with the U.S. is likely to result in more restrictive subsidies codes than Canada would like.

failed in their efforts to secure exemptions from U.S. anti-dumping and countervailing actions during the FTA and NAFTA negotiations. And as a result, Canadian access to the U.S. market has been made "dependent on the goodwill and free-trading instincts of the American political process."[11] This goodwill has not always been forthcoming.

In sum, it's not so much that the existing set of dispute resolution mechanisms is bad, but that U.S. restraint and adherence cannot be guaranteed.[12] As long as we live in two separate nation-states, with two political and legal systems, there is a limit to how much control we can exert over each other's behaviour. Last time I checked, there were no Canadians sitting in the U.S. Congress and Canadians couldn't vote in U.S. elections. In the long run, it may be possible for Canada and the U.S. to develop a better and more predictable model of co-operation on trade—one that falls short of a full-blown institution but that captures some of the elements of the older joint commissions on boundaries and water.[13] But we should not hold our breath.

In the meantime, in order to address the continuing irritants in our relationship with the U.S., we need a dual-track strategy that *combines* bilateralism and multilateralism. First, we should work with the U.S. to carve out exceptions to trade-remedy law wherever we can. The steel sector, which is already highly integrated, is one candidate where such exceptions could be made. And second, where trade disputes cannot be avoided, we should build up precedents and case law through the WTO and the (less effective) NAFTA mechanisms for dispute resolution. The first element of this dual track takes shrewd negotiating; the latter requires patience. But there are payoffs: in May 2003, we saw a major step forward in the softwood lumber dispute with a WTO interim ruling in Canada's favour that questioned how the U.S. calculates its punitive duties. This was followed by a NAFTA ruling in April 2004 that called upon the U.S. Commerce Department to reduce its anti-dumping duties, and by a NAFTA panel discussion in August 2004 to reject the U.S. claim that its lumber industry is facing "material injury" from

95

Canadian lumber exporters. For many in the industry, these rulings prove that the U.S. case for duties is beginning to erode and that Canada was wise not to cave in to U.S. pressure to negotiate a deal.[14]* Similarly, in February 2004 a WTO panel ruled that the Canadian Wheat Board, whose existence has been challenged by the U.S. since the early 1990s as giving an unfair advantage to Canadian farmers, does not contravene international trade rules.

Above all, we need to remember that *we are not alone.* U.S. trade remedies also negatively affect other countries—so much so that they have become an agenda item in the current round of WTO negotiations (the Doha Round). In December 2003, European countries scored a major victory in their dispute with the U.S. over steel when the WTO ruled that Europe could retaliate against the Bush administration's efforts to protect the U.S. steel industry. For a president who has taken so much pleasure in wielding U.S. power, the WTO's ability to force a change in U.S. trade policy was doubly embarrassing. Canada needs to take note of this European success story and restore its faith in multilateral institutions as a way of managing trade disputes. Post-9/11, we have been too quick to assume that issues in the Canada-U.S. relationship can be handled only bilaterally.

The second topic on the Canada-U.S. trade and investment agenda is government regulation. Here, steps should be taken to minimize the different regulatory frameworks that exist in our two countries in areas such as product labelling, product approval, environmental standards, and health and safety. These differences—some of which are based on historical factors—force firms to go through regulatory hoops twice, thereby

---

* Prior to the NAFTA ruling, Washington made Ottawa an offer to abolish the 27 per cent duty placed on Canadian softwood lumber shipments in return for Canada's agreeing to a quota system that would see a reduction in our share of the U.S. lumber market, from 34 per cent to 31.5 per cent. While the Martin government was in favour of the deal, largely as a way to smooth Canadian-American relations, the Canadian provinces rejected it.

increasing their cost to operate in the larger Canada-U.S. marketplace. Two options exist for bringing regulatory differences closer into line: harmonization (adopting the same processes and procedures) and mutual recognition (accepting the other side's processes and procedures as sufficient). At the Monterrey Summit, Bush, Fox, and Martin agreed to press ahead in exploring these options for the automobile, food, construction, and consumer goods sectors. For its part, the Canadian government needs to determine which strategy, harmonization or mutual recognition, would best meet the interests of Canadian consumers and businesses in these particular industries. In so doing, we should glean as much as possible from the European Union's long experience of improving regulatory co-operation among its member states; indeed, as the EU enlarges to twenty-five (bringing in countries as diverse as Malta and Poland), there will be even more data to analyze and learn from.

97

The critics of regulatory co-operation will raise the spectre of a loss of Canadian sovereignty. But is this true? Do we cease to be sovereign by choosing to harmonize our standards and regulations with those of the United States? I would argue that this argument represents an old, twentieth-century logic of fear. Regulatory co-operation along the model I've described would in fact *enhance* our sovereignty: we would be exercising it confidently, for the benefit of Canadians.

There are, of course, crucial areas in which a public policy case can be made to retain a particular Canadian approach to labelling, approval, or health and safety. A few examples will illustrate my point. Consider tobacco labelling. Canada has taken a much more aggressive stand than the U.S. in the warnings we put on cigarette packages; based on recent reductions in the number of people smoking in Canada, this appears to be having some impact. Another example is our weights and measures system. I'm from the generation that spent its early years with inches and feet but now records its height in centimetres. As painful as the transition was for some of us, Canada is now comfortably metric, while the U.S. continues to hold on to the imperial system. Finally, even in the highly integrated automobile sector, there are some significant and justifiable regulatory differences. Canada requires daytime running lights on cars, while the U.S. does not. One might want to make a geographic case for this difference; those of us from Saskatchewan know how early darkness comes in the depths of winter. But there is also a straightforward safety argument: by making cars more visible, we reduce the number of head-on collisions.

For the sake of economic growth, we cannot and should not abandon our unique framework in these cases, or our particular view on the role of the state in the economy. Mutual recognition works only when the two sides see their priorities and policy choices as similar and trust in the ability of the other side to regulate to an equivalent standard. In some aspects of Canada-U.S. relations, the gulf between our two philosophies will be too wide to bridge.[15] But the default position should be harmonization and/or mutual recognition—unless a compelling reason for exception can be made. If over 80 per cent of our exports currently travel to the U.S. market, it's only logical that our regulatory regime be sensitive to requirements that exist in that market. We shouldn't reject U.S. standards just because they are American; instead, we should conduct a pragmatic cost-benefit analysis.

A third item on the agenda is rules of origin, which still exist as a result of preferential trade agreements that Canada (and the U.S.) has with non-NAFTA countries. For example, as a product moves from Canada to the United States, U.S. officials need to know the origin of that product in order to decide whether it gets in duty free (which would be the case if the product originated in Canada) or not (which would be the case if the product originated in, say, China, but has been transshipped through Canada). Where it gets even trickier is where a product is an amalgam of Canadian and Chinese components. Under NAFTA, a product has to be at least 50 per cent (or in some cases 60 per cent, depending on the product) Canadian for it to enter the United

States duty free. If there were no preferential trade deals, there would be no need for these rules of origin because all products (by definition) would face the same tariff treatment regardless of their national origin.

Sources estimate that the burden of maintaining a system of rules of origin is 3 to 5 per cent of the delivered cost of the goods—and 2 to 3 per cent of NAFTA GDP.[16] Thus, by moving to harmonize external trade barriers between Canada and the U.S. (and Mexico), we could significantly reduce the administrative costs faced by firms for customs inspections at the border.[17] Again, there may be important exceptions for us to consider. Let's take pickup trucks as an example. While the U.S. currently levies tariffs of 25 per cent on trucks coming from Asia, Canada levies 6 per cent. In this case, it doesn't make sense to harmonize our tariffs just for the sake of having a full customs union. Pragmatism dictates that exceptions should be made. Moreover, the three trade ministers from Canada, Mexico, and the United States rejected the idea of putting a common tariff wall around North America during a meeting in Montreal in October 2003 and stated their preference for concluding a free trade agreement across the western hemisphere. In the words of the former U.S. trade representative Robert Zoellick, "We've always been proud that a free-trade area doesn't necessarily raise a common barrier to the world."[18]

Finally, to enhance Canada-U.S. trade in services, more progress needs to be made on facilitating the movement of skilled labour within our shared economic space. This aspect of our free trade agreements is arguably the key to economic growth in the future. Highly skilled workers (from sectors such as IT, banking, and consulting) are a crucial ingredient in a twenty-first-century knowledge-based economy; constraints on their movement (such as work visas or professional accreditation) make it more difficult to develop new products and markets. Just as eliminating rules of origin would make it easier for merchandise to flow across borders, so addressing current standards and rules on professionals would make it easier to address labour shortages and barriers to labour mobility within the North American market. Canada and the U.S., as relatively decentralized states, face an additional problem: accreditation is in most cases a provincial or state responsibility. Consequently, professionals face almost as many challenges moving within their own countries as between them.

ENERGY

100 It's known as the butterfly metaphor for chaos: our world is so interconnected and so sensitive to small disruptions that a butterfly flapping its wings in Brazil can instigate a chain reaction of events that ultimately results in a tornado in Texas.[19] And so it was at 3:32 p.m. on August 14, 2003, that an overheating electrical transmission line sagged into a tree on the outskirts of Cleveland, sparking off a chain of events that culminated in the greatest power failure in North American history.

The failure of that one transmission line in Ohio proved critical because it produced a series of unusual power surges on neighbouring lines. These surges then prompted a cascading series of power lines to crash in order to avoid overloading and burning up. Cleveland began to drain huge amounts of power from Michigan and then Ontario, knocking out more power plants and pushing the crisis into New York. The power system in the state of New York responded, in an act of self-preservation, by sealing off its border with Canada, thereby creating a new problem. On that day, New York had relatively light internal demands for power. Without anywhere to send its excess supply, the New York system overloaded itself, leading to a general shutdown that affected close to 50 million people.[20]

A number of lessons have been drawn from the Great Blackout of 2003—about the perils of deregulation, the importance of investing in reliable transmission lines, and the need for fast and fluid communication between the organizations that operate along the electricity grid. But there was a broader lesson for Canadians and Americans: we are all on this grid together.

Canadian and U.S. officials initially clung to the old paradigm of self-contained borders and "national problems." As a result, they resorted to blaming each other for instigating the crisis rather than assuring their citizens with accurate information. As Thomas Axworthy quipped, "As in *South Park*, the knee-jerk response of New York politicians [was] to 'blame Canada.'"[21] But Defence Minister John McCallum also stumbled out of the starting blocks by inform-ing reporters that a fire at a nuclear power plant in Pennsylvania had caused the power outage. Luckily, cooler heads soon prevailed. Two days after the massive blackout, Prime Minister Chrétien and Presi-dent Bush announced the establishment of a joint task force to deter-mine the cause, co-chaired by U.S. energy secretary Spencer Abraham and Canadian minister of natural resources Herb Dhaliwal. The sup-posed national problem had been transformed into a North American problem.

In both Canada and the U.S., the outage has revived public pol-icy debates about the right energy policy for the future. In Wash-ington, President Bush used the crisis to press harder for a comprehensive energy bill that would authorize construction of a 3,600-mile natural gas pipeline, increase oversight of electrical transmission, establish energy reliability standards, and invest in energy production and research. One important element of his strategy is the plan to open the Arctic National Wildlife Refuge to oil drilling, a move that would automatically affect Canada, given geographical realities.

The United States is also slowly waking up to the fact that Canada represents one of its richest and most secure energy sources for the twenty-first century. Currently, we provide 100 per cent of electricity imports for the U.S.; in fact, some American communities are not on the U.S. grid at all, receiving their electricity exclusively from our sources. Canada is also the largest source of petroleum for the United States (at 17 per cent of U.S. imports) and has the second largest oil reserves in the world—ahead of Iraq and Kuwait.[22] U.S. domestic oil reserves, on their own, can supply that country's needs for only three to four more years. And despite some modest moves toward cleaner and renewable sources of energy, the U.S. is unlikely to be in a position to eschew oil imports for several decades—particularly given the lukewarm response of U.S. citizens to calls for energy conservation.

So does Canada represent Washington's new Middle East? Rice University geophysics professor Manik Talwani certainly thinks so. In an editorial in the *New York Times* (ironically, on the same day as the big blackout), he encouraged U.S. politicians to turn away from the geopolitical minefield of the Middle East and invest the capital needed to extract and refine oil deposits from the tar sands of Alberta. "Heavy oil will probably never be as cheap as Middle East crude," he wrote, "but it is much closer to home."[23] It has also made Canada into a rare commodity in the global energy market: a growth region in a market where most producing countries are past their prime or on the verge of declining output. Given the tight global supply of energy, the oil sands of Alberta stand out as a beacon of hope—they hold an estimated 175 billion barrels in recoverable reserves.[24]

After the 1973 energy crisis, when Arab countries imposed an embargo on exports of oil to the United States, Washington claimed it had learned its lesson and would reduce its exposure to such risks. Yet current U.S. dependence on oil imports (a quarter of which come from the Middle East) continues to place its economic and security interests in the hands of forces beyond U.S. control. According to one set of commentators, the problem with U.S. energy policy is reminiscent of Mark Twain's quip about the weather: "Everyone talks about it, but no one does anything."[25] The obstacles to developing a strategic and coherent energy policy are many, but the entrenched interests of the oil and transportation sectors of the U.S. economy are the most significant.

These lobby groups are coming under greater scrutiny, particularly given the U.S. public's growing concern about rising oil prices and the management of U.S. energy supplies.*

The question of *secure* energy access is therefore likely to dominate the U.S. political agenda for some time to come—with significant implications for U.S.-Canada relations. Some Canadian commentators, such as former Reform Party leader Preston Manning, have called upon our government to negotiate a continental energy security pact with the United States. If just a fraction of the U.S. budget spent on securing cheap Middle Eastern oil was devoted to northern gas and oil sands development, Manning argues, the United States would have a more secure petroleum source at lower costs.[26] Others, such as NDP leader Jack Layton, want Ottawa to take advantage of the U.S.'s precarious energy position. According to Layton, the Canadian government should tax U.S.-bound energy exports and use the revenue generated to offset economic losses in the Canadian lumber industry.[27]

How might Canada play its hand? Three facts should drive our policy-making: the reality of energy interdependence, growing concerns about global supply, and the urgent need to change patterns of energy consumption and invest in alternative energy sources. Currently, while the U.S. assumes reliable access to our natural resources, our own resource exporters don't always have secure access to the U.S. market. We need to ensure that openness works *both* ways. In other words, the resource and energy sector (which includes oil, natural gas, electricity, coal, uranium, primary metals, and forest products) should be one area where Canada chips away at U.S. trade remedies and pushes for unfettered and open markets. By appealing to wider issues of access and security, we should strive to convince the Americans to make exceptions in this vital sector and to work with us to develop

---

*A 2004 Ipsos-Reid survey commissioned by the Canada Institute of the Woodrow Wilson International Center for Scholars shows that 76 per cent of U.S. citizens fear they will be affected by a gasoline shortage.

compatible regulation in order to ensure the free flow of energy. This effort can and should include co-operation on energy efficiency, as well as research and development for new and cleaner fuel technologies. But again, the approach must be incremental: we should seek a series of internal bargains rather than negotiating any grand bargain.

And what about water? This is one area where Canadians have traditionally expressed reservations about free trade. It is a symbolic resource that seems to belie the formulas and calculations of the economists. My view is that secure resource pacts with the U.S. can and should exclude water. We can restrict such agreements to commodities where there is currently a high level of activity (such as oil, gas, electricity, minerals, and construction materials). To date, there has been very little trade in bulk water between the U.S. and Canada, and we manage our shared water resources through the International Joint Commission. I see no reason to deviate from this status quo.

Loonies and Sense

So far, my discussion of the Canada-U.S. economic agenda has left out one obvious element. That elephant in the room is our loonie. Is currency union with the United States the right answer for Canada? Before evaluating the arguments for and against currency union, let's be clear about what the stakes really are. The only real option on the table for Canada is dollarization (that is, the adoption of the U.S. dollar), not the creation of a new common currency—with a name like the "amero."

As I suggested earlier, the realities of power asymmetry within North America make the European model of integration of limited relevance here. Moreover, the origins of the euro are fundamentally political, not economic. While economic rationality played its part, the bigger driving force was idealism: the need for European countries to leave behind their history of bloody conflict and deliver greater peace, prosperity, and justice for their citizens. From that initial impetus, the original six member states (France, Germany, Italy, Belgium, Luxembourg, and the Netherlands) worked painstakingly to expand their areas of co-operation. Only when a political union had been created, under the 1991 Maastricht Treaty, was currency union seen as an achievable goal. All along the way, European leaders have been conscious of the unique organization they are building: one that is made up of nation-states that have their own individual interests but also share institutions that are concerned with furthering the interests of Europe *as a whole*. This sense of community makes the prospect of giving up strong national currencies, with long historical pedigrees, much more palatable.

Canada's situation is much different. We are not being asked to create something new and bigger with our North American partners. Instead, we are contemplating taking on the currency of our powerful neighbour. An analogy would be asking Poland to adopt the German mark.

The case in favour of letting go of our national currency has shifted somewhat since the (relatively) recent appreciation in the Canadian dollar, but its proponents are as determined as ever. Four main arguments stand out in the public debate.

The first argument raises concerns about the volatility of the Canadian loonie vis-à-vis the U.S. greenback. If you're a regular viewer of CBC's *The National*, you're used to seeing the regular instalments of the loonie soap opera. In the summer of 2002, it fluctuated around the 63-cent mark. One day it would creep above 64 cents U.S.; the next we would hear that it had been a "bad day for the dollar" and it had slipped somewhere into the low 62s. In the spring and summer of 2003, the loonie began its spectacular rise, reaching the peak of 85 cents U.S. in November 2004. (At the time this book went to press, the loonie had settled back to roughly the 79-cent mark.) The boost in value was due largely to the sluggish performance of the U.S. economy in the first half of 2003, to the massive and growing U.S. trade deficit (which reached US$42 billion in March 2004), and to the differences between Canadian and U.S. interest rates (something I will address later).*

Some argue that a low value of the loonie compared with the U.S. dollar isn't all bad. After all, it makes Canadian exports, such as cars, wheat, and lumber, cheaper for others to buy—thereby giving us a competitive advantage in trade. In 2001, our weak dollar also made it easier for Canadian companies to weather the economic downturn after September 11. For example, while the Canadian economy created almost 170,000 jobs during the first quarter of 2002 (100,000 of them in manufacturing), total U.S. employment in this period *fell* by 53,000.[28] Even in the first half of 2003, when Canada experienced the fallout from the SARS crisis, our healthy job growth rolled on. Since the rapid appreciation of the dollar, Canada has seen a drop in exports (especially in the automotive industry). This has led some to argue that Canada should dollarize in order to prevent the negative fallout from any further appreciation of the Canadian dollar.

On the other hand, a low loonie, relative to the U.S. dollar, makes imports more expensive for Canadians. This has been particularly costly in the all-important high-tech sector, which accounts for a large portion of our imports. The lower value of our dollar also makes it more costly for Canadians to take part in a global economy. Many of us have been there; travelling abroad, we find that our dollars translate into less purchasing power. If you have a penchant for shoes like I do, you stand outside the shop windows in Manhattan trying to rationalize how you can really spend *that* much on those great strappy sandals.

---

* It is important to note that the appreciation of the Canadian dollar is not occurring in a vacuum: European currencies have also been rising in value vis-à-vis the U.S. dollar since January 2002.

Canada's Robert Mundell, the acclaimed Nobel laureate in economics, was the first to point out that the cost of having a flexible
exchange rate (such as the current rate between the Canadian and
U.S. dollars) is a decline in real income for those with the weaker
currency. Imagine how you would feel if your wage rate were suddenly cut. Would you take it lying down? Or would you protest in
front of Parliament or use the next election as an opportunity to
voice your opposition? Mundell argues that Canadians have been
quietly accepting an equivalent kind of loss for the past twenty-five
years. During that time, our loonie has dropped from a rate above
parity with the U.S. dollar to one that, until recently, was barely
two-thirds of its value. In the process, our standard of living compared with the United States has eroded. Twenty years ago our
income was US$2,000 per person less than that of Americans; by
the year 2000 the gap had widened to US$7,600. The Conference
Board of Canada estimates that by 2010 that gap could rise to
US$12,000.

The view of many economists is that the low value of our dollar
hides deeper problems: our productivity gap with the United States
and our tendency to shield weak sectors of the economy. If Canada
and the U.S. had a monetary union, hiding our competitive weaknesses would no longer be possible and the cost of supporting unpro-
ductive industries would increase. Had Canada shared the U.S.
greenback over the past decade, economist Don McIver argues,
"more people would have been employed and regional labour migration would have increased. In a nutshell, the Canadian economy
would have been more like that of the United States."[29] Monetary
union with the U.S., so the argument goes, would force improvements in productivity and remove control over monetary policy from
the Canadian government.

The second argument for dollarization is about "spillover." Since
the Canada-U.S. economic relationship is already quite dense, isn't

currency union the next logical step in this process? As the Europeans argued, having free trade leads at some point to a common market, and having a common market leads at some point to a common currency.

Thanks to the Canada-U.S. Free Trade Agreement, goods, capital, and people frequently and easily cross our common border. In fact, given the tendency of companies to disaggregate their production processes, some goods pass back and forth several times at different points in the production cycle; automobiles are the most obvious example. Several Canadian-based companies already price their products in U.S. dollars and sell more of their product in the U.S. than they do here. Gaining even a small percentage point in market share in the U.S. can mean millions for a Canadian company. Given this level of integration, some argue, a common currency seems the only rational way forward.

In particular, economists have focused on something called "transaction costs": the costs incurred in exchanging currencies when travelling, trading, or conducting financial transactions across sovereign frontiers. Different currencies mean different interest rates. These rates often fluctuate, affecting the value of assets and liabilities. Insurance against those fluctuations comes at a price; trade and investment suffer from this added cost. A common currency would mean that those annoying American Express service charges and the premiums charged in debt markets would be wiped away. Investment and trade would become even easier.

The third argument in favour of currency union is that the world's foreign exchange markets are inherently prone to crisis. This leads to the kind of economic instability we saw during the Great Depression and the Asian financial crisis of 1997. Wouldn't it be far better to lock into a stable regime, with fewer managed currencies? The days of headaches and constant worrying, and the temptation to hide money under our mattresses, would be gone.

Finally, there is the current distrust of many in the Canadian elite of government management of the economy. These critics argue that our weak loonie buffers our economy from the effects of bad government policy—including taxation, regulation, and labour market policies. All of these policies, the argument goes, hold back Canada's competitiveness.[30] Rather than leaving the Canadian economy vulnerable to the possibility of poor leadership, it would be better to impose discipline from the outside through a fixed exchange rate system.

Is this case against our dollar watertight? I think the arguments can be challenged—keeping the loonie still makes the best sense for Canada. In fact, an in-depth 2002 report from the C.D. Howe Institute (usually noted for its pro-business orientation) questioned both the logic and the evidence that is presented in favour of abandoning our dollar, and concludes that "a separate, floating Canadian dollar is the best monetary choice for Canadians."[31] The counter-arguments I give below should remind us that none of this is a foregone conclusion: Canadians still have a *choice*.

To begin, let's remember that focusing on currency rates takes us only so far. Our lower living standard vis-à-vis the U.S. is not due primarily to a dysfunctional exchange rate. Instead, it is a function of two factors. The first is the greater weighting of primary commodities (such as oil, lumber, and metals) in Canadian output and trade. In other words, our reputation as "hewers of wood and drawers of water" is somewhat deserved. As a share of gross domestic product (GDP), the production of these commodities is about three times higher here than it is in the United States. Moreover, while Canada is a commodity exporter, the U.S. is a net *importer*. Although the Canadian economy has moved gradually away from the traditional dependence on the resource sector, it continues to be vulnerable (and, in particular, more vulnerable than the U.S.) to downward trends in the prices of these resources. The loonie has fluctuated as a result. The second factor behind our relatively weak dollar is what Conference Board of Canada CEO Anne Golden calls the "magnet effect" of the U.S. economy.[32] Up until 2002, the U.S. dollar appreciated against *every* major currency and was attracting investors from all over the world. The greenback is the major currency used for other countries' foreign reserves (especially in Asia), and 50 per cent of the world's trade is denominated in U.S. dollars. The Canadian loonie, like many other currencies, simply couldn't compete with the U.S. greenback in the world of highly mobile capital.

As for the argument about lagging Canadian productivity, we need to keep several things in mind. First, a common currency and fixed exchange rate will not necessarily solve the productivity problem. In Europe (where there is a fixed exchange rate), this has yet to occur. Similarly, countries that have dollarized (such as Panama) have not enjoyed the increased private-sector competitiveness that pro-dollarization economists predicted. Others, such as Ecuador, have suffered from the low exchange rate that was set for them, resulting in lower real wages for Ecuadorian citizens.

We also need to examine our alleged productivity gap with the U.S. a little more closely. The biggest differences in the productivity performance of our two countries are in the machinery and electronic equipment sectors. However, these sectors are relatively larger in the U.S. and have seen outstanding performance in recent years. Without correcting for this anomaly we risk distorting the problem. As the C.D. Howe Institute puts it: "Elsewhere, Canadian firms sometimes do a little better than their U.S. competitors and sometimes a little worse, but nowhere is the difference stark, particularly when allowance is made for the uncertainties that cloud the measurement of productivity."[33] In addition, Canada's productivity level fares very well when compared to countries other than the U.S., especially those in Europe.

Above all, we need to ask ourselves whether the U.S. productivity standard is really the one we aspire to. Let's understand what the productivity measure is: the business sector's output divided by the number of (declared) hours worked. This aggregate number, while useful, ignores other important economic and societal factors. Take the role of ideas and innovation: these may contribute to improved products and services, but because they can't be measured they are excluded from the equation. Aren't we interested in *quality* of output, rather than just quantity? Moreover, how do we adjust for the impact of technology? The party line in the U.S. is that productivity gains over the past decade are another benefit of the "new economy": the corporate world, by using technology, can squeeze more value out of the average worker. But this thesis should be taken with a grain of salt. How can we measure value added in the services sector, which in the U.S. employs almost 80 per cent of the private work force? For the services sector, the numerator in the productivity equation is measured by the salaries and compensation packages of workers, which is a questionable proxy for output. But the denominator is even more problematic: units of work time. The U.S. Labor Department has estimated that in sectors such as financial services, the average workweek has remained unchanged, at 35.5 hours, since 1988. But what planet have these statisticians been living on? With the development of laptops, cell phones, and Blackberries, today's service workers are always on call. The Labor Department has grossly underestimated the time actually spent on the job and overestimated productivity gains.

In reality, the U.S. productivity boom is "driven more by perspiration than by inspiration"[34]—a phenomenon that is increasingly having negative effects on the health of the U.S. labour force. In addition to burnout, the productivity measure provides incentives for downsizing. While the staggering productivity statistics in the United States are partly a result of solid output growth, the dominant factor is a decline in the number of labourers used. According to McGill business professor Henry Mintzberg, these kinds of corporate practices are virtually killing the American economy: "A sizeable portion of American business is now rotting from within, while the economy becomes more productive."[35] The workers who haven't received pink

111

slips are left to do more, often with less support. Yet it is the owners of company stock, rather than hard-working employees, who have reaped the real increases in standard of living increases. Does Canada really want to champion this model?

Beyond these issues of measurement and comparison, there is a second important argument against monetary union: the different economic priorities of Canada and the United States. To illustrate this point, recall the strong economic performance of Canada in 2002 and 2003. In both of those years, Canada's economic outlook was the strongest in the Group of Seven (G7) leading industrial countries. In particular, Canada's economy outperformed that of the U.S., as we finally reaped the benefits of a painful decade of deficit-cutting. While Ottawa has been running budget surpluses since 1998, Washington's deficit exceeded $150 billion in 2002, largely as a result of tax cuts and big spending increases. Astonishingly, it reached $412 billion in the fiscal year 2004. No wonder Jean Chrétien couldn't resist gloating over Canada's economic track record at the G8 summit in Evian, France, in 2003. Under a Republican administration, U.S. economic growth has slowed and unemployment has been on the rise. Thus, although Canada's unemployment rate is still slightly higher than that of the U.S., the gap is the smallest it has been since the early 1980s. Indeed, Canada's unemployment rate is at a level not seen in thirty years. These trends demonstrate that Canadian and U.S. economic cycles do not necessarily overlap: our government and central bank need the flexibility to make independent policies.

Part of the reason for Canada's economic success, according to Bank of Canada governor David Dodge, is our traditional preference for moderation. Because Canada's investment boom in the 1990s was not as high as that in the U.S., our economy did not have as far to fall or as much to recover.[36] In May 2002 Canada's financial renaissance was given the seal of approval by the powerful New York–based Moody's Investors Service; it upgraded Canada's credit rating to a top-notch triple A (a level our rating hadn't reached since it was downgraded in 1994). After years of hearing economists lament over how much "Canada sucks," it is nice to bask in some glory. In fact, the Economist Intelligence Unit declared in July 2003 that Canada will be the best country in the world in which to do business over the next decade. In the same survey, the United States tumbled out of the top spot into fifth position due to major imbalances in its economy, and weakening public finances.

This variation in economic performance explains why we saw the interest rate policies of Canada and the U.S. diverge in the post 9/11 period. Those who favour monetary union have a hard time accounting for this example of Canada's "monetary sovereignty." While the Bank of Canada (wisely) raised interest rates to slow down our economy, the U.S. Federal Reserve continued to let rates drop—down to an unprecedented 1 per cent. This aggressive rate-cutting led currency analysts in the summer of 2002 to suggest the unthinkable: that the era of the strong U.S. dollar might be ending.[37] Deficit spending, falling U.S. stock prices, and a ballooning trade deficit all combined to fuel a decline in the American dollar against currencies like the euro.

In sum, Canada's current monetary system (a national currency, flexible exchange rate, and Bank of Canada management) provides us with a robust toolbox to manage different economic performance levels and priorities. Do we really want to give up this important political and economic lever? The exchange rate allows us to adjust to shocks in the wider system, whether they are changes in the price of resources, fluctuations in productivity, or movements in international capital. It is no coincidence that the frontiers of currency markets are roughly analogous to the contours of sovereign countries.

As for informal dollarization (that is, Canadian workers or firms using the U.S. greenback), we need to be careful about exaggeration. As the C.D. Howe report shows, the degree of dollarization in Canada is actually quite modest. While it increased in the 1990s to about 10 per cent—largely as a result of the Free Trade Agreement—dollarization was actually higher at some points during the 1970s than it is today.[38] Furthermore, its increase seems to have levelled off. Interestingly, the depreciation of the U.S. dollar since 2002 has led some Canadian businesses to hold their assets in euros rather than U.S. dollars—even though they do almost no business with Europe. For their part, Canadians still by and large pay one another in Canadian dollars. And, of course, we still have an obligation to pay our taxes in loonies.

My third argument against dollarization draws on the different approach that Canada has taken to financial supervision. While this might seem like an obscure point, it has important implications for how banking and insurance are organized and regulated. For example, U.S. deposit insurance covers up to US$100,000 for each owner of an account, while Canada's insurance system covers only up to CDN$60,000 and is more restrictive in the amounts allowed to individual depositors. Experts believe that the U.S. approach is more vulnerable to "moral hazard"—that is, bad loans—and has given rise to crises such as the 1980s savings and loan scandal. Yet in a currency union with the U.S., Canada might have to adopt an inferior U.S. system.[39] It's also important to highlight the different institutional structures of the Canadian and U.S. central banks. The Bank of Canada is a federal Crown corporation that oversees a heavily concentrated banking industry; the U.S. Federal Reserve, by contrast, is made up of twelve district banks that in turn oversee hundreds of financial institutions. Given the American aversion to concentration in banking, Canada would again be pressured to give in.

A fourth element of the case against currency union relates to political accountability. Monetary policy matters to our everyday lives, whether we recognize it or not. Interest rate changes make mortgages more or less attractive, lines of credit more or less costly, and saving more or less lucrative. Given this impact, it seems reasonable that those who make the decisions about our dollar and our interest rate are accountable (even if indirectly) to Canadian voters. If Canada entered into currency union with the U.S., it is unlikely that the particular features of our economy would be taken into account in New York and Washington. We therefore risk being subjected to stimuli and depressants that are suitable to the U.S. economic context but not to our own.

At present, Canada's monetary system rests on the pillar of the Bank of Canada, which is answerable to Canadians through their elected representative, the minister of finance. For example, the finance minister and the Bank governor jointly set the current inflation targets of the Bank. So even in a world where the performance of the Bank of Canada was mediocre, there would still be good reasons to resist handing this mechanism over to a foreign body such as the United States Federal Reserve. The reality today, however, is that the Bank of Canada's performance is stellar and its credibility has never been higher. For the past six years, the Bank has consistently delivered on its promise to minimize inflation. This achievement—combined with the Canadian government's budget surplus, strong employment growth, trade surplus, and payment against the debt—makes the case for change hard to sell. The facts suggest that Canada has actually done a better job in recent years than the U.S. in managing fiscal and monetary policy. While the U.S. Federal Reserve has been struggling to restore investor confidence, its rate-cutting exercise seems to have had little of the stimulating effect on the U.S. economy that was expected.

These facts have not been lost on the Canadian public, which seems by and large happy with current monetary arrangements. An Ekos survey conducted in 2001 showed that only 21 per cent of Canadians believed that using the U.S. dollar would be advantageous, while 75 per cent indicated their preference to maintain the Canadian loonie.[40] Similarly, an Ipsos-Reid poll in April 2002 showed that while 66 per cent of Canadians viewed close economic ties with the

United States as a positive trend, only 23 per cent favoured entering
into monetary union with the United States. Seventy-two per cent of
Canadians indicated that they are content with the status quo: Canada
as an independent country with its own monetary policy.[41]

The final and strongest argument against dollarization has to do with
the United States government. It's simply not interested in monetary
union with Canada (or Mexico), and has absolutely no incentive to
change from its current position. American public opinion is similarly
unimpressed. In a spring 2002 survey by the NFO CF Group, 84 per
cent of American respondents rejected the idea of a new common currency for North America.[42] As the C.D. Howe report shows, this lack of
American interest means that Canada would have to sacrifice something to the United States in negotiation to achieve dollarization: "If
Canada seeks monetary integration with the United States, then it will
do so as a demander, and the United States will have no motivation to
make concessions to Canada in the monetary area without something
else being on offer."[43] Our water? Our cultural industries? This kind of
bargaining amounts to unconditional surrender. Small inflation-
plagued countries such as Ecuador and El Salvador have been willing to
make those kinds of concessions to the United States. But Canada—a
large, industrialized country with a stable banking sector and a skilled
central bank—has a wider array of options it can employ to produce
economic stability. For its part, the U.S. currently benefits from its
informal monetary hegemony, and its government sees little payoff in
formalizing monetary union, even with a country like Canada.

In conclusion, the only sensible path for Canada is to keep its loonie
and current monetary policy. We should be confident in this choice
and take note of the countries in Europe that have chosen to remain
outside the euro: Britain, Sweden, and Denmark. While it is still early
days, there is no evidence that these countries have suffered economically as a result of their decision to retain their own currency. Holding
to the loonie, however, doesn't mean clinging to the status quo.

Alongside this choice, we must continually improve our fiscal policy. We also need to invest in our global competitiveness in other ways—particularly by endowing the quality-of-life factors that make us attractive to investors, educated workers, immigrants, and refugees.

This distinction between quality-of-life and standard of living is an important one for Canadians to remember. An alternative measure to standard of living is the United Nations Human Development Index. Although Canada occupied fourth place in this index in 2004, it still ranked very near the top in the composite measure of life expectancy, education, and income per person. In particular, Canada was praised for its ability to minimize income inequalities through social policy. While countries in the OECD have increased incomes over the past two decades, most have also seen a widening gap between rich and poor. This is particularly true for the U.S., which placed sixth in the ranking.[44] Similarly, the Conference Board of Canada's *Performance and Potential* report shows that while the United States is a leader in standard of living among OECD countries, it has the highest rate of poverty, the highest crime rate, and one of the lowest rates of life expectancy.[45]

For those who truly aspire to the levels of wealth that exist in the United States, there may ultimately be limits to what Canadian policy-makers can do to provide for them. At some point, those individual desires must be reconciled with the objectives of a national community. I believe an obsession with having as high a standard of living as the U.S. blinds us to Canada's true mission as a country. It focuses us on getting rich, rather than on our shared history, culture, and traditions. That doesn't mean we shouldn't strive for the very best—to have globally competitive businesses, to engage in cutting-edge research in our universities, and to produce world-class cities to live and study in. But it does mean developing our own standard of excellence, one that encompasses all those measures of well-being, safety, and success that Canadians value. For those who remain committed to a country with a different approach to taxation, defence, immigration, health care, criminal justice, the environment, and much more, a lower per capita income than that which exists in the U.S. may be the price we have to pay for our choice. And to me, the price is well worth it.

A New Security Perimeter

It's become commonplace to describe today's U.S. government as obsessed with security. What we tend to forget is how relatively new this obsession is. Prior to the terrorist attacks on New York and Washington, the United States was reaping the benefits of its Cold War victory and its emergence as the world's only superpower. The most likely challenger, China, was still years away from amassing the kind of power resources possessed by the U.S., and the spectre of a monolithic Islamic threat was viewed by many as premature and exaggerated. With the discipline imposed by the communist threat now removed, the mantra of the Clinton White House was "It's the economy, stupid."

While terrorism had been identified as a security challenge for the U.S. well before 9/11,[46] the U.S. government responded to the attacks in an unprecedented way by placing threat at the forefront of Washington's policy-making. In fact, fear and threat—rather than power— are the main factors that have shaped the administration of President George W. Bush. There have been two main aspects to the U.S. response. The first, counterterrorism, has largely revolved around the new Department of Homeland Security—a mega-ministry of twenty-two previously existing agencies—and has produced policies in the areas of domestic intelligence, immigration and refugees, and policing. But counterterrorism has also had a more traditional foreign policy dimension, as evidenced by the campaign to root out al-Qaeda from Afghanistan in the winter of 2002. The second aspect, pre-emptive regime change, is a subject I deal with in later chapters, when I consider the implications of Washington's new foreign policy for the role of Canada in the world.

A LEAKY BORDER?

The television screen depicted Canada in an unusual light. The diverse ethnic neighbourhoods of Montreal and Toronto were portrayed as dark and dingy breeding grounds for terrorists. In place of fiddle music from the Maritimes, faint and meandering Arabic music served as the backdrop for a deep voice predicting future attacks on U.S. cities.

This was the 60 *Minutes* segment entitled "Al-Qaeda in Canada," which aired on CBS In April 2002. The program was a powerful illustration of the fear that permeates post-9/11 U.S. society and of the determination of its government to tackle any and all potential threats. In this broadcast, the source of those threats was us—the neighbour to the north. The program disparaged Canada for having the "most generous refugee system in the world" and for providing a sanctuary for foreigners on the run. It depicted our immigration policy as "ultra-liberal," criticized our social welfare system for tolerating abuse by criminal elements, and accused Canadian politicians of catering to the "immigrant vote."

The conclusion of 60 *Minutes*—that "liberal" and "generous" are synonymous with "security threat"—was too simplistic. It also demonstrates that our southern neighbours continue to misunderstand the nature of Canadian society and our sense of responsibility to the global community. Some of the concerns raised in the program were valid. Prior to September 11, Canadian officials did fail in their efforts to track and detain three North African men linked to terrorist activities, including Ahmed Ressam, the Algerian-born former Montreal resident who was later convicted in a U.S. court of plotting to blow up Los Angeles Airport. However, it is a stretch to draw the inference that Canada was somehow responsible for the breaches of security around

119

9/11. As John Manley correctly pointed out during the television program, the U.S. system itself is far from failsafe. All of the nineteen hijackers involved in the 9/11 attacks operated from a U.S. base. Manley was too polite to remind CBS that it was also the U.S. immigration system that mistakenly processed the visas of some of those terrorists—*after* they had already perished in the flames of the World Trade Center.

Canada should also resist any suggestion that it has failed to take counterterrorism seriously. It was Canada, after all, that pioneered a system in 1996 to place immigration control officers at airports abroad to prevent those with false documents from boarding aircraft. Other countries, including the U.S., have now followed suit. Since September 11, Canada has taken a number of positive steps, in cooperation with the United States, to decrease the vulnerability of our citizens to acts of terrorism. Border management has been the focus of that collaboration.

Immediately after September 11, delays at crossings along the 49th parallel stretched to twelve hours (and much longer in some places), forcing some manufacturers to temporarily shut down production in Canada. Billions of dollars were lost,[47] and border communities found their livelihoods in ruins. From this point onward, counterterrorism moved to the top of Ottawa's policy hierarchy. This was symbolized by the creation of the ad hoc Cabinet Committee on Public Security and Anti-Terrorism (chaired by Manley), as well as $7.7 billion of new funding in the 2001 federal budget to finance measures related to immigration, intelligence gathering, and border controls. In the period following 9/11, the Canadian government has taken a series of steps to decrease our country's vulnerability to internal and external threats while at the same time preserving vital economic links with the outside world: it has passed new anti-terrorism legislation, established a new process that can trigger the seizure and freezing of money and assets from suspected individuals, created new criminal offences for those who support terrorists, developed new tools to refuse or revoke charitable status for organizations with terrorist links, issued new

Canadian identification documents (including a Permanent Resident Card) to improve the chances of detecting terrorists seeking entry to Canada, and made improvements to port, border, and maritime security. The policy changes emanating from the Smart Border Declaration, signed in Ottawa on December 2001,[48] are particularly crucial to Ottawa's post-9/11 policy: five new Integrated Cross-Border Enforcement Teams including police, immigration, and customs officers; a huge infusion of cash to improve the infrastructure at Canada's busiest border crossings; a pilot project to fast-track the crossing of trucks carrying commercial cargo into either the U.S. or Canada (which later became known as FAST); and the NEXUS program, a series of fast lanes for low-risk, pre-cleared travellers who display digitally imprinted "smart cards."

Under the leadership of Prime Minister Paul Martin, further policy changes have been made, including the creation of a new Public Safety and Emergency Preparedness Ministry (headed by Anne McLellan), which oversees intelligence and security functions and co-ordinates border operations. Coming on the heels of Auditor-General Sheila Fraser's scathing report on the failure of federal government departments to collaborate on counterterrorism and emergency response, the establishment of this new ministry has been accompanied by intense scrutiny and high expectations. While much progress has been made, Fraser's analysis revealed that Canada's security apparatus continues to be plagued by inefficiency, bureaucratic overlap, and inadequate funding. In April 2004, McLellan's department tabled Canada's very first National Security Policy, which sets out an integrated strategy for meeting current and future threats to Canadians. The National Security Policy provides a blueprint for action in six key areas (intelligence, emergency management, public health, transportation, border security, and international security), and has invested over $700 million in a host of new initiatives—including the much anticipated Passport Security Strategy, which calls for facial recognition biometric technology on our passports.[49] The policy also recognizes that addressing twenty-first-century threats to Canadians will require the federal government to partner with the provinces, municipalities, the private sector, and key allies around the world.

A key impetus for all of these moves was undoubtedly economic: the potential loss in trade for Canada from a long-term border disruption is monumental. It had become clear that the mood in Washington, and Washington's attitude toward Canada, had fundamentally shifted and required a tangible response. A U.S. State Department report released in May 2002 claimed that one suspected terrorist per week had tried to cross the border from Canada into the United States.[50] But Ottawa's activism also reflects a recognition that all Western societies are to some degree vulnerable to terrorism. After all, Canada (along with other U.S. allies) has been expressly cited by Osama bin Laden in two audiotaped messages issued since 9/11. Finally, Canadian officials have been forced to admit that many of the world's terrorist groups, including al-Qaeda, have adherents in our country. In the words of former CSIS director Ward Elcock, "Our proximity to the United States, the openness of our society for the movement of both people and money, and our multi-ethnic population make our country one in which terrorists may seek to find a haven."[51]

As I showed in chapter 2, many in the Canadian elite condemn Canada's approach to dealing with the American giant as naive, fragmented, and too little too late. According to the grand bargainists, Canada's survival in a post-9/11 world demands that we offer up a new North American security perimeter aimed at preventing terrorists from penetrating the continent, in exchange for guaranteed access to the U.S. market.[52] What the example of the "smart border" tells me, however, is that Canadians already have the ideas, talent, and initiative to negotiate effectively with the U.S. More importantly, we can *lead* that bargaining process when changes south of the border threaten our vital interests. More of this kind of proactive policy-making will be needed in the twenty-first century as our relationships with our partners in North America become more dense and intricate. The challenge for our public servants and politicians is to ensure that measures to enhance security and maintain economic welfare do not jeopardize the "Canadian way" or the well-being of Canadian citizens.

The now legendary case of Maher Arar shows just how important it is to be vigilant about the potential downsides of the U.S. approach to immigration and counterterrorism. The Syrian-born engineer had been a Canadian citizen for more than a decade and had been travelling to the United States for business purposes for a number of years. But on a trip back to Canada in the fall of 2002, Arar passed through a New York City airport, and even though he was travelling on a Canadian passport, U.S. officials interrogated him for nine hours (without a lawyer present), held him overnight in an airport jail cell, and then transferred him to a detention centre in Brooklyn, where he was placed in solitary confinement. Shortly afterward, citing "reasons of national security," the U.S. government charged Arar on counts of immigration violations and belonging to a terrorist organization. He was deported to Syria, where he was jailed for ten months and allegedly subjected to torture. In January 2004, after Paul Martin and George Bush met at Monterrey, the Canadian and U.S. governments exchanged diplomatic letters, in which the latter formally pledged that, going forward, it would inform Canadian authorities immediately whenever a Canadian citizen is detained in the U.S. on security grounds. But this has been cold comfort to Arar, whose case was the subject of a lengthy judicial inquiry. Indeed, he argues that the Canada-U.S. consular notification agreement would not have changed what happened to him and still leaves Canadians vulnerable when they travel to the United States.

Some argue that a trade-off between sovereignty on the one hand and security and prosperity on the other is inevitable for Canada in a post-9/11 world. To me, it all depends on how we conceive of sovereignty. If being sovereign means absolute autonomy and independent decision-making, then clearly we have moved significantly away from that ideal. Under this definition, only Burma and North Korea could really be considered sovereign, since they have chosen to maintain absolute autonomy and independence in decision-making by shutting themselves off from the outside world. But if we adopt a twenty-first-century conception that acknowledges the need for interstate collaboration on joint problems and the possibility of shared interests and values, then the gains from co-operation need not come at the expense of sovereignty. Recent counterterrorism moves in the airline industry illustrate how we can achieve this balance.

Following 9/11, Washington asked Canada (and Mexico) to provide the U.S. with passenger lists for all flights coming from abroad into our country. In other words, these lists were to include not just those passengers who intended to transit into the U.S., but *everyone* landing in Canada—even if they never intended to travel to the United States. The concern in Ottawa, according to a well-placed civil servant, was sovereignty-related: we were being asked to share data on individuals, including Canadian citizens, who might never during their lifetime cross the border into the United States. In addition, the request gave the impression that Canada wasn't capable of taking care of its own security; Washington would have to step in for us.

The solution derived by Canadian and U.S. officials—which became fully operational in the spring of 2004—addresses these concerns. Canada continues to institute its own advance passenger information tracking system. Ottawa and Washington jointly agree on targeting criteria for high-risk passengers, but each country applies those criteria to its own data. When a particular individual's score places him or her in the high-risk category, information is automatically shared between Canadian and U.S. officials. So, for example, the United States gathers data on Joanne Smith, arriving in Boston, and determines (on the basis of intelligence information and past flights) that she is high-risk and should therefore be interviewed. This information is automatically passed on to the Canadians. In the event that an individual is close to but not over the risk threshold, the Canadian and U.S. systems communicate to determine if the other country has data on the individual that would put that person over the critical score level. The bottom line? Data is not shared between Canada and the U.S. except in cases of passengers in the high-risk category. Sovereignty concerns—not to mention privacy concerns—are met in a way that results in an equally good security outcome. This is a textbook case of how our countries can constructively work together without Canada compromising its citizens or its values.

Thomas d'Aquino, president of the Canadian Council of Chief Executives, would like the 49th parallel to become simply an "internal checkpoint" between the U.S. and Canada.[53] In other words, a North American security perimeter would present a hard shell to the outside world but have a soft and porous middle at the 49th parallel. But as long as we want two distinct political communities to exist— and Canadians loudly and clearly state that they do—we cannot have a perfectly seamless frontier. Nor can we provide a guarantee to the U.S. that our security provisions will operate successfully 100 per cent of the time. According to the Conference Board of Canada, "one successful terrorist, having crossed into the United States from Canada, would do immense damage to the American perception of a secure northern border."[54] This may well be true, but such fears cannot and should not dominate our policy-making.

The name of the game is risk management: not eliminating terrorism altogether—a goal that is ultimately unattainable—but significantly reducing its incidence and impact by marshalling the latest technology and using our limited resources to their fullest capacity. In the words of John Manley, "If our target is terrorists, then we are essentially trying to find a needle in a haystack. Part of the answer is to make the haystack as small as possible."[55] This is what security means in the twenty-first century.

Shrinking the haystack also requires us to rethink how borders operate in an interconnected world. George Haynal, an experienced Canadian diplomat with a deep knowledge of the Canada-U.S. agenda, describes it as "pushing the border outward": instituting new measures that will confront risks where they originate, well before they reach North America. This means enforcing global legislation on terrorism and crime, and sharing information with a variety of states about high-risk people and goods. Under this scenario, the Canada-U.S. border becomes one node in a global perimeter against threats to peace and prosperity.

It will always be easy for U.S. politicians to claim that security threats can come from Canada; there is no definitive way to disprove this. But what we can do is to continue to build trust in our risk-management procedures and to demonstrate that we are doing our share. In short, a zone of confidence rather than a security perimeter.

During the summer of 2003, in an incident widely reported in the U.S. media, Canadian officials detained nineteen students and immigrants from Pakistan on suspicion that they were part of an al-Qaeda sleeper cell. An investigation determined that the men had used fraudulent documents to obtain immigrant status and that one of them was taking flying lessons at a school near an Ontario nuclear power plant. "Based on the structure of this group, their associations and connected events, there is a reasonable suspicion that these persons pose a threat to national security," the official documentation recorded. Commentators in the U.S. applauded the work of the Canadian government. At the same time, however, a Toronto lawyer representing two of the suspects claimed that the police action was based on inconclusive evidence and smacked of racism: the men happen to be Muslim. (In the end, no terrorist-related charges were laid.) These contrasting views speak to the challenges that Canadian policy-makers confront as they seek to maintain a fine balance between addressing a more perilous security environment and welcoming those from outside our borders who seek safety and prosperity. Immigration and asylum-seeking is the policy sector where the balance between sovereignty and security will be the hardest—but most important—to maintain.

In a discussion with refugee workers and claimants in downtown Toronto in 2002, I was reminded of Canada's humanitarian tradition and reputation as an open society. The meeting, inside Massey College's beautiful Round Room, brought together a number of recent refugees from troubled zones such as Zimbabwe, Eastern Europe, and Columbia, all of whom had explicitly sought out Canada as their refuge. Some of the participants came from what the United States labels "terrorist countries." But from the harrowing stories I heard—most from women—there is little doubt that most fulfilled the internationally accepted definition of a refugee: a person with a well-founded fear of persecution based on race, religion, nationality, or political opinion.

    At the end of June 2002, Canada's new Refugee and Immigration Protection Act came into force. With its adoption, our government was given new tools to prevent those who pose a security threat from settling in Canada, including increased authority to arrest, new grounds for inadmissibility, and more resources for deportation. In addition, the negotiations spearheaded by Manley and Ridge produced a number of joint Canada-U.S. initiatives on immigration. Examples include information sharing on refugee claimants and asylum seekers, and the creation of common databases for immigration. The most significant initiative to date is the new Safe Third Country Agreement, which deals with the issue of refugee migration from the U.S. into Canada. In the year 2002, for example, 72 per cent of refugees making claims at our border crossings and airports came here from the U.S.—a significant increase from the previous year. The reasons these refugees cite for their movement? For some, it is a safer and faster asylum process in Canada; for others, it is an express desire to live in Canada, whether based on family ties or on perceptions of Canada as a safe and stable home. The new agreement means that most refugees who land first in the United States—recognized as a safe country—must apply for refugee status there. Those who come northward to Canada will be sent back to the United States.*

The Safe Third Country Agreement has been a policy objective of Canadian officials for some time and has reciprocal effects. Just as refugees arriving in Canada from the U.S. will now be turned back, so too will those arriving in the U.S. from Canada. For those in favour of the agreement, the major benefit is that it offers an opportunity for Canada to focus its refugee and asylum policy on those facing *imminent* threat, and to direct more of its energies to identifying the most needy refugees abroad. In short, refugee and asylum policy could become an integrated part of Canada's overseas aid and humanitarian policy.

From the point of view of refugees, however, this agreement has three major problems. First, it is far easier to travel to the United States from abroad than it is to Canada; there are many more direct flights to U.S. airports. This means that even if your final destination is Canada, you often access it from the south. Second, as Canada learned when it backed away from a similar agreement in 1996, U.S. Customs and Immigration actively uses detention as a means of deterring those seeking asylum. As one Canadian civil servant told me, "the U.S. immigration system is stuck in the nineteenth century. It's guns and sheriffs all over again." Those who arrive without documents are jailed—often in the same cells as people who have been convicted of major crimes. A highly critical report from the U.S. Justice Department's own inspector general concluded that the roundup of hundreds of illegal immigrants in the months after 9/11 was riddled with errors and led to many people with no connection to terrorism languishing in jails for an average of eighty days in unduly harsh conditions.[56] Finally, as refugee advocates in Canada have noted, the U.S. refugee system is more subject to the political biases of

---

* The agreement makes exceptions for people who have relatives in Canada, for those who make a claim at an airport or inland office, and for children.

the U.S. government, particularly with respect to those coming from South and Central America. According to critics of the agreement, refugee claimants will now have an incentive to enter Canada illegally from the United States, often putting their lives at risk. Refugee advocates are particularly concerned that the Niagara River will be a focal point for desperate attempts to cross into our country.

Measures such as the Safe Third Country Agreement bring into sharp relief just how difficult it is to balance security, prosperity, and sovereignty in a post-9/11 world. On the one hand, the terrorist attacks have reminded Western societies that openness and freedom of movement have a price. Today's security threats are more varied and more diffuse. Some of the plotters of deadly attacks on our citizens live among us or have crossed our relatively open borders. In response, most governments in the Western world, including our own, have put in place new legislation to make their own national citizens feel more secure. On the other hand, countries such as Canada have a reputation for opening our borders to those fleeing persecution in their homeland and to those seeking a new start. Furthermore, in the face of a rapidly aging population and a tumbling birth rate, Canada has an economic incentive to maintain an accessible system for would-be immigrants. The 1993 Liberal Red Book—the bible of the party's election victory—called for an increase in annual immigration levels in Canada to 1 per cent of the population, or 300,000 annually. During the past ten years, we have fallen short of that target. In 2002, for example, the goal set was lowered to 210,000 to 235,000 new immigrants. Some commentators insist that the current system will deliver the right size population for Canada in the next few decades.[57] But for those of us under forty, who have been paying into the CPP with little hope of being able to draw on it later, the spectre of a shortage of skilled workers and a shrinking tax base gives us the shivers. Not only will we be forced to pay more to support the baby-boom bulge, but there is also increased likelihood that there will be fewer Canadians in twenty-five years to support us.

Finally, there is the glaring hypocrisy of globalization: we welcome the free movement of goods, services, and capital, but not of people (unless, of course, they are investment bankers). In fact, historians have shown us that in terms of immigration, our societies are less open now than they were at the turn of the twentieth century.[58] Given the ever-growing inequalities in our global commons, isn't there also a moral case to be made for more free movement?

In the wake of 9/11, President Bush demanded an end to neutrality: you're in or you're out. If Canada gives in to the notion of a security perimeter and transforms its policies on immigration and refugee policy and on law enforcement, we are effectively putting ourselves inside the tent. As University of Waterloo political scientist Andrew Cooper writes, such a move sends out a signal to the world beyond North America—"one of contraction and a sense of identity that favours the depiction of a firmer 'us and them' view of the world."[59]

In the midst of the debate about North American security in the twenty-first century, some are tempted to forget our connections and commitments to those outside of this country and this continent. At times it can sound as if Canada's relations with the United States are not *really* foreign at all, but rather a natural extension of our domestic policy. But Canada's distinct refugee and immigration system reflects our nation's commitment to generosity, openness, and diversity. It has not only provided us with some of the building blocks of our country, it also continues to sustain and refresh it. There is no doubt our procedures could work better than they do—implementation of the strategy is far from perfect. But the overall direction is right. We must remain confident in this "Canadian way": it is a competitive advantage, and there is no compelling evidence to suggest that our procedures are less secure than those that exist in the United States. On this dimension, there can be no trade-off. Canadians are at home in the world, and the world is at home in Canada.

CHAPTER FOUR

A Middle Power?

D URING his first visit to Kabul, Christopher Alexander was
overcome with impressions, all of them unforgettable: a lat-
ticework of mud-wall houses; endless knots of young
children, with too much time on their hands; wall-to-wall poverty
and destruction; a surfeit of new building projects; and the raw, arid
beauty of the Hindu Kush. But one early observation had a special
significance for him: there were weapons everywhere. The city was
home to more than 500 operable tanks, artillery, armoured vehicles,
and missile launchers, most of which were outside national army
control. This is in addition to the countless burnt-out hulks—some
gathered together in football-field-sized scrap heaps—that testify to
the carnage wreaked by decades of combat.

At the ripe old age of thirty-five, Chris Alexander is Canada's
ambassador to Afghanistan—a job that is either enviable or unenvi-
able, depending on your risk threshold. A key element of his brief was
to oversee Canada's participation in the International Stabilization
Assistance Force (ISAF), the NATO-led effort to protect Afghanistan's new regime, led by Hamid Karzai, against the remaining warlords and Taliban forces who oppose him. When Canada joined ISAF
in July 2003, the task of demilitarization (an important requirement
of the Bonn Agreement, which established Afghanistan's post-
Taliban order) had not yet been addressed. Former commanders of the
Northern Alliance, a group that had waged a long battle against the
Taliban, were now prominent members of the government and continued to maintain units loyal to themselves within the bounds of the

city of Kabul. Most of these units possessed heavy weapons. Their aggregate strength went well beyond any force the new Afghan National Army could field and thus represented a challenge to the proposition that new state institutions in Afghanistan are now running and self-sustaining.

After detailed consultation with the Afghans and NATO allies, ISAF went to work on an inventory of heavy weapons in Kabul. This inventory was produced primarily by Canadian staff officers, using a variety of tools. By December, the first heavy weapons had moved into cantonment (storage) as part of a pilot project for downsizing. By the middle of June 2004, over three-quarters of the original 500 heavy weapons were in cantonment. As Alexander explains, the power of the warlords is based on the military force they command. Therefore, "heavy weapons cantonment strikes at the heart of their power and deprives them of the ability to threaten communities with the kind of devastation visited upon Kabul during its long civil war."

But the impact of disarmament and weapons cantonment goes even further. The process also has implications for the political calculus in Afghanistan: warlords who agreed to decommission units and to give up heavy weapons would expect political rewards during the country's upcoming elections (which have been postponed twice due to security concerns). On the other hand, those who refused to disarm would risk either censure or irrelevance to Afghanistan's future. Second, demilitarization of principal regions beyond Kabul, such as Jalalabad, Kandahar, and Gardez, might be destabilizing in the absence of Afghan National Army units to deploy in those areas. In sum, the disarmament process would be complex, would require sustained commitments of resources and policy co-ordination among ISAF members, and would have a direct bearing on the new political landscape.

Within this confusing mix of forces, it was clear for Chris Alexander what Canada's contribution would be. With Japan the lead nation for disarmament overall and the United States set to be a key source of finance, Canada—with its previous efforts in heavy weapons canton- ment, its key place in ISAF, and its lead-nation role on mine action— would naturally take on a major part in the peace-building script. But, in Alexander's words, "the challenge would go well beyond any- thing our soldiers and military-political analysts had faced in the Balkans, Africa, or elsewhere in the world." In short, this is a peace- keeping exercise that Lester Pearson would barely recognize. Canada's participation in the Afghan mission is symbolic of the new roles we are being called on to play in the post-9/11 security environment. 133

Diplomats like Chris Alexander are the heirs to a precious tradition in the annals of Canadian foreign policy: the tradition of Canada as a mid- dle power. It was after World War II, when the tectonic plates of the international system shifted and a bipolar division between commu- nism and capitalism emerged, that the term "middle power" became a standard feature of the diplomatic lexicon. The United Nations Security Council formally recognized the great powers of that time— the United States, the Soviet Union, Britain, France, and China—by giving them veto-bearing permanent seats. But this put the status and relevance of "second-rank" states, such as Australia, Canada, India, and Mexico, into jeopardy. If the world after 1945 was made up only of great and small powers—a view that enjoyed a certain popularity with the Permanent Five—then how could those with a past reputation for and interest in international governance justify their seats at the table?

For the past half a century, the "middle power" tag has been Canada's answer to this dilemma. Our country lacks the economic and military capabilities of a great power. We do not seek superiority over our neighbours, nor do we inspire jealousy and suspicion. But neither are we at the bottom of the heap. To put it another way, while we cannot do some of the things that great powers can do, we can do things that smaller powers cannot do.[1] By taking advantage of this ambiguous position within the international hierarchy, Canada has gone a long way. The language and practice of middle power diplomacy has justified our country's attainment of disproportionate influence in international affairs and has given us a distinctive national foreign policy brand.[2]

Post-war history illustrated that Canada, through skilful diplomacy, can punch above its weight and exert a degree of influence on the international stage. Whether it was introducing the very first UN peacekeeping force in the Sinai desert in 1956, designing a new aid program for the Third World in Colombo in 1952, participating in the talks that led to the General Agreement on Tariffs and Trade, or being present at the creation of NATO, Canada's early post-war diplomats—whom Andrew Cohen aptly calls the "Renaissance Men"[3]— pulled our country out from under the shadow of the British empire and established it as an independent force in international politics. Lester B. Pearson, our most famous foreign affairs minister to date, epitomized this middle power practice. "Wherever he went in the world," Cohen writes, "the lisping, bow-tied Pearson was the embodiment of the Helpful Fixer and the Honest Broker."[4] By 1967, Canada's centenary, our new reputation and identity had been solidified. As the *Economist* (one of the pillars of British journalism) would proclaim in that year, "The community of nations has learned that it needs an active Canada."

During the frosty decades of the Cold War, the role of a middle power seeking to find a niche between the United States on the one hand and the Soviet Union on the other made a lot of sense for Canada. It might even have had a degree of utility in the early years of the 1990s, as the world was adjusting to the breakup of the Communist bloc, focusing on the world economy, and building new forms of international collaboration. But it is time for Canada to finally shed its middle power syndrome. The transformation of the international context, combined with changes within our own country, has made this depiction of our place in the world anachronistic. More importantly, the essence behind middle powers (the origin of the term can be found in the Italian *potenze mediocre*[5]) is second best. Mediocrity. Canada has been far too self-conscious as an international actor, regretting rather than accepting its inability to be a great power. The result has been an endless quest to prove our good international credentials. In this new century, Canada must think less about whether it is a great, middle, or small power, and more about the kind of power we wield, where we can best wield it, and for what purposes.

135

2005 vs. 1995: A Changing Global Context

A decade ago, the Department of Foreign Affairs and International Trade in Ottawa engaged in a full-scale review of our country's foreign policy. Entitled *Canada in the World*, the 1995 study took stock of the global contextual changes that had accompanied the end of the Cold War and identified three key goals for Canada to pursue internationally: the promotion of prosperity and employment, the protection of Canadian security within a stable global framework, and the projection of Canadian values and culture abroad.

There is a whiff of idealism, even triumphalism, about *Canada in the World*. Written soon after the West's victory over communism, its language is a quaint reminder of the trends and assumptions that dominated the 1990s.[6] Most significant among them was the phenomenon of globalization and its two associated tenets: first, that economic power rather than military might would define international politics; and second, that authority was draining away from the nation-state as its prerogatives and functions passed to subnational and supranational actors. The document rightly noted that the old bipolar world had disappeared in the wake of communism's collapse but that a new world order had yet to take hold. New centres of power and influence seemed to be emerging, such as the economic "tiger states" of Asia, and the agenda of international relations was believed to centre on creating a better, freer, and fairer environment for trade and commerce.

Some of the predictions that shaped this foreign policy review have come to fruition, while others have been challenged by the events of 9/11. There are myriad developments and forces that have arisen in the past decade, including the growth and diversification of non-state actors, the acceleration of the technological revolution, and the changes in the nature and conduct of war. But I will focus on five main changes in the global landscape since the publication of *Canada in the World* that will have a particular impact on the shape of our foreign policy. They have to do with security, power, governance, allies, and empire.

IT'S SECURITY, STUPID

Bill Clinton's campaign for the U.S. presidency in 1992 employed a now famous phrase in its attack on George H. Bush: "It's the economy, stupid." While Bush had waged a successful war to oust Saddam Hussein from Kuwait, the U.S. economy had sputtered through his time in the White House. The American people punished him on election day for (literally) failing to deliver the goods. Clinton's move into the Oval Office coincided with the biggest economic boom in the U.S. since the Second World War, with ramifications for economic growth around the globe. According to the drafters of *Canada in the World*, influence in international affairs now depended increasingly "on the strength of economic relations." The industrialized West had struggled through a painful recession (in fact, Canada had endured two of them) and was now set for a decade of prosperity.

Coinciding with this focus on economic power was a love affair with the private sector. Business, not government, was the centre of the action. The story goes that in the first year of Clinton's presidency, his feisty campaign manager, James Carville, claimed that if he were reincarnated he would want to come back in the next life not as the president or the pope, but as the bond market—because that was what really ruled the world.[7] During the 1990s, millions of citizens in Western democracies opted for private solutions to their retirement needs by investing in mutual funds (for the more prudent) and the stock market (for those with a higher "risk tolerance"). Many of them saw unprecedented returns on their investments. But in addition to fuelling a massive rise in living standards in the Western world, the private sector served as the model for how to structure organizations and societies. Workers from the public and non-profit sectors sat through endless seminars on how to infuse their departments with efficiency and entrepreneurialism. Economists drafted elaborate plans for how to bring the market economy—the magic solution to all political and social ills—to the societies of the former Communist bloc.

As we entered the new millennium, the halo around the private sector and the free market began to show some cracks. The first was the bursting of the dot-com bubble and the accompanying plummet in stock market value. The second was the uncovering of scandal and corruption within some key players of U.S.-style capitalism. Questions began to be asked about the foundations of global capitalism, the purpose and leadership of corporations, and the role of the state in Western liberal democracies.

The events of 9/11 served as the biggest "correction" to the 1990s obsession with globalization and wealth creation. There is the obvious fact that the terrorists targeted the seat of economic power in the U.S.—the financial district of New York City. And they did so by turning all of the celebrated tools of globalization against us: airplanes, electronic banking, and e-mail. But more significant was the ascendancy of security to the top of the hierarchy of public concern.

The scenes of firefighters and police officers rushing into the World Trade Center to rescue pinstriped traders and investment bankers was a poignant reminder of the critical safety net that is provided by *public* institutions. In the end, no amount of wealth can buy security.

While the public policy pendulum has swung back toward security, we are finding ourselves on rocky terrain. The current security agenda is focused largely on so-called new threats, particularly those emanating from global terrorist cells. In contrast to the twentieth century, when security threats came in the form of an adversary's army amassing on your borders or building up its conventional or nuclear arsenal, the perpetrators of today's challenges are largely non-state actors. As U.S. secretary of defence Donald Rumsfeld continually reminds the American people, the war against terrorism is a completely new kind of battle, where the enemy is everywhere and nowhere and where action is required on a variety of fronts: cutting off financial flows to terrorist groups, beefing up intelligence-gathering, building new political coalitions, and investing in niche military capabilities to root out terrorists from their hiding places. In addition to terrorism, a host of other security threats have been identified as priorities in the twenty-first century: organized crime, weapons of mass destruction, "failed states," mass migration, and international disease.

In reality, these "new threats" are not so new at all. Terrorism has been a force in international politics at least since the early 1970s—and arguably before. Living in Britain during some of the darkest years of the conflict in Northern Ireland, I experienced my share of evacuations from movie theatres and underground trains and kept a watchful eye for stranded suitcases in railway stations. In addition, during my time in the Policy Planning Staff of our Department of Foreign Affairs in 1993–94, countless documents crossed my desk warning of the security challenges posed by criminal organizations, the spread of nuclear, chemical, and biological weapons, fractured and collapsed states in the developing world, illegal migration, environmental degradation, and virulent strains of viruses, such as HIV/AIDS.

Academics, policy-makers, and politicians were aware of the changing nature of security well before 9/11. But we failed to act upon that knowledge. Government departments and international organizations were still largely designed to counter the old threats—as the scathing assessments of the CIA and FBI after September 11 have since revealed. As a result, the danger posed by international terrorism became even more ominous during the course of the 1990s, while particular features of globalization, such as improved communications technology, enhanced terrorism's organizational and destructive powers. Today, our lumbering bureaucracies are finally adjusting to the realities of this globalized and networked world, where power and violence are no longer organized in the familiar hierarchical ways and where our opponents no longer need states in order to act on the international stage.[8] Though the names applied to policy-making still carry twentieth-century overtones (consider, for example, the National Security Strategy of the Bush administration), the twenty-first-century framework for thinking about security is what those in the field call "intermestic" (a combination of international and domestic factors). Security concerns that were previously considered national, such as policing and immigration, are becoming increasingly central to our foreign and defence policies.

Even though the threats to our security are new and more menacing, some of the fronts we are battling them on hark back to the past, when defence policy meant the protection of our own territory. Prior to 9/11, few analysts of foreign affairs predicted an attack on North American soil. Security was something we pursued and projected "out there," beyond our shores. But in the aftermath of the terrorist attacks, the entry points to the U.S. and Canada have once again become a key focus of our concern: border crossings, seaports and airports, even the Arctic frontier. This re-engagement with what the U.S. calls "homeland security" has reminded citizens that threats to security can be both local and personal.

A NEW DISTRIBUTION OF POWER

The second key contextual change since 1995 relates to the layout of our international chessboard. The gap in power between the world's greatest power, the United States, and all the others has become so wide that we have entered into a structure unprecedented in the history of the modern states system: unipolarity. Even the great powers of previous centuries, such as Britain, never enjoyed the kind of power currently possessed by the United States. In its heyday, for example, Britain had a smaller army than those of its continental neighbours and was therefore always vulnerable to challenge. Today, depending on which measure you believe, U.S. military spending exceeds that of the next *twenty* countries combined. In addition, the U.S. economy is the largest in the world, and the main source of technological innovation.

What is even more striking about our unipolar system has been our reluctance to acknowledge it. Charles Krauthammer, a neo-conservative columnist for the *Washington Post*, heralded the "unipolar moment" in 1990, shortly before the collapse of the Soviet Union.[9] But at that time, his description of the international system was rejected as overly optimistic and tinged with American exceptionalism. At the beginning of the 1990s, scholars and pundits were predicting instead a new multipolar world, with states such as Japan, Germany, and China rivalling the United States.

The 9/11 attacks and their aftermath snuffed out any remnants of the multipolar thesis. As Krauthammer reminds us, three phenomena in the days and months following the terrorist attacks on New York and Washington confirmed—for those with any remaining doubts— the reality of U.S. dominance. The first was the bold demonstration of

American military power in the campaign against the Taliban and al-Qaeda in Afghanistan. Even in the Kosovo War of 1999, which the U.S. fought with its NATO allies, the Pentagon had not fully unleashed its war-fighting potential. But in December 2001, it left nothing to chance. While victory was never in doubt (who, for example, was really impressed by the U.S. claim on Day 3 of the campaign that its forces had achieved "air superiority" over a poor and isolated country like Afghanistan?), the display of America's destructive power was stunning. A medieval society and infrastructure was bombed into the Stone Age. Second, September 11 illustrated the "recuperative power" of the United States. Its economy rallied, symbolized by the reopening of the New York Stock Exchange, and its politicians united to provide financing and leadership for the new war on terror. Finally, America's circle of allies was substantially widened. Those who had shown a degree of ambivalence toward the U.S. during the 1990s, including China, Russia, India, and Pakistan, realigned themselves toward it after September 11.[10] Not only was the U.S. the world's unrivalled superpower, but it also convinced some of its traditional enemies to support its hunt for al-Qaeda.

Of course, the change in the distribution of power that has produced unipolarity does not tell us everything about our twenty-first-century world. The structure of the game goes only partway to predicting or explaining how the players conduct themselves. We must also consider what sort of superpower the United States is likely to be, and who will define its objectives. Will it be an assertive power, which is blind to the views and interests of its allies and which acts in defiance of international institutions, or will it be more of a multilateral leader, which is sensitive to allied concerns, builds consensus, and works through institutions?[11] To date, it is the Republican administration of George W. Bush that has given shape to U.S. unipolarity. Led by an influential cadre of neo-conservative advisers, the Bush White House has articulated and pursued a variety of doctrines

141

since 9/11: "You are with us or against us," pre-emptive action against states harbouring weapons of mass destruction, and, most recently, regime change. But we must be careful about assuming that this particular flavour of unipolarity is inevitable or permanent. The U.S. will undoubtedly continue to lead in the twenty-first century. *How* it will do so is a topic for deep and considered analysis that avoids simplistic categories such as "rogue superpower."

Before moving on, let me highlight two other facets of the distribution of power that have implications for Canada in this new century. First, there has been a shake-up in the lower ranks of the power hierarchy since 1995. China and India remain important regional, and potentially global, powers and partners for Canada. But some of the new centres of power predicted in *Canada in the World* have risen and fallen with remarkable speed, particularly in the wake of the 1997 Asian financial crisis. Neither Japan nor the so-called tigers of East Asia have proven to be a serious rival for the United States. Similarly, the promise of powerful Latin American states, such as Brazil, Argentina, and even Mexico, has been largely unfulfilled; the late 1990s and the early years of the twenty-first century have seen a reversal of their economic fortunes. And then there is South Africa—the state that was heralded in the mid-1990s as the new superpower for Africa. It too has suffered decline in the past decade, most notably as a result of the devastating HIV/AIDS pandemic.

The second point to underscore is the substantial change in the notion of power itself. According to the dean of Harvard's Kennedy School of Government, Joseph Nye, power—and our measurement of it—has become a contested concept in international relations today.[12] If power is associated with the possession of certain resources (population, territory, military strength, economic size, culture, and so on), then it is clear that the U.S. is the world's unrivalled superpower. But it is less clear how we should categorize other states. While some might be considered great in economic terms (such as Germany) or in population (such as India), they may not necessarily be granted that label in military terms. Similarly, while certain components of "hard power" remain essential to superpower status (such as nuclear weapons), other features of what Nye calls "soft power" are becoming more decisive as states seek to convert their power resources into effective influence. Just look at the track record of the United States in post-war Iraq: to "win the peace," the U.S. has had to show as much skill in using soft power as it did in using hard power to win the war.[13] As Nye demonstrates, the most effective power is often not commanding or coercive, but rather indirect or co-optive: getting others to want what you want.[14] Nye believes that the Bush administration's National Security Strategy focuses too heavily on using the U.S.'s hard power to force other nations to do its will and pays too little heed to the soft-power resources that will help prevent terrorists from recruiting new supporters and that will help us deal with the global problems that require multilateral co-operation.[15] Some Canadian commentators, such as former foreign affairs minister Lloyd Axworthy, extend this logic and argue that Canada should seek to develop and harness its soft-power resources. But as I will show later, we cannot rely on soft power alone. A more sustainable strategy for Canada is to reinvest in certain military, hard-power resources marshalled against a new set of civilian objectives.

A CRISIS OF LEGITIMACY

The third important contextual change is the current crisis of legitimacy in international organizations. For Canada, a country that prides itself on multilateralism, this development is especially worrying. Many of the tried and true organizations that defined Canadian foreign policy for the past fifty years—including the United Nations, NATO, and the WTO—are facing uncomfortable questions about their relevance, effectiveness, and accountability. Consequently, it is no longer good enough to describe our country (in the words of *Canada in the World*) as a "champion of constructive multilateralism" if our current multilateral structures are in trouble.

The first target was the WTO. At the Battle of Seattle in 1999, the efforts of trade officials to complete the next round of trade liberalization came up against an angry crowd of protestors who questioned not only the substance of that agenda, but the right of the WTO to set it. Increasingly, the WTO is issuing regulations that directly affect the domestic politics and societies of its members. Yet it does so in a highly secretive and politicized setting where there are disparities in negotiating strength and unequal access to information and specialist advice during the conduct of trade talks.[16] As the non-governmental organization Christian Aid points out, at the WTO meetings held in Doha the European Union had over 500 delegates present, while Haiti had only one. Critics insist that the "democratic deficit" within international organizations—that is, their failure to reflect and serve the interests of all the world's citizens—is jeopardizing their authority and capacity to govern the global commons. The breakdown of WTO talks in Cancun in September 2003 saw developing countries, for the first time, band together to challenge the West's domination of the trade liberalization agenda.

Criticisms about accountability and transparency also surfaced during the diplomatic crisis in the UN over Iraq in the spring of 2003. One of the major roles of the United Nations in international society has always been that of collective legitimizer.[17] States (particularly democratic ones) not only take great pains to justify their foreign policies to their domestic population, but also are conscious of the need for broader approval for their actions. British-led efforts to obtain a second Security Council resolution authorizing the use of force against the regime of Saddam Hussein are a powerful illustration of this trend. Nonetheless, a number of factors have created a tension between the Security Council's legal authority (as laid out in the UN

Charter) and its legitimacy in the eyes of international society. These include the slowness of Security Council decision-making; the under-representation of key regions on the council, such as Africa, South Asia, and Latin America; the right of the Permanent Five to veto actions that affect their national interests; and the secretive political bargaining that occurs in the hallways of the UN's offices in New York. Interestingly, some commentators suggested that even if the second resolution on Iraq had been approved by a majority of Council members in 2003, the horse-trading and political coercion necessary to achieve this result would have damaged the resolution's legitimacy. In other words, the *quality* of votes—including how they are achieved—is as important as their quantity.[18] Recent allegations on the part of states such as Mexico that the U.S. and Britain may have been spying on meetings where compromise solutions to the stalemate over Iraq were being discussed only adds to the view that UN processes are in need of rewiring.

Finally, there is the nagging question of why we should put so much stock in the endorsement of an organization that is populated by states that may not share our values. After all, the UN Security Council is only as good as the states that compose it. And the states that sit around its table—the victors of the Second World War—carry their own national interests and values with them. Charles Krauthammer puts the point even more provocatively: "Why it should matter to Americans that their actions get a Security Council nod from . . . the butchers of Tiananmen Square is beyond me."[19] A similar kind criticism was levelled at Prime Minister Chrétien when he withheld Canada's support for the U.S.-led war against Iraq in light of the failure to get a Security Council mandate. According to some, Chrétien was effectively saying that if China—a state with a less-than-stellar human rights record—supported the action, so would Canada. For proponents of the U.S.-led war against Saddam Hussein, the diplomatic manoeuvring that tried to avert it was a thinly veiled attempt to thwart America's legitimate ambitions. And those who led that effort, according to *National Post* columnist Andrew Coyne, no longer deserve to share a seat with the U.S. in multilateral forums: "The United States is prepared to listen, in other words, to those who have earned its trust: who have shown they mean it no ill, are prepared to work with it constructively, and have something to offer in return. The United Nations can no longer serve as an effective sounding board, for it is composed, in the main, of countries that meet none of these criteria."[20] Coyne's alternative, a "Council of Free Nations," would admit as members only those states committed to democracy and human rights, willing to contribute to the defence of the free world, and prepared to acknowledge U.S. leadership of the international system.

146

The critique of today's international organizations can be answered. There remain good reasons, as I show later, why Canada should continue to invest in and work through them. But the old answer— "because we are good multilateralists"—just won't cut it any more. We need to explain to others, and to ourselves, why we seek to work through international institutions such as the WTO and the UN. We also need to be willing to work outside them, or to lead efforts to reform them, when they fail to meet the challenges of the twenty-first century.

A DIVIDED WEST

The fourth major change in the global landscape since 1995 is the transformation of what we have traditionally known as "the West." Some of this change was bound to occur. The discipline of the Cold War bound the liberal democracies of Europe and North America together, submerging their differences under a broader banner of anti-communism. It was the West's solidarity, coupled with its attractive model of freedom and prosperity, that proved such a powerful magnet for the former satellite states of Central and Eastern Europe. But could such a high level of consensus survive the fall of the Berlin Wall?

In the early years of the post–Cold War period, the unity of the West remained largely intact. Big projects needed our concerted effort: the reunification of Germany, the expansion of NATO, and the intervention against the forces of nationalism and tyranny in the former Yugoslavia. But as the twentieth century gave way to the twenty-first, the gulf between the two sides of the Atlantic seemed wider than ever. In spite of the genuine outpouring of sympathy and support from Europe after September 11, relations between the U.S. and its European allies became increasingly strained. Bones of contention included U.S. steel quotas, peacekeeping arrangements in Bosnia, U.S. opposition to the Kyoto Protocol and the International Criminal Court, the treatment of al-Qaeda detainees at Camp X-ray, and, of course, the U.S.-led war in Iraq. It is the different views on the best strategy for combatting global terrorism, according to former U.S. secretary of state Madeleine Albright, that have had the greatest impact on transatlantic relations: "Osama bin Laden has been able to do something that forty years of communism were not able to do, which is to divide Europe from the United States." A year after the conclusion of military hostilities in Iraq, European dissatisfaction with U.S. foreign policy remains. Indeed, research shows that Europeans' lack of trust in the commitment of the U.S. to democracy and freedom is growing rather than diminishing, and that there is greater support for a European foreign and security policy independent of the United States.[21]

The rift over Iraq—played out in front of the TV cameras in New York and Brussels—gave rise to unprecedented levels of name-calling on both sides of the Atlantic. While France and Germany accused Washington of recklessness, the U.S. began an active campaign after the war to "punish" those states that refused to join its coalition to unseat Saddam Hussein. Anti-Europeanism joined anti-Americanism as a disturbing feature of transatlantic relations. As British scholar and journalist Timothy Garton Ash has noted, there is strong sexual imagery associated with the current transatlantic skirmish. "If anti-American Europeans see 'the Americans' as bullying cowboys," Garton Ash writes, "anti-European Americans see 'the Europeans' as limp-wristed pansies. The American is a virile, heterosexual male; the European is female, impotent, or castrated. Militarily, Europeans can't get it up. (After all, they have fewer than twenty 'heavy lift' transport planes, compared with the United States' more than two hundred.)"[22]

148   Above and beyond the rhetoric, Europeans and Americans are also pursuing different policy agendas. As the United States finishes its war in Baghdad, Europeans debate admitting Iraq's Muslim neighbour, Turkey, to the European Union. While Washington supplies Israel with loans and sophisticated weaponry, the European Union underwrites the Palestinian Authority and pays the salaries of its new police force. And as American soldiers attempt to flush out the remnants of the Taliban from the mountains of Afghanistan, Europe (with Canada) manages the International Stabilization Assistance Force in Kabul and draws up plans for nation-building.

For many observers in the United States, such as Robert Kagan, this diversion in practice stems from a massive asymmetry in military power between the U.S. and Europe. In terms of international politics, Kagan argues in his seminal article on transatlantic relations, the United States is "making the dinner" and the Europeans are "doing the dishes." Because America is powerful, it can dominate the other actors and institutions in international society, acting like a latter-day sheriff, "trying to enforce some peace and justice . . . often through the muzzle of a gun."[23] Europe, on the other hand, because it is weak, has largely rejected military force as a means of influence in world politics. What is more infuriating, according to Kagan, is that Europeans are attempting to make a virtue out of necessity. Rather than humbly and gratefully admitting that U.S. power underwrites European security and prosperity, Europeans are propounding their own, alternative view of international affairs. This alternative view is founded on the centrality of international institutions, on the rule of law, and on the role of military force as the last resort of international diplomacy. For Kagan and his neo-con friends in Washington, such thinking smacks, at best, of naive idealism. At worst it represents a desire on the part of the Europeans to undermine American security. In their eyes, Europeans are using the institutions and rules of international society, such as the UN Security Council, as a mechanism for taming U.S. power.

In reality, the causes of the feud within the Western camp go beyond the simple dichotomy of power and weakness. Contrary to the current view in Washington, Europe's commitment to international law and institutions is not just a smokescreen for its "free-riding" on American military might. (The GDP of the European Union, particularly following its enlargement, would allow for spending on an American scale.) Rather, after slowly devising a new approach to international relations within the European continent, which sees only a limited role for force, Europeans are *choosing* to be militarily weak. In the case of the Iraq war, the breakdown in consensus between the U.S. and its European allies stemmed from different assessments of the imminence of the threat posed by Saddam Hussein's regime and from different views on the appropriateness of force in international politics.

For key European states, particularly those that endured the destruction and instability of the Second World War, military force must always be a last resort. Its devastating and unforeseen consequences, which often include crimes against humanity, necessitate that it be used reluctantly and only in extreme cases. War represents a failure of diplomacy. This explains Europe's painstaking efforts to rid the continent of the scourge of war through the process of integration—a process that now includes members of the former Soviet empire. It also explains the desire of France and Germany in March 2003 to give the UN weapons inspectors more time to complete their job in Iraq, in the hopes that such an effort would convince Saddam

Hussein to take the necessary steps to avoid war. Thus, we cannot say that Europe simply disagreed with the *means* of getting rid of Saddam Hussein. The substance of the disagreement is more fundamental. For the Europeans, war cannot be a tool of foreign policy just like any other. It has its own distinct and lethal properties.

For the U.S., military intervention has always been an important tool of statecraft. As Michael Ignatieff puts it, "American foreign policy largely consists of doctrines about when and where to intervene in other people's countries."[24] Frequently, the use of force has been attached to noble, almost missionary objectives, such as Woodrow Wilson's crusade to "make the world safe for democracy" during World War I, Harry Truman's and Lyndon Johnson's interventions to prevent the spread of communism, George H. Bush's campaign to halt starvation in Somalia, and Bill Clinton's intervention to restore democratic rule in Haiti. Underlying all such military interventions is the belief that war can be transformational—that it can be a force for good. Hence, in the run-up to the Iraq war, advisers to President George W. Bush spoke of the historic opportunity to "remake the Middle East" and establish a beachhead for democracy in that historically troubled region.

Of course, this depiction fails to acknowledge the divisions within both the United States, where there has always been an anti-intervention party, and Europe, where the governments of (but not the broader public in) Britain, Spain, and Italy supported the U.S.-led war against Iraq. In fact, Donald Rumsfeld has devised an explicit policy of "disaggregation" vis-à-vis Europe: driving a wedge between what he calls "Old Europe" and "New Europe" (the states of the former Soviet bloc) and building alliances with those who are willing to provide the U.S. with the things it needs to wage its interventions abroad. Consequently, it is Poland (not France or Germany) that has led the peace-building efforts in northern Iraq—a reward for its decision to support Washington in its military campaign to unseat Saddam Hussein.

Nevertheless, the main contours of the split between the U.S. and Europe remain. Europeans have comprehended more quickly than their American cousins that, in the words of the EU's commissioner for external relations, Chris Patten, the United States, while "invincible, is not invulnerable."[25] The West is confronted not only by a new threat, but also by a qualitatively new *kind* of threat. Limiting vulnerability in an age of cheap technology requires more than a massive buildup of conventional and nuclear weaponry. It also requires that more attention be given to the sources of hostility, to the possibilities for preventive diplomacy, and to long-term reconstruction of zones of conflict. Though the United States is loath to admit it, many countries around the world believe it is Europe that is the more positive force at work in solving global problems.[26] In Kagan's terms, it appears that the world needs saloon keepers every bit as much as it needs sheriffs.

151

Where is Canada in this current transatlantic divide? We have liked to think of ourselves as a hybrid of the best of the United States and the best of Europe. Yes, we are a New World country with American-style football, wide-open spaces, and a sophisticated consumer culture. But we also have a European-style welfare state, profess to be officially bilingual, and eschew the gun-toting culture of our southern neighbour. In fact, a 2003 poll taken by SES Research showed that Europe slightly edges out the U.S. in the eyes of Canadians. Though we admire the way Americans do business and show their national pride, we would rather be European on issues such as diversity, education, social programs, and culture.[27] In terms of foreign policy, Canada also seems to prefer European ends and means and the attention Europe has paid to building up its soft-power resources. While we have been prepared to fight shoulder to shoulder with the U.S. (as our participation in the combat phase of the Afghan campaign demonstrates), we have more often found ourselves collaborating with European allies on conflict prevention and peacekeeping.

Well-known scholars of Canadian foreign policy, such as Denis Stairs, J.L. Granatstein, and Kim Richard Nossal, have suggested that focusing on the Canadian-European connection no longer makes sense and that the only real imperative is Canada's relationship with the United States. In their view, our government made a mistake in siding with "Old Europe" over Iraq. The idea that Europe could serve as a counterweight to U.S. power for Canada, they argue, "is as dead as the dodo."[28] But although this analysis comes from some of the sharpest minds writing about Canada's role in the world, it strikes me as off the mark. The key point about Europe is not its hard-power resources or its capacity to act as a counter-weight to the United States. Instead, Europe's approach serves as an alternative (though related) way for mature liberal democracies to conduct their foreign relations. And for Canada, this alternative is becoming even more compelling. Arguably, it is the European way—the promotion of democracy and development through trade and foreign aid—rather than the American way—the reliance on military might—that could prove critical in the reconstruction of Iraq.[29]

As this first decade of the twenty-first century unfolds, Canada will need to re-evaluate its commitment to and role in the transatlantic alliance. In particular, we must recognize that old alignments and partnerships are shifting and may be ill suited to new objectives. There is a natural role for Canada as interpreter for both sides in the transatlantic divide, given our hybrid characteristics. But we must also consider the impact of changes in our demographic makeup: while European immigrants helped to build our country and remain an important part of our multicultural character, the new citizens of Canada in this century come from other parts of the globe, particularly from Asia.[30] This transformation could have profound implications for our foreign policy priorities in the coming decades.

EMPIRE IS BACK

The final change in the global context that impacts Canadian foreign policy is the return of empire. At the end of the Cold War, the U.S. and its Western allies hoped to reap the peace dividend by decreasing military expenditures and bringing their soldiers home. Even where interventions did occur—such as in Iraq in 1990–91 and Somalia in 1992–93—the focus of military officials was on designing the right "exit strategy." The prevailing motto was "Go big, and go home."

The United States was attracted to short-term military engagements, given the still painful experience of its Vietnam quagmire. Any talk of nation-building, which would require the long-term commitment of soldiers and civilian personnel, sent shivers down the spines of the country's political leaders. In fact, during the 2000 presidential campaign, candidate George W. Bush was openly critical of the use of U.S. military resources for nation-building, insisting that the purpose of the army was to fight and win wars. His campaign adviser on foreign policy, Condoleezza Rice, was particularly scathing about the nature of U.S. troop deployment in the Balkans: "Carrying out civil administration and police functions is simply going to degrade the American capability to do the things America has to do. We don't need to have the 82nd Airborne escorting kids to kindergarten."[31] Even after the attacks of 9/11, during the buildup to war against the Taliban, President Bush reiterated this position by claiming that "we're not into nation-building, we're focused on justice."[32]

As 2001 turned to 2002, however, U.S. attitudes toward nation-building began to shift. This evolution was a result of two factors. The first was a greater willingness to consider the breeding ground for terrorism. The breakdown of order in Afghanistan and the success of the Taliban in filling the void were vivid illustrations that state failure can have consequences far wider than poverty and lawlessness for a state's own population. Second, as the military campaign against the Taliban progressed, it became clear that international support for U.S. action depended in large part on whether that action could secure a better deal for the Afghan people. The Bush administration therefore drew two lessons: first, that if more had been done to induce or compel the Taliban regime to protect the Afghan population, Afghanistan might have proved a less inviting haven for al-Qaeda; and second, that once the U.S. removed that regime from power, it had a responsibility (shared with the UN and other countries) to leave Afghanistan a better place than it had found it.[33] Acting on these lessons in future cases—such as Iraq—would require a combined strategy of military action and civilian reconstruction.

154

In truth, the U.S. was late in learning these lessons. Starting in the 1990s, traditional peacekeeping—which Canada has always considered its niche market—was dramatically transformed, as the UN took on ever-widening responsibilities in the reconstruction and administration of war-torn territories. Whereas peacekeeping missions had demanded a relatively light footprint and had restricted themselves to keeping warring factions apart, the new "peace-building" mandates concerned themselves with the deeper causes of conflict. The trend began in Cambodia in 1991–93, when the UN's efforts to restore stability involved not only stationing Blue Helmets, but also supervising elections, policing, and exercising a degree of civilian authority. In the more recent cases of Kosovo and East Timor, the UN's level of involvement is even deeper; in attempting to develop the institutions of government, it has assumed most of the sovereign powers of these fragile states (albeit on a temporary basis). It's beginning to look a lot like empire.

Mounting a sustained international presence, while crucial to creating lasting stability, raises thorny questions for peace-building states such as Canada. The first is about legitimacy. How do the UN and the states that act on its behalf justify exercising their semi-colonial powers? With the dissolution of colonial empires after 1945, the principle of self-determination—that all peoples have the right to self-government—became a defining principle of the UN system. Running countries in the style of the British Raj and remaking them in one's own image was supposed to be passé. Furthermore, as Ignatieff has noted, there is a profound contradiction between imperial reconstruction, particularly when spearheaded by the United States, and democratization.[34] The challenge for the international community—a challenge nothing short of Herculean—is to ensure that the takeover of government functions is effective but also short-term. But this leads to a second question: when is the job done? How does the international community determine the right moment to hand over control to the local population? In the case of Iraq, this issue of local ownership has been particularly controversial. Then again, is the selection of local leaders the sine qua non of successful nation-building? Or should the threshold also involve establishing institutions and conditions that make the resumption of conflict unlikely?[35]

155

In sum, it is no longer enough for peace-building countries, such as Canada, to define the mission in terms of freedom and democracy. In fact, these terms are themselves the subject of intense debate. Whether and how the two notions of freedom and democracy fit together in nation-building missions has become a burning question for the international community in the twenty-first century. This is only the beginning, not the end, of the exercise.

Canada's New Identity Crisis

What do all of these changes mean for Canada? Andrew Coyne once referred to Canadians as the "Unitarians among peoples": we are always questioning our faith. Defining the Canadian national identity became a cottage industry in the 1970s, 1980s, and 1990s, especially as our country endured two referenda on whether we should continue to exist as a coherent entity.

The post-9/11 era has been quieter on the national-identity front. There is a segment of Quebec society that still desires sovereignty, and there are significant rumblings in Western Canada about the inequities in our confederation. On balance, however, national cohesion is more robust. After so much time and energy invested in creating and revising the Canadian constitution, many citizens of this country are relieved that the "C-word" has largely dropped out of policy and dinner-table conversations.

On the other hand, Canada's identity vis-à-vis the outside world is a topic that cries out for discussion. There is both the perception and the reality of Canadian decline on the international stage. We are resting more and more uncomfortably on our past reputation as the helpful middle power. Measured in terms such as the size of armed forces and of development-assistance budgets, Canada has less and less meat to put on the international table. And, as Andrew Cohen reminds us, such foreign policy downsizing has a cost: "We are no longer the world's necessary angels, and the unfinished country has become the diminished country."[36] As a result, we are experiencing "status anxiety."[37] We wring our hands about where we haven't been able to "make a difference." We constantly look around the world to see what other countries are doing, and ask why *we* can't or won't do it.

At this point in our national history, we need to be asking ourselves some tough questions about the world beyond our frontiers. What do we want to do on the global stage? What do we want to stand for? What kind of world do we want to build? Are we willing to put our money where our mouth is? As our policy-makers and citizens debate these challenges, the "middle power" mantra will have very little utility.

The first set of problems is conceptual. What does it mean to be a middle power in the twenty-first century? A concept like middle power is relational: it requires great and minor powers to inhabit the weigh scales as well as middle ones. With the emergence of the U.S. as the dominant power, the global context has changed dramatically. We no longer live in an international system where great powers are pitted against one another and where smaller powers like Canada work skilfully to find a path through the middle. Instead, we live in a world with a single ruler that, on the one hand, requires fewer friends to get the job done but, on the other hand, is demanding stronger demonstrations of allegiance. These changes have made the tactics of "middlepowermanship" much trickier to employ.

157

Even under a more sophisticated conception of middle powers, such as that offered by the University of Waterloo's Andrew Cooper, it is clear that the areas amenable to innovative diplomacy have narrowed. Scholars like Cooper define middle powers less in terms of their size and geographic location and more in terms of their "technical and entrepreneurial capacities."[38] Their argument is that during the short-lived—and now heavily debated—period of U.S. decline in the late 1980s,[39] the absence of clear leadership in the international system opened up alternative potential sources of initiative and innovation in international politics. The current international context, however, has filled this void: it does not lack for leadership. There is a direction, whether we approve of it or not. And while opportunities for niche diplomacy remain, the importance of having U.S. support for one's initiatives is often critical. Prime Minister Tony Blair's campaign to restart the Israeli-Palestinian peace process after September 11 is a telling example. Without the full backing of George W. Bush, the (now defunct) "road map" of 2003 would never have gotten off the ground.

Second, the logic behind the notion of middle powers can only partially explain how an individual state will behave. In the academic terminology, it is a "systemic explanation"—one that focuses on the way that the global chessboard is laid out, rather than on the kinds of players that take part in the game. To put it simply, a systemic framework treats states as though they were black boxes.[40] To call Canada a middle power—and then to describe its behaviour accordingly—is to miss all of the domestic and societal influences on our foreign policy. Clearly there are factors beyond Canada's position as a middle power that explain our country's traditional propensity to co-operate in multilateral institutions and to seek the peaceful resolution of disputes. Indeed, there are other countries positioned in the middle-power ground that do not exhibit these tendencies. Canadians need to understand that our past foreign policy behaviour was based not just on our place in the global balance of power or on some innate desire to do good, but also on a careful consideration of our interests. So, for example, we tend to gloss over some of the less noble deeds of the quintessential middle-power era, such as our government's use of quotas and high tariffs on goods from the developing world in order to protect particularly sensitive Canadian industries (particularly those concentrated in Ontario and Quebec). As John Holmes famously quipped, there is often a "moral arrogance" to the whole middle-power exercise.

Third, the concept of middle power is mostly about process; it lacks substantive content. Middle powers are defined through their tactics: compromising, building coalitions, participating in international organizations, forging consensus, and maintaining international order. But as Denis Stairs has pointed out, this middle-power commitment to international order is inherently conservative. It rests on the assumption that you are happy with the status quo as it is and do not seek to change or improve upon the current international order to pursue other goals, such as greater justice. The middle power, Stairs writes, "has to care more about ensuring that problems are peacefully settled than about the terms upon which the settlements themselves are based."[41] In short, tactics can provide only the shell, not the filling. As defined by its originators—and as expanded upon by subsequent

scholars and diplomats—middlepowermanship is a *way* of conducting foreign policy. It doesn't tell us very much about what we want to
achieve through those means. But values and purpose have become all
important in our post-9/11 world. People want to know what we
stand for.

This leads to a final drawback: the middle-power identity is unin-
spiring for our younger generations. Canada 25, a non-profit organization that seeks to bring the ideas of Canadians aged twenty to
thirty-five to our country's public policy discourse, exemplifies the
global ambition of our country's future leaders. The formative experiences of young Canadians, particularly their exposure to global media
and the borderless World Wide Web, have made them inherently
internationalist. Now they passionately believe that they will do great
things in the world.[42] To be a middle power is to settle for mediocrity.
The former *New York Times* correspondent in Canada, Anthony
DePalma, may like to call our country the "Danny Kaye of nations,"[43]
but is this all we want to be?

Beyond these conceptual problems are the concrete policy choices
that flow from a middle-power identity. Since 1945, the middle-
power vocation has encouraged Canada to become a "serial joiner."[44]
Today, our country is part of a network of international organizations
that range from big ones, such as NATO or WTO, to those below the
radar screen, such as the Organization for Security and Co-operation
in Europe (OSCE) or the World Meteorological Organization. We
have been obsessed with joining institutions and pursuing the tactics
of middlepowermanship; in so doing, we've lost sight of what we are
trying to accomplish both on the North American continent and in
the wider world.

We can no longer be part of international clubs simply for the sake of
membership. All too often, these institutions themselves begin to
drive our foreign policy agenda. As one foreign affairs official described
to me, "The minister's policy agenda, his time, and his international

contacts are driven principally by events, organized by multilateral organizations over which we have very little scheduling control. As these events become more elaborate, and more 'scripted,' the principal benefit is frequently found in meetings at the margin—outside in the halls rather than in the main room. These might be useful, but only produce a shadow of what sustained attention could bring in terms of Canadian interests." Given that fiscal responsibility is here to stay, governments need to be precise and efficient in their international commitments. That means continually reviewing our institutional affiliations to determine whether we want to continue to invest in them. In some cases, this may result in a scaling back of Canadian commitments, but in other cases it could mean greater involvement in new kinds of conflict prevention and peace-building activities.

Over a decade ago, Denis Stairs hinted at what I have described in this chapter as the middle-power syndrome. "Canadians are the citizens of a middle power," he remarked in 1993, "and in the time-honoured custom of most members of the middle class, they will try to pretend the result of their tailoring is finer finery than it really is."[45] Let's shake off this mindset. It has led us down the garden path of too much process and not enough substance.

The real challenge for Canada is to understand and clearly define the new and pressing threats to international peace and security in the twenty-first century: terrorism, the proliferation of weapons of mass destruction, humanitarian crises and mass flows of people, failed states, and infectious disease—to name the most prominent. Does Canada, for example, support the U.S. move toward a right of pre-emptive self-defence against regimes that possess weapons of mass destruction? How far are we willing to go in relaxing the norm of sovereignty to intervene in situations of oppression—are human rights violations on their own enough (suggesting that we should intervene in Zimbabwe), or must there be evidence of ethnic cleansing and genocide, as there was in Kosovo and Rwanda? Should Canada work to reform international institutions to give them greater legitimacy in the eyes of the developing world and global civil society? How intrusive are we willing to be with respect to the AIDS epidemic, the greatest scourge in Africa in modern history? What does Canada propose to do about the global energy crisis, which encompasses not just shortages of supply but also threats to current energy sources? Above all, how can Canada pursue its goals in an era of U.S. dominance? These are the pressing problems that face Canadians of my generation. The next step is to develop a clear view on how we, with like-minded partners in the wider world, can best respond to them.

161

CHAPTER FIVE

Contending Visions for Canada

J OANNA KERR'S first day of teaching wasn't exactly easy. Here she was, a thirty-something woman from Canada, facing a roomful of South Asian Muslim men. "I hope you're not bringing us feminism," one of them scoffed. "What if I was?" she shot back. "It doesn't work here," he replied. "It will take centuries for our societies to change with respect to women. You can't rush it."

As the Executive Director of the Association for Women's Rights in Development (AWID), Joanna splits her time between downtown Toronto (where the organization's head office is now located) and the rest of the world. AWID's mission is to inform, connect, and mobilize women's rights activists worldwide. But it also provides guidance and training to institutions around the globe that are trying to move away from traditional, patriarchal models. As Joanna's experience in Pakistan shows, this is painstaking work. "These guys didn't like me," she recalls, "but they tolerated me. And they kept on asking me why I tried to look like a boy by having short hair."

Joanna and her colleagues are fully aware of the entrenched views that exist in many countries about the role of women in society. But AWID—along with countless other civil society organizations—remains committed to bringing about evolutionary change. This requires patience and a willingness to compromise. In the case of the South Asian pupils, it meant talking in terms of dollars and cents. "In the end," Joanna explains, "they were businessmen. They began to see the practical case for addressing gender inequality. In the short term, it would make their organization more attractive to funding agencies. In the longer term, I believe it will make their projects, and their societies, work better."

The image of Joanna teaching disgruntled students about gender equality seems a long way from the middle-power diplomacy of Lester Pearson. But it also raises the question of what Canada's international vocation should be in a "post–middle power" world.

To put the question even more provocatively, why have a foreign policy at all? Given the limited room for manoeuvre in a U.S.-dominated world and the pressure on public funds to sustain important social programs such as health care and education, this isn't a rhetorical question. It urgently needs answering. If the response is the old nationalist one—that we need a Canadian foreign policy to help us feel different from the United States—then we are in serious trouble. This approach is unsustainable in a world where other policy priorities vie for the public purse—and for the skills of talented Canadians like Joanna.

Why Not Be Switzerland?

We could, for example, follow the lead of Switzerland—a country that places emphasis on being a great place to live, rather than engaging in international activism. Though Switzerland recently joined the United Nations, the Swiss have a reputation for neutrality and opting out of arrangements for interstate co-operation, most notably the common European currency. Swiss military expenditures are a third of Canada's (US\$2.55 billion compared with US\$7.86 billion).[1] After all, governing is all about making choices, and Switzerland's choices

163

have focused on a social safety net that is broad and deep. Could Canada also choose to direct its efforts internally?

As tempting as the Swiss model is, there are a number of factors that require Canada to be and do more. The first and most basic one is geography. Because of its location and its massive coastline, Canada is both isolated and exposed. Couple this with only one neighbour—a very powerful one—and you have an argument for developing a wide set of international relationships. The second factor relates to the size and nature of our economy. Canada's GDP is four times that of Switzerland, and our impressive rates of growth and budget surpluses during these first years of the twenty-first century have made us a valued member of the G8 and a potential contributor to international initiatives. In addition to size is the nature of our economy: it is highly dependent on free trade with other countries (most notably the U.S.).

But there are two more significant reasons that Canada has aspired—and should continue to aspire—to a greater global role. Our immigration and refugee policy, combined with our changing ethnic makeup, constitutes one of these key drivers. Canada has quite literally opened itself to the world, and many parts of the world live within our borders. Canada's net migration rate is 6.0 migrants/1,000 population, compared with 1.37 migrants/1,000 population for Switzerland. A gap also exists between Canada's rate and that of the U.S. (3.5 migrants/1,000 population).[2] Thus, while 10 per cent of the U.S. population is foreign-born, that figure is 18 per cent for Canada.

The other salient factor is our history and national identity. Though the story of Canada's presence as an independent actor on the international stage is relatively short, it is a compelling tale of contribution and sacrifice. I am reminded of it every year on November 11, when members of my family stop to pay tribute to my father's two brothers, Lawrence and Victor, who died within a year of each other during the Second World War. During the Dirty Thirties on the Canadian prairies, there wasn't much by way of work or economic prospects to keep these Welsh boys at home. Both of them signed up for the army before the legal age. Neither of them had ever left Saskatchewan, let alone Canada. But away they went and never came back. I've often wondered what our family would have been like, and how much bigger it would have been, had they not served. Today we have a permanent tribute to their contribution in the form of two bodies of water in northern Saskatchewan named Welsh Bay and Welsh Rapids. I've also accompanied my father to Harrogate, in northern England, where Lawrence's body is buried in a Canadian war cemetery. Victor, who died somewhere over North Africa, was never found.

Canada's experience in the international arena hasn't been limited to war fighting. As chronicled by Andrew Cohen in *While Canada Slept*, the history of our contribution also includes the creation of NATO and the GATT, the development of UN peacekeeping, and the establishment of the International Criminal Court. In short, we were a player on the international stage. The Canadian citizenry continues to believe that we should be. In 2002, when Ipsos-Reid asked a sample of Canadians whether they wanted our country to take an active part in world affairs, a whopping 70 per cent agreed.

Internationalism has also become a defining feature of the new Canadian identity. Indeed, surveys indicate that Canadians believe our country has a moral obligation to the world. Our past involvement in activities such as peacekeeping and multilateralism is a major source of pride for our citizens. As a consequence, Canadians—to a greater degree than Americans—want more spending on overseas development assistance, more engagement with the UN, and more involvement in trade agreements.[3] The problem, however, is that Canadians have not been asked to make difficult trade-offs in spending: if more money is to be given to these externally focused policy areas, what are we willing to spend *less* on? An additional problem is that the degree of support demonstrated for internationalism is way out of proportion with the facts on the ground. Today, the gap between the expectation of what we *should* do and the reality of what we *are* doing is growing wider and wider.

Foreign Policy as Canada-U.S. Relations

Given the public's enthusiasm and the government's recent spending trends, just what should Canadian foreign policy look like in this new century? One of the contending visions is a regional foreign policy, based on what Allan Gotlieb calls "the paramountcy of Canada-U.S. relations."[4] Gotlieb argues that in our post-9/11 world, all foreign policy issues and initiatives need to be examined within the framework of Canada-U.S. relations. This view rests on two premises: first, that Canada will not be able to contribute significantly to international peace and greater justice without being able to influence the United States; and second, that our influence in other important countries and organizations is directly correlated with how much we have the ear of Washington. Gotlieb believes that our best foreign policy years were those in which we enjoyed a close relationship with government officials in Washington. The now legendary fondness between Brian Mulroney and Ronald Reagan is the most obvious example, but Gotlieb argues that Pierre Trudeau and Richard Nixon also held each other in high regard. The trust we earned in the U.S. through these relationships allowed us to "collateralize our bilateral assets" and enjoy greater influence beyond North America.[5]

Some maintain that a foreign policy based on leveraging a healthy bilateral relationship with Washington has been pursued, with great effect, by British prime minister Tony Blair. Blair enjoyed an extremely close personal relationship with U.S. president Bill Clinton. The two leaders collaborated on important international initiatives such as the 1999 war to stop ethnic cleansing in Kosovo and the enlargement of the NATO alliance, as well as on a strategy of "new progressivism" to tackle the domestic challenges facing liberal democracies. Blair's and Clinton's ideological views were so similar that they co-branded those views as the Third Way—a model of Western democracy that avoids both the bureaucratic, top-down form of government traditionally favoured by the left and the aspirations of Reaganites and Thatcherites to dismantle government altogether.[6] What has surprised so many is Blair's ability to sustain these close ties with the White House after the election of George W. Bush, a man who in many ways is Blair's complete opposite.

Tony Blair experienced the attacks of 9/11 as though he were an American, and he was watching from the balcony as Bush gave his historic speech to the U.S. Congress, launching the war on terror. The British prime minister also backed the U.S. strategy of using military force to disarm and unseat Saddam Hussein, and he argued passionately for its legality (against the advice of many of the best legal minds in Britain). In fact, Blair's eloquent case for war was much more convincing than the one mounted by the Bush White House—so much so that polls taken during the lead-up to the war showed that the American public trusted Britain's political leadership more than it did its own. Meanwhile, back in Britain, Blair had placed himself on a collision course with both his party and his electorate. The criticism of his Iraq policy has continued since the conclusion of hostilities, as the search for weapons of mass destruction comes up empty and the rationale for putting British soldiers in Iraq starts to look thinner and thinner. The two foundations of Blair's case for war—intelligence reports on Iraq's weapons and the legal advice of his attorney general—were both questioned during the British election of 2005 (an election that saw Blair's majority in parliament sharply reduced).[7]

So why did Blair risk so much to side with Bush? The answer is simple: because he believes that Britain's interests in the world are best secured by a close relationship with the United States. Following on from this, Blair is convinced the best way to influence the course of U.S. foreign policy is, in the words of one British government adviser, to "hug the Americans close." On a rhetorical level, there's no doubt that this warm embrace has paid dividends. During his visit to London in November 2003, President Bush spoke of the "alliance of conviction and might" between the U.S. and the U.K. and declared that the U.S. was lucky to have Britain as its "closest friend." But in terms of real results, we need to ask two questions. First, what tangible benefits did the British government receive in return for its loyalty and support? And second, was Blair really able to influence the direction of U.S. foreign policy?

On the first question, the answer is mixed. While Blair's advisers claimed that the prime minister wasn't expecting any "goodies" from the U.S. during Bush's state visit to London, there was hope for movement on a series of thorny issues dividing the two allies: the status of nine British citizens being held by U.S. forces at Guantanamo Bay, the fate of the Israeli-Palestinian peace process, the plans for Europe to develop its own defence and military capability outside of NATO, and U.S. tariffs on imports of European steel. Blair saw some movement on the first and last issues; Secretary of State Colin Powell indicated U.S. willingness to release the Britons held at Guantanamo so that they could be tried in British courts, and President Bush announced he would lift steel tariffs in late 2003. But with respect to the rest of the items on this list, the Bush administration held firm to its differences of opinion with its European allies.

The second question, about influence, is harder to measure. Blair had some success in convincing President Bush to put new energy into the "road map" for peace between the Israelis and the Palestinians. Even if the process itself has stalled, the re-engagement of the U.S. in 2002 can be partly explained by Blair's insistence that a program for stability in the Middle East cannot focus on Iraq alone and must involve some resolution to the historic stalemate between Israel and the Palestinians. It is also widely accepted that Blair was largely responsible for convincing Bush to work through the UN in the autumn of 2002 with respect to Iraq—a course that was strongly opposed by many of the President's advisers.[8] Although the UN path ultimately ran into roadblocks, the fact that it was pursued at all owes something to Blair's personal interventions. As it turned out, the British prime minister didn't have to push that hard on the question of UN involvement: once the U.S. had decided on a "heavy option" for Iraq, it needed some time to build up its forces in the region. Finally, Prime Minister Blair leveraged his good reputation in the White House to win support for a more comprehensive approach (read, beyond brute force) to the reconstruction of Iraq and for a faster handover of control to the Iraqi people. In the end, however, the United States had 95 per cent of the decision-making power in the Coalition Authority in Iraq, and the United Kingdom only 5 per cent.[9]

Even if we take a favourable view of Blair's impact on the White House, it doesn't mean that copying his approach to foreign policy is the right path for Canada. Britain's influence comes from more than close personal relationships. It derives from a sixty-year history of investing in a "special relationship" between the United States and Britain, one that has seen the Americans supporting British actions such as the war in the Falklands, and the British backing risky American ventures in Grenada and Panama. It also emanates from the sheer power of the U.K.—its large and well-trained military, its strong economy, its seat on the UN Security Council, and the global reach of its activities (largely a hangover from its empire). Above all, Britain matters to the United States because of its place in Europe and its ability to influence the direction of the ongoing project of European integration.

This leads to a final point. Drawing on the Blair analogy to argue for a Canadian foreign policy focused on the U.S. risks distorting the true nature of British foreign policy. While Blair devotes a considerable amount of time and energy to the Anglo-American alliance as a key way to advance British interests, it is not the only game in town. There are other avenues for Britain to project its power and values, most notably through the European Union. Indeed, Blair knows that the White House is interested in Britain *precisely because* of its place in Europe; with an ally in Brussels, the U.S. hopes to have some influence over the course of EU policy. Britain has also chosen to involve itself in a series of initiatives that either do not concern the United States (such as the conflict in Sierra Leone) or diverge from U.S. preferences (such as the Kyoto Accord). In short, the British have not chosen the U.S. at the expense of everything else, and neither should Canada.

Foreign Policy as Trade Policy

A variation on the Gotlieb approach has been forwarded by former Canada-U.S. free trade negotiator Michael Hart. Hart argues that, given the size of Canada's population and our dependence on trade, our foreign policy should effectively be about our trade relations.[10] Given that the U.S. is by far Canada's largest trading partner, it logically follows that foreign policy can be reduced to our relationship with the United States.

Not surprisingly, Hart is critical of the Lloyd Axworthy era and what he calls its "romantic quest" to chart a foreign policy course independent from the direction being taken in Washington. Policies under Axworthy, he contends, drew us away from the United States and therefore reduced our influence. For Hart, the "relationship with the United States is the indispensable foundation of Canadian foreign policy in all its dimensions."[11] To muster support for this view, he quotes Rodney Grey, the chief negotiator for Canada during the 1970 GATT talks: "If a small country dissipates its foreign policy bargaining power on issues that concern it primarily as a member of the international community, it might not have the resources, the credibility, or the leverage to protect its trade policy interests."[12] In other words, pursuing initiatives like the Ottawa Process on Landmines or the International Criminal Court might make us feel good, but they are in conflict with our *real* interests.

Hart's argument makes perfect economic sense. But that's precisely its problem: it conceives of the Canadian government as solely a profit maximizer and of the Canadian public as motivated predominantly by the desire for greater prosperity. The realities of government decision-making and the aspirations of the Canadian people are much more complex.

Think back to the early weeks of the referendum campaign in Quebec in 1995. The strategy of the federal government in Ottawa was to emphasize the economic costs of Quebec independence. The only rational course of action, Quebeckers were told, was to remain part of Canada. A vote for sovereignty was a vote for corporate relocations, job losses, and a lower standard of living. But the argument fell like a lead balloon. The debate raging inside Quebec wasn't primarily about dollars and cents. It was about belonging and collective purpose. Thankfully, the federalists caught on before it was too late, and tapped into this discourse during the last week of the referendum campaign. The "no" side squeaked through because it offered another, ultimately more powerful vision of belonging—to the idea of Canada.

I see the same danger in Hart's proposal for "foreign policy as trade policy." Canada does not exist only to buy and sell goods and services with other countries. Its national purpose is not all about getting rich. If that were so, we would have become the fifty-first state a long time ago. Indeed, the very existence of Canada as a political entity that runs east-west defies the cool rationality of the economists. It stands as a testament to a broader set of political and social objectives. And a Canadian foreign policy must continue to reflect those goals.

There is also a more hard-headed case against conceiving of foreign policy solely as trade policy. While Hart's argument may have had some resonance during the 1990s, when the West had won the Cold War and was enjoying an unprecedented level of security, the post-9/11 era presents a host of new threats to international peace and security and to our way of life. Canadian foreign policy must actively address these threats, in collaboration with other actors on the international stage. In short, we must do more than buy and sell. We must contribute to the creation of new rules and structures to manage global problems. We must build capacity in other members of the international community so that they too can contribute, both economically and politically. And if the Canadian view on how to address new threats and problems differs from that of the United States, we must be willing to go our separate ways. In the words of Paul Heinbecker, Canada's permanent representative and ambassador to the UN until January 2004: "We should not shrink from disagreeing with U.S. administrations when they are wrong any more than we should shrink from agreeing with them when they are right. We should call them as we see them."[13]

Finally, Canadian policy-makers must dare to entertain the notion that the United States will not be the world's only superpower forever. This is not to invite decline or ruin for the United States. Rather, it is to do some prudent long-term planning. Canada's interests are best served if future superpowers are firmly embedded in international institutions and have been "socialized" to co-operate with others in the management of common problems. This will require us to remain engaged in the world beyond North America's shores and to monitor the development and policy direction of emerging giants such as China and India.

Reliving the Glory Days

A competing vision for Canadian foreign policy in this new century is one that takes us back to the "Golden Age," when Canada gave its blood and sweat in the First and Second World Wars. The nostalgia for this kind of role is palpable in much of the recent hand-wringing about Canada's so-called decline. In the infamous *Time* magazine article "Where Has Canada Gone?" journalist Steven Frank compares Canada to a child hiding in tangled underbrush: "You know it's there, but you just can't find it."[14] Frank exemplifies the view of many commentators, including Canadian historian J.L. Granatstein, who see the decrease in Canadian defence spending as a key driver of our marginalization in international relations. "In the cut-throat realm of international relations," Granatstein proclaims, "power still comes primarily from the barrel of a gun, not from the ranks of social workers that Canadians believe they send abroad. The weakness of the Canadian military has played a part in limiting its ability to operate on foreign fields as well as in destroying the country's reputation in global capitals."[15]

Compared with a decade ago, Canada's troop numbers have declined by 20,000, and we rank near the bottom of the list of NATO countries on the measure of percentage of GDP devoted to defence (1.1 per cent vs. the NATO average of 2.2 per cent) Similarly, while we were once at the centre of UN peacekeeping and contributed 10 per cent of the world's peacekeepers, we now rank thirty-fourth on the list of contributor countries and have had to turn down a series of requests to send our forces to war-torn countries, such as the Democratic Republic of Congo. In the current international system, it is Britain that is the true leader in peacekeeping. In Kosovo, Macedonia, Sierra Leone, and Afghanistan, Britain was able to deploy its troops quickly and to provide a common structure for force contributions from a variety of states. Today, while the British can deliver a brigade headquarters into the field within forty-eight hours, it would take Canadians several weeks to do the same thing.[16]

Critics of Canadian foreign policy during the Chrétien era, such as former Ontario premier Mike Harris, believe that these trends undermine Canadian values and compromise Canadian interests: "The international reputation of our military isn't peacekeeping—it's hitch-hiking. This is a betrayal of what Canadians stood and died for at Vimy Ridge and Juno Beach."[17] But is it? As tempting as it is to recall the sacrifice of those like my uncles, Lawrence and Victor, the reality is that Canada cannot and will not return to the era when we boasted the world's fourth-largest military. While the Canadian public, post-9/11, has shown a greater willingness to invest in the military,[18] there are limits to the range of spending increases that it would tolerate. In a poll sponsored by the *Globe and Mail* and the Dominion Institute, published on Remembrance Day 2002, Canadians demonstrated reluctance about increasing the military budget at the expense of other big-ticket items, such as health care. Furthermore, given decades of shrinkage, there is no realistic prospect of returning Canada's military to an all-purpose force capable of undertaking its traditional defence and combat roles, whether at home or abroad. Restoring and sustaining such core capabilities would require, in the estimates of some experts, an infusion of $50 billion over the next fifteen years, amounting to an annual increase of $5 billion. This figure is difficult to square against calls for more spending on health care, urban infrastructure, and education.

Numerous studies conducted over the past five years have reached the same conclusion: the Canadian military is facing a commitment-capabilities crisis. The starkest report—entitled *Canada without Armed Forces?*—argues that not even a major increase in expenditure can halt the pending crisis in equipment, personnel, and supportive infrastructure that will befall us in the next five to ten years. Even if we had the money (and this is a huge assumption), we don't have enough time to turn things around—"[The] downward slope of the capabilities curve is too steep, and the slide is too fast." More time is required to recruit new personnel, train leaders, build and acquire equipment, and design new operational capabilities. To put it bluntly, we have already sealed our fate. At best, the report concludes, "the next government might set the Canadian Forces on the road to recovery, but that intent still leaves unfilled the immediate, critical needs of foreign and national defence policies."[19] Canada is entering a period when our government will be without effective military resources—even for domestic purposes, such as surveillance and disaster relief.

Such reports make sobering reading. Even if you were to argue—quite rightly—that other Western governments reduced military spending after the end of the Cold War, few have seen as dramatic a decline as Canada. In Britain, while there have been decreases in the percentage of GDP devoted to defence, there has also been a concerted effort to redesign the military to meet the challenges of a new international environment. Hence the attention being paid to making the British military, in the words of its Ministry of Defence, "versatile, adaptable, and deployable." Canadian governments over the past fifteen years have neither invested nor redesigned. Nor have they given much intellectual energy to defence policy (the last government White Paper on defence was written in 1994 and makes virtually no mention of threats from non-state actors, such as terrorists). The relative security and stability of the 1990s largely afforded them the opportunity to place other priorities ahead of our armed forces. But today we are experiencing the consequences. Scrambling to acquire essential equipment (such as night-vision goggles) to support the mission in Afghanistan. Renting Ukrainian-made cargo planes to transport personnel and equipment on overseas missions. Putting our soldiers into the field in jeeps that crumple under the pressure of exploding land mines.

Rather than lamenting this condition, which will serve only to further demoralize the committed men and women who serve in our military, it's time to turn our gaze to the future. The February 2005 federal budget nudged us into the right direction with a $12.8 billion increase in military funding over the next five years. But the debate cannot simply be about money. We urgently need a national conversation about how to transform our armed forces into the best small army in the world—one that may never fight or win a battle on its own but that can fulfill the basic functions of "homeland defence," disaster relief, and joining with others in keeping and enforcing the peace internationally. Our new chief of defence staff, General Rick Hillier, has already kick-started the debate with his vision for a transformed and modernized military that can meet twenty-first century threats.[20] Canadians themselves are ready for this shift. In the 2002 survey mentioned above, while half of those polled (53 per cent) said that they would opt for "a better-funded and equipped all-purpose armed force capable of undertaking traditional defence and combat roles at home and abroad," most of the remaining respondents (32 per cent) already indicated a preference for this newer concept of a force that has been "downsized and reconfigured as a small but well-equipped peacekeeping and disaster-assistance force."[21]

A reconfigured Canadian military of this kind will not allow us to relive the so-called glory days. Canadians of my generation are already learning to accept this fact. But it will open up new opportunities for impact and heroism. In an era when the greatest threats to our security are mass epidemics, pockets of terrorists, collapsing states, environmental catastrophes, and the proliferation of nuclear, chemical, and biological weapons, the priorities for spending by the Department of National Defence (DND) should look different from the ones that guided them during the Cold War. Making a difference in the international community isn't limited to sending troops to liberate a country, as visible and symbolic as that might be. More importantly, we need to recognize that, increasingly, homeland defence has extended beyond traditional military functions. The new Department of Public Safety, rather than DND, may play the more significant role, requiring us to reallocate the "defence" spending envelope among a much broader array of government departments.

The change in threats that marks our new century is matched by new realities about the efficacy of military power. While the use of force remains an important policy tool in key instances, the post-war situation in Iraq has illustrated its limits. Even though the $400 billion defence budget of the U.S. (which accounts for 40 per cent of all the world's military spending) allowed the United States to "shock and awe" the Iraqi military, the U.S. has faced serious obstacles in achieving its ultimate objective. As one British commentator aptly puts it, "The U.S. possesses a fine hammer. But the challenges it confronts are not all nails."[22] All the smart weapons in the world cannot produce a stable and democratic Iraq—unless, of course, the U.S. intends to bomb every Iraqi citizen into submission. While coalition forces in Iraq numbered, at their height, more than 150,000, expert opinions suggest that twice that many were required to give Iraqis a sense of personal security.[23] But the structure of the U.S. army and its policy of force rotation simply could not fulfill this requirement. Even the mighty U.S. is confronting a problem that dogs every Western democracy: a limited capacity to put "boots on the ground."

Canada: The New Norway?

Another foreign policy model being championed in some Canadian circles is the Norwegian approach. During the past fifteen years, Norwegian governments have developed a niche foreign policy personality that plays well both internationally and domestically. As represented by the 1993 Oslo Peace Accords between the Israelis and the Palestinians, the Norwegian niche is the area of mediation and conflict resolution.

In late 1999, Norway was invited to play the role of mediator in Sri Lanka's ongoing internal struggle between the government and the

Liberation Tigers for Tamil Eelam (known as the LTTE or Tamil Tigers). Sri Lanka's president, Chandrika Bandaranaike Kumaratunga, had tried to broker a peace agreement on her own in the mid-1990s, but there was a breakdown in trust between the two sides and a resumption of devastating terrorist attacks. Norway (like Canada) is home to Tamil refugees, some of whom have become active in Norwegian politics. In addition, a number of Norwegian non-governmental organizations have been active on the ground in Sri Lanka. These two factors led to the belief that Norway would have a good "feel" for the situation in Sri Lanka and would therefore be an effective mediator. While Norway's early efforts failed to produce results, its second brokering attempt, launched in February 2002, led to a ceasefire agreement and the establishment of a monitoring mission. At the time of Norway's overtures (in 2000 and 2002), some Canadian commentators suggested that our traditional role as "helpful fixer" had been usurped by the Scandinavians. The Norwegians were upstaging us at every turn and outperforming us in their ability to mediate and consensus-build.[24]

But let's look at the facts a little more closely. Yes, Norway responded to Sri Lanka's request and enjoyed its fifteen minutes of international fame. In the autumn of 2003, however, the head of the monitoring mission was sent back to Norway on the orders of President Kumaratunga, having been accused of feeding crucial military information to the LTTE. In fact, throughout the peace negotiations there were rumblings that Norway's demographic makeup (that is, its Tamil population) and past NGO involvement in Sri Lanka put its objectivity into question. That crucial characteristic of a peace broker—impartiality—had been irreparably damaged.

Should Canada have tried to play mediator between the conflicting parties? And would we have fared any better? I think "no" is the answer to both questions. Despite the warm and fuzzy images we have of ourselves as "honest brokers," the reality is that Canada would also encounter difficulties in sustaining the appearance of impartiality in this dispute—in fact, probably to a much greater degree than Norway. Canada's Tamil community numbers approximately 200,000 (one of the largest outside Sri Lanka), and Canada has been one of the principal support bases for the LTTE. An example will help to illustrate how these realities complicate our ability to play a mediating role.

In the spring of 2000, then finance minister Paul Martin was invited to attend a dinner in Canada to celebrate the Tamil New Year. Martin's office accepted before inquiring into the origins of the group that had issued the invitation but later ran a check on the organization through the Canadian high commissioner in Colombo, Sri Lanka. The high commissioner, Ruth Archibald, discovered that the group was indeed a front for the LTTE and urged Minister Martin in the strongest possible terms to decline the invitation. She argued that the presence of a high-ranking Canadian official at such an event would have grave effects on the Canadian–Sri Lankan relationship, and at a time when the LTTE was locked in a military altercation with the government in Colombo. Martin nevertheless chose to attend the event, against the high commissioner's advice, claiming that it would have been "un-Canadian" not to accept an invitation from one of Canada's key immigrant communities. The high commissioner was summoned by the president of Sri Lanka and dragged across the carpet, and Martin's attendance made the front pages of every daily newspaper in that country.

As Canadians, we need to recognize the limits to our potential as peace broker. In some situations it may be possible and appropriate, but in many others it may not. Even if the individuals who get involved as negotiators are impartial, our country's larger liberal immigration policy—which on its own is to be celebrated—makes it difficult for us to give the appearance of being fair in the internal disputes of other countries. Our open policy toward immigrants and refugees is a major feature of who we are, and we cannot and should not abandon it. Indeed, our diasporas "are us." But we must also recognize the implications of our heterogeneous makeup.

But this example of Norway's involvement in Sri Lanka should give us pause for another reason. The tendency for Canadian commentators to compare our country with Norway and lament what they see as our loss of influence reflects an unhealthy preoccupation with the "Hollywood" approach to foreign policy. Desperately trying to have a prominent role. Making a big splash. Enjoying the media spotlight for a few days. While I don't necessarily believe these were the motivations of the Norwegian government, I do detect them in some corners of the Canadian foreign policy world.

Rather than seeking to grab a headline, which might require us to devote an inordinate amount of human and financial resources to one flashy foreign policy venture, Canada should pursue an activist strategy that looks for opportunities to partner with others. There will be times—when there is a glaring gap in hardware, money, human power, or ideas—that we must take the initiative. This is precisely what Canada did during the Mexican, Brazilian, and Asian financial crises of the late 1990s, when the G7 proved to be an insufficient tool to address the problem. Under Canadian leadership, the G20 was created, as a forum including not just the world's top industrialized countries, but also crisis-ridden countries such as Thailand, Indonesia, and Brazil. But we shouldn't scan the world looking for ways in which we can initiate. We are not, as has been said of the United States, "bound to lead."[25] Contribution is itself a noble task. In fact, contributing is perhaps the most positive role that a country like Canada can play in a world where problems are increasingly communal and no one country's actions or resources can be decisive.

A Foreign Policy of "Soft" Power

A final vision for Canadian foreign policy is one that strives to exercise soft power in the international arena. This approach, which enjoys a high degree of support in academic and policy-making corridors, was practised by Lloyd Axworthy during his tenure as foreign affairs minister from 1996 to 2001. Soft power, as its founder Joseph Nye defines it, is the ability to entice others to "want what you want"—without the explicit use or threat of force.[26] According to Nye, soft power ultimately rests on the ability to set the agenda in international institutions and political debate. It derives not from the size of one's military, but rather from the attractiveness of one's values and culture.

The term "soft power" has also been used to refer to the tactics used to bring about a desired policy objective. In the case of Canadian foreign policy under Axworthy, these tactics were twofold: sophisticated practices of negotiation and coalition-building, and the use of civilian talent and non-governmental organizations to gradually build an international consensus. In Axworthy's words, the soft-power approach "drew upon the culture of compromise we use to govern a vast, diverse, multiracial, bilingual country. And it relied upon the skill and talent of Canadians to negotiate, advise, organize and create, solve problems peaceably and look for practical solutions."[27] In addition, it recognized that the revolution in communications and technology made it more difficult for states to control flows of information and influence. This opened up opportunities not only for interaction between national civil societies, but also for the creation of a global civil society that could push for change on controversial issues such as child soldiers and land mines.

While Axworthy was a convert to the doctrine of soft power, another main driver of his approach was the brute fact of federal government downsizing. During the mid- to late 1990s, the Department of Foreign Affairs and International Trade (DFAIT) lacked the raw material with which to build a traditional international agenda. As minister of foreign affairs, Axworthy responded to this constraint in an entrepreneurial fashion: he started up a new game of foreign policy, based on the idea that soft power, rather than hard power, was *the* new currency in international relations. Not everyone took the bait. Axworthy was criticized by some for resorting to self-righteous moralism and by others for trying to wage foreign policy on the cheap. But it is hard to deny that his approach produced some very impressive results. Under his stewardship, DFAIT initiated the Ottawa Process on Landmines (which led to the December 1997 creation of a convention to ban land mines), took a lead role in the preparatory meetings for the creation of the International Criminal Court, used Canada's stint as a non-permanent member of the Security Council to garner a UN resolution on the protection of civilians during wartime, and launched an international commission to analyze the legitimacy of military interventions for humanitarian purposes.[28] The Axworthy years proved that, sometimes, effective persuasion and advocacy can convince states to do the right thing. But can a foreign policy based on soft power sustain us in this new century?

In my mind, it all depends on credibility. Credibility is a prized but somewhat intangible possession in contemporary international relations. What makes a country's promises and pronouncements credible? It is partly about past behaviour: you deliver on what you said you would deliver. It is also partly about resources: your promises seem commensurate with your abilities.

We therefore come back to the question of material capabilities. Soft power has worked so well for the United States precisely because of the economic and military power that it holds in reserve. As Nye himself states, hard power and soft power are intimately related and reinforce each other. "A country that suffers economic and military decline," he writes, "is likely to lose its ability to shape the international agenda."[29] If soft power ultimately depends upon hard resources, then it is more difficult than Axworthy suggests to apply the concept to a country such as Canada, whose coercive capacities have eroded so significantly. This is not to say we can have *no* impact through the use of soft power. It is simply to question whether soft power is a sufficient basis for Canadian foreign policy. As my Oxford colleague Neil MacFarlane argues, it is not enough to have attractive values and ideas. You also need the capacity to disseminate and, more importantly, implement them. And this requires the commitment of real resources: "Agreement that the use of child soldiers constitutes an unacceptable infringement of the rights of children," for example, "must be accompanied by efforts to demobilize and reintegrate the large numbers of young people involved into normal social and economic life." Similarly, "implementation of an agreement that ethnic cleansing is impermissible may require the deployment of substantial military forces to end it where it is occurring."[30]

183

As a final point, we need to consider the viability of a soft-power strategy in the current international environment. I would wager that when we turn the clock ahead and regard the decade of the 1990s as history, it will appear as the exception rather than the rule. Unprecedented economic prosperity, geopolitical stability, massive reductions in military spending—all of these things are conducive to soft power. But in a world where security is again precarious and threats are unfamiliar and unpredictable, the currency of hard power appreciates.

This new context also raises questions about the main purpose of soft power during the Axworthy years: the promotion of "human security." Both in and out of office, Axworthy has argued for the need to expand the notion of security "beyond the level of the state and toward individual human beings."[31] In so doing, he has added his voice to those who believe that armed territorial security is not the only responsibility of state leaders and that attention must be paid to the plight of human beings, whether they reside inside one's national frontiers or elsewhere. Tactically, the promotion of human security has been an excellent way for Axworthy, and others, to elevate issues traditionally thought of as within the realm of "low politics," such as the environment or human rights, to the top of policy agenda. Once a problem becomes "securitized," its status is enhanced and it becomes worthy of more focused attention, more resources, and faster resolution—perhaps even by military means. To put it more crudely, changing the debate about security has real influence on the distribution of money and power.[32]

On the practical side, however, the idea of human security has created dizzying complexity for policy-makers. Even if we limit the notion to protecting individuals from violence and repression, we still have a lot of discretion in how we choose to define thresholds—how much repression justifies action?—and the appropriate response. Moreover, we risk putting too much on the agenda at once. The notion of repression takes policy-makers beyond immediate safety into larger questions about governance and the rule of law. Does securitizing the individual really make human security issues more urgent, or do we simply end up designating everything as urgent? Which individuals do we choose to give our attention to today (assuming that we cannot give equal amounts of attention to every individual on the planet)? As one commentator claims, "It is like the airline company giving a priority tag to everyone's luggage, with the result that the bags come out in a completely random order."[33] We still need criteria to help us determine which individuals are in the greatest peril and which cases are most suited to action on the part of the international community.

In the absence of such criteria, we risk creating a further problem: setting up false expectations on the part of suffering people around the world. During the past decade, the international community has intervened with military force to save Kosovars from ethnic cleansing and East Timorese from the wrath of the Indonesian militia. But it has left other civilians, such as those in Chechnya, Zimbabwe and the Durfur region in Sudan, to combat repression on their own.[34] Axworthy's own recounting of the story of Eastern Zaire and Canada's inability to launch a military force there to protect civilians in peril attests to this problem of false hope.[35] Despite Prime Minister Chrétien's desire to act, Canada lacked both intelligence data and the capability to mount and support a humanitarian mission. Thus, proclamations that individuals have become the focal point of security have done very little in concrete terms to improve the lives of those who are most affected by violence. Which part of the international community are they supposed to appeal to—a UN agency? a non-governmental organization? It has even been suggested that setting up a vague right to human security has made things worse: individuals in conflict-ridden societies look to the international community rather than to local political processes, which are likely to be more effective and consistent in providing for security.[36]

This leads me to a final observation, which I first heard made by the great moral philosopher Tzvetan Todorov in his 2001 Amnesty International Lecture: the inhabitants of most countries in the world, whether democratic or non-democratic, still enjoy many more rights as citizens of a state than they do as citizens of the world.[37] In some of his writings and speeches, Axworthy comes close to demonizing states, as though sovereignty were the greatest threat to international peace and security.[38] In so doing, he seems to forget that the original purpose of states, if we consult history, was to provide greater security and predictability for individuals. Security may ultimately make sense as an objective of individuals, but it can be achieved only in a collective, political process.[39]

Axworthy also errs in setting up a collision between sovereign states on the one hand and the international rules promoting and protecting individual human rights on the other. This alleged tension, which was fashionable to highlight in the 1990s, is less and less convincing in the twenty-first century. As Todorov argues, "a human right not guaranteed by the laws of a country and its state apparatus is not good for much."[40] In other words, it is states, much more than the ambiguous "international community," that make the real experience of human rights possible. And it is states to which we must look for the provision of security for

185

individual human beings. That doesn't mean that all states currently provide this security. Collapsing and failed states constitute one of the biggest threats to international peace and security. But our primary goal, as one of the healthiest countries in the world, should be to build the capacity of weak states to protect and provide for their citizens. This is the most productive and effective way to deliver human security.

CHAPTER SIX

Canada: Model Citizen for the Twenty-first Century

THE IDEA was born in a coffee shop. Two engineering-school buddies, Parker Mitchell and George Roter, were meeting to compare notes about life after graduation. While Roter had gone on to pursue a master's degree in biomedical engineering, Mitchell had joined a management consulting firm as a business analyst. Both, however, had been passionate about international development during their student days, and were looking for a way to apply their problem-solving skills to issues such as poverty and hunger. They suspected that many of their engineering colleagues felt the same way. As twenty-seven-year-old Mitchell remembers, "We scribbled down a business plan on a napkin, came up with a name, and Engineers Without Borders was launched."

Mitchell and Roter's hunch—that Canadian engineers are passionate about contributing to alleviating problems of underdevelopment—proved to be right. Four years after the coffee-shop summit, Engineers Without Borders (EWB) has over 6,000 members and has sent more than 100 Canadian volunteers to work on more than 50 projects in 25 countries around the world. When most of us think of engineers, we think of bridges and roads. The reality, however, is that EWB focuses on small-scale projects in areas such as water and sanitation, agriculture and food processing, information and communications technologies to assist development, and small-scale rural energy systems. EWB volunteers have worked alongside locals to repair rice-milling facilities in Ghana, to build household water purifiers in Cambodia, and to improve hygiene practices in Madagascar in order to reduce child mortality. The organization's mission is the product of deep soul-searching by Mitchell and Roter about the most urgent challenges facing developing communities and about the most effective role that "outsiders" can play in assisting them. In the end, EWB has chosen to focus less on big and visible projects, and more on building local capacity. As Mitchell explains, "We measure our success not by how many big wells we leave behind, but by how many technicians we have trained."

Travelling around the globe in his capacity as co-CEO of EWB, Mitchell has also rethought Canada's place in the world and what it is that makes him proud to be a Canadian: "To me, it's all about the values that Canada represents. Tolerance. Inclusiveness. Acceptance." But for Mitchell, these values serve a broader purpose than just making us feel good. They can also make us more effective in our activities abroad. It's the respect that others have for these values, he argues, that gives Canada a potential competitive advantage in international development: "Compared to a 'given' Western country, Canada is better placed to give aid, and will have more development impact, dollar for dollar. And all because people are more receptive to the inclusive Canadian model."

Mitchell's story demonstrates that as Canada manoeuvres its way through this new century, it must resist the temptation to fall back on familiar but outdated roles. While our military must be retooled and reformed, it will never again resemble the force that grew out of the ashes of the Second World War. Nor should we conceive of our foreign policy in narrow terms—whether through the "soft power" agenda of the 1990s or the foreign-policy-as trade-policy agenda of the continentalists. The challenges we face today require bolder and more multi-faceted solutions. They also necessitate rethinking the very notion of foreign policy, and what Canada can do and be in the world.

In this final chapter, I propose a simple but ambitious vision for Canada's global role: as Model Citizen. Both words—*model* and *citizen*—capture important realities about our contemporary world. First, the notion of a model suggests a different approach to effecting change. A crucial aspect of Canadian foreign policy today is simply *being what we are*: a particular, and highly successful, model of liberal democracy. Our model values pluralism, as reflected in our federal structure, our official policy of bilingualism, and our immigration and refugee policy. It prizes mixed government, by balancing legislative decision-making with an activist court and a robust human rights culture. Our model makes risk a collective problem for society, by establishing a set of state-funded benefits that Canadians can draw upon in their time of need. It seeks a balance between providing greater security for citizens in a world of terrorism and other transnational threats, and respecting hard-won civil and political liberties. The Canadian model is also extremely civil, as seen in our crime levels, the vitality of our cities, and the success of our artists. Most of all, our model of democracy is internationalist, in embracing free trade and multilateral co-operation, but is also confident in our ability to sustain a unique national identity.

All these aspects of the Canadian model are exceedingly attractive. And what is attractive creates a magnetic effect. It induces others to emulate what we do, and to forge better and closer relationships with us. This magnetism, whether we recognize it or not, is a form of foreign policy. While its effects are seen only gradually, they are nonetheless real. Canada as a model democracy effects change in a way not unlike Western Europe did for Eastern Europe in the last years of the Cold War. The very success of Western Europe—and the increasing ability of those in the Eastern bloc to see that success, thanks to the revolution in technology and communication—contributed to the fall of communism as a less viable way of organizing society.

Taken on its own, this recipe for foreign policy is too passive. But "model" is a verb as well as a noun. Therefore, Canada can model in another sense. It can demonstrate how to establish the foundations of a strong society—much as a teacher or consultant might do. This is the underlying philosophy of organizations like Engineers Without Borders. Rather than transplanting our model into other countries, our foreign policy can seek to help others help themselves. To contribute to *regime-building*, rather than imposing regime change. In this task, Canada is ultimately a collaborator or partner, rather than an imperial occupier. To put it another way, we are

claiming to be not *the* model, but *a* model—one that others may find useful and inspiring.

This idea of partnership is captured by my second word: *citizen*. Citizenship is fundamentally a social phenomenon, which implies solidarity with others. It is a status that is given to those who are full members of a community.[1] And with that status come rights and duties, which all citizens—in legal terms, at least—enjoy equally. My vision for Canada's future entails modelling, for other countries around the world, what those rights and duties entail within the global community. But it also involves other attributes of citizenship, such as exercising self-restraint in terms of how we use common resources, like clean air and water. Just as citizens within national communities are expected to exercise personal responsibility in terms of choices that affect their health and the environment, so nation-states must act with the larger "public good" in mind.[2]

Understanding Canada as a Model Citizen helps to steer us away from the problems associated with the traditional discourse of power. As I've suggested, power is inextricably linked with the idea of control: getting others to do what they wouldn't otherwise do. But because the ability to control is often determined by the possession of certain resources, we end up defining power—and debating the status of certain countries as great, middle, or small powers—in terms of those resources (such as population, territory, or military force). Citizenship, by contrast, is an inherently egalitarian concept, better suited to the common problems faced by countries in the twenty-first century. While some citizens are clearly more active than others, we do not think or act in terms of "great citizens" or "small citizens." The language of citizenship also helps us to avoid choosing between "hard" and "soft" power. Citizenship can be exercised in a myriad of ways, depending on the problem or issue at hand; in extreme circumstances, it may require giving one's life for the cause of the community.

Let me make two caveats. In describing Canada as a Model Citizen, I am not ignoring the serious—and growing—cracks in our model. In short, we are far from perfect. The most glaring example is the condition of Canada's 1.4 million First Nations, Inuit, and Métis people, who lag well behind the national average in terms of life expectancy, health, and educational attainment. To date, Canada's profile on the world stage has been largely unaffected by this domestic black mark, but this is likely to change in the coming decade—particularly as Aboriginal groups increase the effectiveness of their lobbying efforts in international organizations. A good example was the May 2004 meeting of the Permanent UN Forum on Indigenous Issues, where Wilton Littlechild, a lawyer from Alberta, shone the spotlight on the disappearance of close to five hundred Aboriginal women in Canada over the past fifteen years.[3] My vision for Canada crucially depends on continuous efforts to address disparities in living standards *within* our borders. Once we begin to think of ourselves as a Model Citizen, the domestic and the international become closely entwined.

Second, in advocating the notion of Model Citizen, versus middle power, I am not leading us off into a utopian sunset. I do not for a moment believe that the world of international relations is, or can be, devoid of power considerations. In fact, many commentators on the Iraq crisis seemed to forget that the United Nations Security Council itself, though an important institution of international society, is rooted in power politics. The vision of the founding fathers of the UN in 1945 was to bring together the world's greatest powers to manage threats to the international system—by making the prospect of their collective response a deterrent to those who sought to destabilize the post-war order. In proclaiming that "the international system must be ruled by law not power," the drafters of Canada's 1995 foreign policy review, *Canada in the World*, are committing us to an unattainable goal. Power is an ineradicable feature of international relations, and will continue to be one of the means that states, organizations, and individuals use to achieve their objectives. In this, Canada is no exception. But this does not mean that power should define everything about who we are, or what we can do, in the twenty-first century.

In order to realize the vision of the Model Citizen, Canada must think more strategically about its role internationally. And a strategy requires choice: Not being all things to all people. Not trying to steal a newspaper headline on every international issue. But choosing those areas where we want to make a contribution and where we are willing to apply our resources (human as well as financial) to make a difference. Designing such a strategy requires three steps: re-examining our values, articulating our interests, and focusing and prioritizing our activities.

Revisiting Canadian Values

I've suggested that one of the main challenges facing Canada in this new century involves our international vocation. The dominant images we've held about ourselves, as a middle power or America's best friend, have been called into question by changes within our borders and in the world beyond them.

To fulfill its promise as a Model Citizen for the twenty-first century, Canada must tackle an even tougher challenge—one that drives to the heart of what Canadians stand for. Even if we haven't always been able to articulate who we are, we have prided ourselves on being able to articulate what we believe in. One of the most impressive statements can be found in our own Charter of Rights and Freedoms, which establishes the rule of law and enshrines our commitment to human rights and democracy. These three values—democracy, the rule of law, and human rights—are also elevated as guiding principles in *Canada in the World*.

It's hard to disagree with this list. All three values have sacred status in most of the world's industrialized countries, and we all want to be "for" them. In early November 2003, in what has become known as his "Age of Liberty" Speech, George W. Bush evoked his predecessors in the White House, such as Woodrow Wilson and Franklin D. Roosevelt, in making liberty and democracy the cornerstones of U.S. foreign policy. "We've witnessed, in a little over a generation," Bush proclaimed, "the swiftest advance of freedom in the 2,500-year story of democracy . . . As the 20th century ended, there were around 120 democracies in the world, and I can assure you more are on the way."[4] Viewed in quantitative terms, the story does look impressive. But the real challenge is to articulate what these notions of freedom and democracy *actually* mean and require—both at home and abroad—in the twenty-first century.

Take, for example, democracy. In the days following the toppling of Saddam Hussein's statue in Baghdad, the first post-war administrator of Iraq, retired lieutenant general Jay Garner, proclaimed that U.S. troops would not stay in that country a moment longer than it would take to get the electricity up and running and to stage free elections. But this minimalist American position was quickly proved wanting. Holding an election, as we have seen in the tumultuous period since the Iraqi vote of January 2005, is only part of what is needed to establish an effective democracy.

Democracy, at its simplest, is government by the people, for the people. It requires three things: regular, institutionalized political debate; a mechanism to involve all citizens of a community in the political process; and the ability of "the people" to hold their government accountable—and to remove that government without bloodshed. In most democracies, this latter condition is fulfilled by representative government, which is established through the mechanism of a general election.

But before any vote by "the people" can occur, someone has to define who "the people" actually are and what kind of government they are choosing. This requires a constitution—which, as we in Canada know so well, cannot be written overnight. In the case of Iraq, constitutional negotiations since March 2003 have been focused on resolving complex questions about the boundaries of the provinces that will make up a federal Iraq and about finding the right form of government to manage the country's distinctive ethno-religious mix. Only when a constitution, complete with elements of federalism, is in place can an election have any chance of producing a fair outcome. Similarly, without protection for a broad set of human rights, such as free speech, freedom of assembly, and freedom of religion, it is hard to imagine a truly competitive election, where Iraqis are exposed to a broad set of ideas about the future of their country.

It's clear, then, that we have already slid into our second and third values: the rule of law and human rights. Commitment to the rule of law is essentially a revolt against arbitrary decision-making. We don't want just any kind of rule in our societies; we want rule that is consistent, general, and constant. But majority rule, whether through direct or indirect democracy, will not necessarily produce this kind of predictability. Only through the presence of general standards, laid down in advance, can citizens develop reliable expectations about how they, and their rulers, will act. Constitutions typically fulfill this function, by stipulating not just the way legislation is made, but also what it can and cannot entail. Joe Heath, professor of philosophy at the University of Toronto, summarizes it like this: "A law is not a law just because the legislature says it is. The law must also satisfy certain constraints."[5] One of the preferred ways to elaborate this check on the legislature is through a bill or charter of rights. A commitment to human rights is a safety net against the so-called tyranny of the majority: it sets limits on what kinds of measures can be taken by the collective (even if it is the majority) by giving individuals, or minorities, a trump card that they can play. At their most basic, human rights are those rights that we have *by virtue of our humanity*. They are said to be both inalienable and unconditional: they cannot be transgressed by any public authority, and they do not depend on a particular role, a particular status, or a particular circumstance.

195

Ideally, the net result of combining these values is a society that can "self-correct."[6] The rule of law sets society's limits on the power of the state; individuals are then given the power to appeal to their judiciary when the legislature is believed to have overstepped its legitimate boundaries. In reality, however, there are a host of challenges associated with putting this theory into practice.

First, there is the key question of how the values of democracy, rule of law, and human rights fit together. Western countries like Canada seem to place great value on a political system's possession of all three attributes. Yet, as political theorist Jeremy Waldron has dared to suggest, these values may not always mesh together so easily. Is it possible for any one of them, or two of them, to exist without the other?[7]

Let's start with the rule of law. In the United States, and increasingly in Canada, final authority over important questions of individual rights and social policy rests with courts rather than with Congress or Parliament. The issue of same-sex marriage, which rose to prominence in the summer of 2003 in Canada, is a case in point.[8] Confronted by a court decision that the prohibition of same-sex marriage contravenes basic equality rights and is unconstitutional, our federal government was faced with the prospect of a conflict between this judicial pronouncement and the will of a majority of Parliament. With Bill C-38 Parliament has followed rather than challenged the court on this issue. Nor is it obvious that this swing in favour of rule of law is a bad thing. After all, public opinion polls tell us that Canadians (and particularly younger Canadians) trust their courts more than they do their politicians.[9] Should we accept the curtailment of human rights, as we have seen in the recent anti-terrorism legislation, as an expression of the will of Parliament at a particular point in history?

If the rule of law and democracy can conflict, so too can democracy and human rights. In his influential book *The Future of Freedom*, Fareed Zakaria has argued that these two values do not always go hand in hand. The most disturbing example is Adolf Hitler, who rose to leadership of the German state via the ballot box. But we can find examples in our own twenty-first century. Across the globe, as Zakaria shows, democratically elected regimes (often ones that have been re-elected or reaffirmed through referenda) are depriving their citizens of their basic liberties.[10] In other words, it is possible to have an *illiberal* democracy, as shown in contemporary Russia. George W. Bush might like to count Russia in his list of 120 democracies around the world, but this country can hardly be called a beacon of individual liberty. According to the international observers who monitored the parliamentary elections in December 2003, the extensive use of the state-owned media to support Vladimir Putin's United Russia party created an unequal playing field among the competitors. The result was an election that was technically free, but not necessarily fair. Even more troubling was the 2003 report by the United Nations Human Rights Committee, which warned of frequent human rights violations both in the case of the beleaguered republic of Chechnya (where the Russian military is accused of torture and extrajudicial execution) and in the case of crackdowns on Russian journalists and broadcasters.

Part of the problem is that the consensus on the content of human rights is still fragile. What do such rights encompass? Some, such as Michael Ignatieff, believe we should concentrate on very basic rights, as laid out in the International Covenant on Civil and Political Rights, since these are part and parcel of any human society. These so-called negative rights include freedom *from* certain things (for example, cruel punishment) and avoid the debate over whether there is a right *to* certain things (for example, subsistence or welfare). This allows us to focus on rights, Ignatieff argues, but in a way that is manageable and morally uncontroversial. Supporting human rights doesn't guarantee that everyone will live a wonderful life; it means only that human beings will be free from cruel, inhuman, or degrading treatment.[11] But others would argue that even this conception of basic rights betrays certain (liberal) values about the importance of individual autonomy. What good is political freedom, they assert, if you don't have a job or food on your plate? Moreover, it is clear that even the so-called right to life is not absolute. When the Taliban stoned women to death for adultery, this was considered a clear violation of a human right to be free from cruel, inhuman, and degrading treatment. But does the U.S. violate a human right when its judicial system sentences people to death? Even defining human rights minimally leads to controversy.

In reality, the model of government that represents Canadian values is what Waldron calls "constitutional democracy"—a very particular constellation that combines representative government, an impartial and independent judiciary, and a charter of civil and political rights that are both negative (for example, freedom from cruel treatment) and positive (for example, the right to due process). While this model includes a very strong democratic component (universal suffrage, regular elections, and a representative legislature), it also relies on unelected experts to resolve important issues of rights and social policy. There are, I might add, very good reasons for this non-majoritarian component. But those reasons cannot obscure the fact that we live under a mixed government, not a purely democratic one, and that it requires careful balancing and fine-tuning.[12] We should be proud of this model, while being very clear about exactly what it entails.

Can this special configuration flourish in countries that have not yet enjoyed democratic institutions? President Bush has suggested that this question smacks of cultural condescension. Every country, he argues, has a passion and a potential for liberty.[13] While this argument may be true, it does not mean that we can't ask questions about how to unleash that potential. Writing in the context of Iraq, Zakaria rightly points out that while Bush and his advisers have found it easy to embrace democracy, they have been less keen about the "long, hard slog" it takes to get there: "It means constant engagement, aid, multilateral efforts and a world, not of black and white, but of grey."[14] It also involves questions about how institutions should be designed, and in what order. Such questioning is not just idle speculation by an academic in her ivory tower. It gets to the root of what we are trying to do when we "build democracy" abroad.

This leads to the second question about this triad of values: whether they can be imported from the outside, or whether they must grow organically from the inside. The great nineteenth-century liberal John Stuart Mill believed that our highest moral duty is to respect the right of peoples to self-determination. It is through the act of self-government that political communities—and, by extension, individuals—experience freedom and develop a civic spirit. According to Mill, outsiders cannot and should not interfere with this process, because it is "during an arduous struggle to become free by their own efforts that these virtues have the best chance of springing up." Consequently, even if foreign armies intervene to help an oppressed population overthrow its tyrannical ruler, they must quickly turn power over to local authorities, since "the liberty which is bestowed on them by other hands than their own, will have nothing real, nothing permanent."[15] But at what point do outsiders disengage? Where is the line between liberation and occupation?

As we watch hundreds of foreign troops—and countless more Iraqi citizens—dying on a daily basis in the name of democracy, these questions become more important and more poignant. In fact, the issue of how to rebuild Iraq caused almost as much dissension in the Security Council as did the war to unseat Saddam Hussein. In order to obtain a UN Security Council resolution authorizing the U.S.-led multinational force in Iraq, the Bush administration needed to demonstrate to key council members—notably France— that it had a plan for handing over power to the Iraqi people. Even though the U.S. said enough on this front to get the requisite number of votes,[16] its plan was still too flawed, in the eyes of countries such as France, Germany, Pakistan, and Russia, to spur any contribution of troops or money beyond existing levels. There remained a deep fear in many quarters within the international community that only an Iraqi government run by Iraqis could secure the loyalty of the people of Iraq, and that the U.S.-led occupation authority would soon lose public support. These fears were realized in the spring and summer of 2004, as coalition forces faced constant challenges from rebel forces. Even after the 2005 election, the Iraqi transitional government continues to be dogged by the perception that it is propped up by "foreign" powers.

My discussions with young Canadians suggest that while we hold the values of democracy, rule of law, and human rights very dearly, we are also deeply uncomfortable with the notion of imposing them on others. This is an aspiration associated with U.S. foreign policy, and one that has resulted in charges of hypocrisy and imperialism. Canadians, it has been said, take other countries as they find them, rather than seeking to transform them. Nor are we confident in our ability to rebuild other societies overnight. Perhaps this derives from our own very gradual experience of building Canada—a process that we see as ongoing. Part of the magic of being Canadian is the recognition that our country is still a work in progress. With this recognition comes a sense of humility, but also a sense of empowerment that an individual can make a difference to the shape of his or her society.

The reluctance to claim the moral high ground stems from an additional value that is becoming increasingly important to a new generation of Canadians: the value of pluralism. Canadians believe in and are committed to the appreciation of difference. It is part of what accounts for our success domestically, and it will define our role as Model Citizen going forward. Attachment to pluralism partly explains the skepticism among many Canadians about the Bush administration's doctrine of regime change. But pluralism cannot become the excuse for inaction on the global stage. Canada, as an outward-looking citizen, has the responsibility to help build stable regimes around the world and an interest in doing so. We also have the ideas and expertise to do it. It is no accident that the Aga Khan has chosen Canada as the site for his new institute for the study of human pluralism, which will enable people in the developing world to access resources, learning, and experience to help them build pluralist societies.

So how would Canada's role in the world reflect this reconsideration of its core values? A concrete example can be seen in a recent initiative for the Middle East that, compared with President Bush's bold aspirations to democratize the region, has gained very little media attention. A group of scholars and public officials, led by Canadians, has come together to facilitate the establishment of a security charter for the Middle East region—along the lines of the Organization of American States (OAS). Currently, the Middle East is the only region in the world without such a charter. The objective is not to impose one particular model, but rather to encourage governments in the region to collaborate in efforts at modernization and reform. Those involved in the exercise recognize that region-building is a slow and painstaking process—one that is unlikely to be fulfilled during a single government's mandate—but believe that the current situation of flux in the Middle East may offer a unique opportunity for progress. They also acknowledge that there is a limit to what Western states can accomplish on their own. "There is clearly some interest in the region," says Janice Stein, one of the key architects of the process, but the most the Canadians can do "is help to facilitate."[17]

Articulating Canadian Interests

The word "interest" doesn't roll off the Canadian tongue very easily. One of the spin-off effects of viewing ourselves as a middle power has been an overreliance on *how* we do things at the expense of thinking about what outcomes we want to achieve. In addition, Canadian foreign policy since 1945 has often had a tinge of moralism about it: while *other* countries have interests, *we* have values. We've given the impression that we float above the grubby world of power politics. Canadian criticism of U.S. foreign policy on values-based grounds has been resented by some in Washington, such as former secretary of state Dean Acheson, who once described Canadians as "a lot of cry-babies."[18] Canada's policy differences with the U.S.—whether the critique of the U.S. bombing of Vietnam or, more recently, our leadership in forging the treaty banning land mines—have been described, at best, as self-righteous and insufficiently appreciative of the complexities and burdens faced by a great military power and, at worst, as armchair criticism by a country that can afford a values-based foreign policy only because the U.S. effectively underwrites our security.

Model citizenship requires some tempering of the "good boy-scout" mentality. As Thomas Axworthy has put it (paraphrasing Ralph Emerson), for Canadians, "virtue is not reward enough."[19] To achieve its goals internationally, Canada must at times be willing to engage with great powers on *their* terms. This means appreciating where vital interests are believed to be at stake and offering constructive solutions to problems, rather than lecturing from afar. Above all, our government must be clear about what Canadian interests are being pursued, whether in a regional or a global setting, and articulate these to the wider Canadian public.

Our involvement in ISAF in Afghanistan illustrates my point. To say that this was a dangerous mission for Canada's armed forces is an understatement. Far from engaging in Pearsonian peacekeeping, our soldiers were warding off attacks by members of the Taliban, who, having regrouped in Pakistan, continued to challenge Afghan leader Hamid Karzai's hold on power. As former defence minister John McCallum describes it, "the international forces of which we are a component are the only thing standing between Afghanistan today and falling back into that failed-state status that would allow the re-emergence of al-Qaeda and the risk of further terrorist attack."[20] During a visit to Afghanistan in November 2003, McCallum tasted these dangers first hand. Acting on a tip given to a Canadian Forces patrol, soldiers found two 107-millimetre rockets in a palace near Camp Julien (the base where Canadians are stationed in Kabul), set up and ready to launch. Only minutes before McCallum arrived at the camp, sirens sounded and soldiers took cover in concrete bunkers until receiving the "all clear" signal.

The responsibilities of our government in this uncertain context were twofold: to explain to Canadians why we were in Afghanistan, and to give our soldiers the tools to do the job. Putting aside the second issue for later, how did our government fare in its first responsibility? Returning from an earlier visit to Afghanistan in September 2003, McCallum proclaimed that Canada's participation in ISAF represented a happy coincidence between altruism—our instinct to "keep the peace"—and our self-interest—the need to prevent another September 11. But let's analyze this expression of Canadian interests more closely. How does the presence of Canadian peacekeepers in the limited area in and around Kabul protect our citizens from terrorist attacks? And how would the Canadian public have reacted to a larger number of deaths than the seven that we experienced over the course of the mission? Given the stakes, Canada's role and interests in stabilizing Afghanistan—and other troubled regions in the future—need a fuller explanation. Above all, it must be made clear that missions such as this are not peacekeeping, in Canadians' nostalgic understanding of the term. They involve the use of force, and they expose our military to the potential for large-scale casualties. In order to sustain the necessary public support for such missions, our government must be clear about why we should assume those risks.

Some might interpret my appeal to the national interest as a return to Pierre Trudeau's approach to foreign policy, as articulated in the 1970 federal government review, *Foreign Policy for Canadians*. For Trudeau, this document represented a rebalancing of Canada's priorities, away from boy-scout activism and back toward "what is good for Canada." The shift under Trudeau has been portrayed by historians as a triumph of interests over values and as a retreat from the internationalist agenda that Canada had pursued under Pearson. In the current post-Iraq war context, many are advocating a revival of this kind of approach to Canadian foreign policy—one that would that put what they call "hard-headedness" ahead of "wishful thinking." According to J.L. Granatstein, Canada must not mistake "its loudly professed values" for its national interests. "Moral earnestness and the loud preaching of our values," Granatstein warns, "will not suffice to protect us in this new century."[21]

But as tempting as the interests-before-values mantra is, we cannot abandon a values-based agenda. We live in a democratic society, where the values and principles we stand for *must* form a critical part of our activities in the international arena. Such values help to forge cohesion across a huge territorial mass and diverse population, and make collective action possible. In fact, one of the by-products of the end of the Cold War has been a move away from ideological justifications for action, based on the traditional groupings of left and right, in favour

203

of an ethical framing of policy initiatives that can achieve a broader degree of consensus. We see this not only internationally, but also domestically, in policy areas such as health, education, and citizenship law. Furthermore, the values we project globally help to define who we are. Foreign policy is partly an exercise in forging national identity. Rather than trying to deny or hide this fact, we should recognize this as part and parcel of our contemporary world. Consider the United States, which portrays itself as the leader of the free world, or China, which defines itself as the guardian of the developing world.

I believe we should stop trying to juxtapose interests and values, as if the former were selfish and narrow and the latter ethical and internationalist. In reality, values and interests work much more in tandem. "What is good for Canada"—to use Trudeau's phrase—involves more than just the pursuit of the well-being of Canadian citizens within our national borders. Furthermore, this nexus between values and interests is something that the United States instinctively understands and employs in its own foreign policy. Despite the widely held view that President Bush's famous National Security Strategy was a defence of "realism" and unilateralism, the document lacks any careful articulation of U.S. national interests. Instead, it is dominated by the notions of freedom and democracy, and links these historical themes of U.S. foreign policy with a new willingness to use power to project them.[22] Thus, far from being an "irritant" to Washington, as those such as Granatstein suggest, values-based perspectives (as opposed to rhetorical jibes) can make an impact in the Canada-U.S. relationship. During Canada's latest term on the UN Security Council in 1999–2000, our representatives pursued policies that were grounded in Canadian values, such as the creation of the International Criminal Court. While our perspective clashed with that of the U.S., our two governments agreed to disagree and did not allow these differences to overshadow the larger set of issues on which Canada and the U.S. concur.[23]

British prime minister Tony Blair provides further evidence of how values and interests can be fused together in foreign policy-making. One of Blair's strategies has been to expand and deepen the traditional notion of the "national interest." For example, during the Kosovo crisis in 1999, British representatives contended that a response to ethnic cleansing could be compatible with the national interest once the notion of "nation" was widened to include the principles Britain stood for. Britain, as a "civilized nation," had an obligation to respond to and to demonstrate horror in the face of "uncivilized" action. In a similar way, Blair's New Labour government has argued that changes in the international system, driven by the forces of globalization, have necessitated a wider conception of the national interest. As Prime Minister Blair proclaimed in his speech to the Labour Party Conference in 2001 soon after the terrorist attacks on the U.S., "The critics will say: but how can the world be a community? Nations act in their own self-interest. Of course they do. But what is the lesson of the financial markets, climate change, international terrorism, nuclear proliferation or world trade? It is that our self-interest and our mutual interests are today inextricably woven together."[24]

There are two consequences of this kind of thinking: first, transnational forces (such as crime, the drugs trade, terrorist networks, people-smuggling, or weapons proliferation) become part of each country's *national* security agenda; and, second, pursuit of the national interest requires steps to minimize the causes and effects of political and economic instability around the globe. In the end, values and interests start to merge.

Applying this logic to the case of Afghanistan, a compelling explanation of Canadian involvement might have looked something like this: First, Canada's security—and the security of its allies—is enhanced by addressing the problem of failed states such as Afghanistan and preventing them from becoming a source of instability or haven for illegal activities in the future. Canada is an example of a nation-state that thrives in the current international system; it therefore has an interest in maintaining this framework of stable, sovereign entities. Second, Canada has both an interest in contributing and a responsibility to contribute to the rehabilitation of societies that have experienced military intervention. In terms of interests, the rationale is similar to the one articulated above: building a durable peace will help to prevent conflict from recurring, with the potential to harm civilians and to spread insecurity beyond the borders of that state. The responsibility is less obvious, but equally important. Too often in the past, Western states have focused only on the short-term target of intervention (for example, the removal of a dictator) and have mismanaged their exit from the country. But military force has a series of damaging and destabilizing effects on local people and institutions. Therefore, those that have undertaken the intervention have a responsibility to address these negative consequences. Third, as a member of the NATO alliance, Canada assumes a series of duties. If we are to benefit from the security provided by such an institution, we must also be willing to contribute our share. Finally, Canadian foreign policy has traditionally been committed to working with "like-minded states" to protect and enhance our values—democracy and human rights— around the globe. Participating in the international force to stabilize Afghanistan is another manifestation of this long-standing objective. This multi-faceted explanation for Canada's contribution to ISAF, which draws on my concept of the Model Citizen, takes us beyond an appeal to altruism, which (however noble) cannot justify such a large-scale commitment of Canadian forces. It is also this kind of reasoning that has led Prime Minister Martin to commit Canada to a continued, albeit scaled-back, military presence in Afghanistan after the formal withdrawal of our ISAF contingent in August 2004.[25]

The strategy of widening the national interest, however appealing, does have limits. They arise primarily from the need to set priorities in the face of budgetary constraints and competing social objectives. Choices still need to be made as to which problems Canada will seek to solve. Not all relate to the national interest to the same degree—no matter how strong the ethical pull—and not all can be addressed with the current state of our resources. In the end, while we have important obligations to those who live beyond our borders, these obligations are not as strong as the obligations we have to one another as Canadians. And we should never forget that promoting the well-being of over 30 million Canadians is a noble pursuit.

The Model Citizen Agenda

The final step on the road to becoming a Model Citizen is the establishment of a focused agenda for Canada on the international stage. This is the toughest task of all. Canadians generally like to shy away from choices: we are reluctant to accept that when we declare a focus in one area, it means that we must downplay something else. For large chunks of our history, our relative prosperity has meant that the choices haven't been that difficult. We've been able to defer declaring our allegiance to one priority at the expense of another. Indeed, Hugh Segal, president of the Montreal-based Institute for Research on Public Policy, claims that Canadian political culture excludes hard choices by its very nature.[26] Governments that have dared to choose have often paid the price on election day.

We must dare to change that culture. Spreading ourselves thinly across multiple priorities is no longer sustainable. The cracks are already starting to show. Our soldiers are showing up on the battlefield without proper equipment. Our foreign aid expenditures, relative to our promises, are coming up short. Upon taking office as prime minister, Paul Martin announced that our top two national priorities would be securing Canada's social foundations, particularly in the realm of health care, and reforming democratic decision-making. But what about our global priorities? The April 2005 International Policy Statement, long awaited, has delivered an answer.[27] Now the challenge is to see whether there is political will to implement it. The priorities set out in the statement are bound to disappoint a certain segment of the Canadian policy elite or general public. This is the reality of setting a strategic course. But the benefit gained is more concentrated effort on the chosen priorities and greater return on that investment.

The Model Citizen agenda I outline here is based on three considerations: the importance of the issue (both to Canadians and to the health and prosperity of the world community), the degree of Canadian skill or expertise that can be brought to bear, and the potential to fill a gap in the level of attention being directed toward this particular problem. After balancing these factors, I believe the following four priorities constitute a compelling vision for Canada, as Model Citizen, in this new century.

208

REFORMING GOVERNANCE

It has often been said that while the United States is a country of ideas, Canada is a country of institutions. Though we might lament the ongoing tinkering with the shape of our confederation, for others the Canadian system of governance is a laboratory full of intriguing experiments. Governance and institution-building have also been key themes in our foreign policy at least since the Second World War. Yet, as we have seen clearly over the past five years, many of the institutions that have defined our role in the world—particularly the United Nations—have been subject to serious scrutiny and criticism.

In the case of the military campaign against Iraq, the UN couldn't win. For those states that went to war, the UN's failure was in not authorizing the use of force. President Bush's prophecy in the autumn of 2002—that the UN was on the verge of irrelevance and risked becoming nothing more than a debating society—seemed to have been fulfilled. But for many other countries (particularly in the developing world), the real failure was the UN's inability to stop the war from occurring. In their view, the UN managed to salvage a sliver of dignity by refusing to give in to U.S. bullying and to rubber stamp a war that—as we now know—had been planned by the White House as early as November 2001. Thus, for them the choice was less about relevance or irrelevance and more about complicity.[28]

This fierce questioning of the UN added to the trauma that Canadians experienced in the lead-up to war in March 2003. According to public opinion expert Matthew Mendelsohn, "All of our beliefs about how the world should work, and particularly the role of the UN, were shaken by the Iraq crisis. I think many Canadians are still recovering from that psychological angst."[29] Those Canadians who didn't feel the trauma joined others around the world in questioning the UN's utility. A study by the Pew Global Attitudes Project in June 2003 found that only 43 per cent of Canadians considered the UN important in dealing with international conflicts, as compared to 50 per cent who said it was no longer so important. While the results in favour of the UN were still higher than they are for most countries, they still mark a significant change and should be a cause for concern among our diplomats and foreign policy-makers.[30]

Nevertheless, the UN retains a vital role in world politics. The cliché is true: if it didn't exist, we would need to invent it. While the rift within the UN over Iraq played out under the glare of the media spotlight, the organization remained seized on a variety of other fronts that affected the fates of thousands in countries such as the Congo and the Ivory Coast. Furthermore, in a hotspot of direct interest to the United States—Afghanistan—the UN has been engaged in a variety of activities, including peace-building, de-mining, famine relief, and the management of refugees and displaced people.[31] But if you need even stronger proof, consider the Bush administration's own about-face after the end of military hostilities in Iraq in May 2003: it sought a UN Security Council resolution to establish the Coalition Authority, and subsequently sought UN assistance in managing the handover of power to the Iraqi people.

The real question about the future of the UN is whether it is equipped to confront new challenges and threats. It is time to recover from the Iraq trauma and get on with the job of reforming and strengthening the architecture that will manage issues of peace and security in this new century. I can think of no more pressing task for those of my generation. We face a moment akin to that which confronted policy-makers in 1945. Old ways of doing things need to be reconsidered, and new solutions crafted to deal with problems that weren't envisaged by previous generations.

As a first task, Canada—in collaboration with others—needs to reiterate the case for international institutions in today's international arena. Simply saying "We need to go through the UN" is no longer sufficient. We also need to explain the value of co-operative mechanisms like the UN, and why it is worth investing the time and political capital to generate a consensus. In making that new case, Canada should emphasize that multilateralism is not a "soft" ideal: it is also backed up by a healthy dose of pragmatism. Multilateral co-operation, as the U.S. found in Iraq, is a crucial way of sharing burdens and risks. Going it alone is not only costly in terms of dollars and lives, but also makes a country the target of resentment and the bearer of responsibility for all negative consequences. Second, working through an institutional framework makes it more likely that an international policy will be motivated by a broader set of interests and concerns—as opposed to the narrow economic or ideological goals of any one state—and is therefore likely to be seen as more legitimate. Third, multilateralism provides a degree of predictability: if there is an established mechanism to deal with issues and crises, countries can invest more in actual problem-solving and less in worrying about process. Finally, and perhaps most importantly, multilateralism is the only way to tackle some of the world's most pressing problems, whether we think of environmental degradation or the management of global finance. One state, acting on its own, cannot make much of a dent in such problems.

Many Canadian foreign policy experts, such as former foreign affairs minister Lloyd Axworthy, believe one of the main benefits of multilateral instruments like the UN is that they provide a forum in which we can "punch above our weight."[32] In my view, this strategic rationale is less and less convincing. It isn't clear to me that Canada is alone in reaping this benefit; for every state (even the U.S.), international diplomacy offers a platform on which it can demonstrate that it matters. The more important argument is that multilateralism allows Canada to have a hand in creating the international rules that Canadians are governed by, and in formulating the policies that Canadians are inevitably affected by. Whether we get noticed or are seen to be having influence is beside the point. Without a seat at a multilateral table, Canada becomes subject to the whims of the more powerful, who can establish the rules of the game with little or no consideration of the implications for us. At present, most of the world is fixated on the United States as that most powerful state. But we must be farsighted enough to imagine a world in which a new superpower (or superpowers) could dominate, such as China or India. For me, this scenario gives added urgency to the task of solidifying the legal and institutional structures that underpin our multilateral international order. We need to lock in *today* the principles and processes we want to govern generations in the future.

So how might we retool the United Nations for this new century? The UN plays two major functions in the field of peace and security, both of which require reform. First, the UN is an institution that *acts in its own right*. It has its own resources and capacities, and it engages in a range of activities from imposing sanctions, mediating conflicts, and sending in peacekeeping forces to co-ordinating the delivery of humanitarian assistance, overseeing referenda and elections, training civil servants, and prosecuting war criminals. Scores of books and reports have been written with recommendations on how to improve upon each of these operational dimensions. But there are two areas in which Canada already has experience and ideas to contribute. The first is toward improving the UN's capacity to prepare for military interventions and peace-building missions *in advance* of Security Council authorizations, which would require member states of the UN to make available battalions and civilian police officers for rapid deployment. These troops and officers would not only enforce or keep the peace, but also help to protect humanitarian workers, assist in disarmament efforts, and provide an investigative arm for criminal tribunals. In his visit to Canada in the spring of 2004, UN Secretary-General Kofi Annan subtly reminded Members of Parliament that of the more than 35,000 troops deployed in UN missions in Africa, only thirteen were Canadian.[33] The stark reality today is that it is developing countries that are doing most of the "heavy lifting" in the realm of peacekeeping, given that many Western industrialized states have substantially downsized their armed forces. The second priority for Canada is to promote more creative ways for the UN to work with regional organizations, such as NATO (of which Canada is a member), the new African Union, and ECOWAS (the Economic Council of West African States, which has led recent missions in Liberia and Sierra Leone). While the original UN Charter made provisions for regional arrangements in collective security, it left unresolved who was to bear overall responsibility for missions or how consultation between the UN and regional bodies would take place.

At the end of the day, however, when we say that the United Nations "acts" or "pronounces," we must remember that it is a state-based organization: it is only as good as the individual member countries that comprise it. In the words of Sir Jeremy Greenstock, former British ambassador to the UN during the Iraq crisis, "The UN doesn't have power unless those who have power switch it through to the UN as a matter of choice."[34] Consequently, the bulk of Canada's reform efforts must be directed at persuading states to fulfill commitments and dedicate resources.

The other—and I would argue more significant—UN role is as the key site for "daily socializing" by members of contemporary global society.[35] The UN is ultimately a forum where actors (both state and non-state) co-operate, compete, and persuade. Within this forum, policies are developed and new norms of behaviour are codified. The UN's market niche can be defined as the world's chief repository of authority: it is the best arbiter we have of legitimate conduct for the global community. Through its resolutions—whether on terrorism, war crimes, weapons of mass destruction, refugees, or (most importantly) the use of force—the *collective* approval or criticism of its members is expressed.

The UN's capacity to confer legitimacy is an asset that must be safeguarded. Without reform, it could all too easily be squandered. Already, a number of factors have damaged the legitimacy of the Security Council in the eyes of global society: the slow pace of its decision-making, the under-representation of key regions on the Council, the increased use of "informal consultation" in backrooms and corridors, the ability of permanent five members (P5) to shield themselves from intervention, and the political nature of many P5 vetoes.[36] Canada's priority, working in concert with other states, must be to improve the representativeness and transparency of the Security Council so that the UN can continue to enjoy its market niche. More specifically, Canada should support the current proposals for Security Council reform, which would see the Council's membership increase to twenty-four (from fifteen) and greater representation for key regions such as Asia and Latin America. Since the Security Council was established almost sixty years ago, the membership of the UN has increased from 51 to 191. Considerations of democracy and fairness demand that the Council's lopsided composition be redressed, and new power realities be acknowledged.

213

But such institutional changes will be tough and slow. Furthermore, even the perfectly designed institution will fail unless it can
deal with the most pressing issues facing its users. Thus, Canada must
also be at the forefront of efforts to rethink the criteria for the use of
force to address new security threats and the spectre of even more devastating weapons. When the UN's creators drafted the Charter in
1945, they could not foresee that wars *within* states, rather than
between them, would mount the most serious challenge to world
peace, or that the instability resulting from economic stress and bad
governance would complicate traditional ideas of collective security.
To these new circumstances has been added a further complication:
global terrorism. In the aftermath of September 11, many observers
suggested that this threat posed such a novel challenge that the existing legal restraints on the use of force against state and non-state
actors had become outdated.

In September 2003, partly in response to these criticisms,
Secretary-General Kofi Annan announced the creation of a High-
Level Panel to examine twenty-first-century challenges to peace and
security, and the contribution that collective action can make in
addressing them.[37] The panel's findings, released in December
2004, call for a new collective security system that better responds
to the threats and challenges of 2005—and beyond. Most significant
among them is the reaffirmation of the need for rules to limit the
right of states to resort to military force. Legal rules provide a framework against which states' reasons for going to war—and exposing
individuals and societies to the risk of disruption and harm—can be
debated and assessed. Without such a baseline, we return to self-
serving arguments and the law of the jungle. Canada, as a society
committed to the rule of law, must support the panel's recommendations not only to reassert the importance of legal rules, but also to
reform them in crucial areas such as the right of anticipatory self-
defence against states that harbour or promote terrorism and the

right of collective military intervention to address humanitarian emergencies.

My focus on the United Nations should not preclude us from thinking about governance in a broader and looser sense. Institutions in today's global arena go beyond the visible "bricks and mortar" type. They also encompass the complex networks that exist between different layers and functions of government—such as judges, central bankers, or health and safety regulators. The challenge of reforming governance at the global level means considering both formal bodies, like the UN, and less formal ones, like the G20. Indeed, as Prime Minister Paul Martin has suggested, these informal settings are sometimes more effective, as they allow officials to engage in concrete problem-solving away from the pressures of high diplomacy.[38]

215

PROTECTING AND PROMOTING HUMAN RIGHTS

While the entrenchment of human rights is a long-standing concern for Canada, today it needs a new infusion of energy and ideas. States have spent much of the last fifty years securing agreement on human rights covenants: now we need to implement these lofty declarations. The implementation imperative is particularly salient in a post–September 11 world, as governments all around the world experience the temptation to sacrifice rights in the name of the "war on terror." As part of its Model Citizen agenda, Canada must demonstrate to others how liberty and security can be balanced. It is undeniable that one of the most fundamental tasks of a government is to protect its citizens. In fact, the classical political philosopher Thomas Hobbes tells us that this is why human beings invented states. Yet since Hobbes's time, many states around the world have evolved into post-industrial liberal democracies. And the true test of a democracy is how it treats it citizens in times of crisis.[39]

After the terrorist attacks on New York and Washington, Bush administration officials insisted that the U.S. would continue to be vigilant in its advancement of human rights. In the words of National Security Adviser Condoleezza Rice, "Civil liberties matter to this President very much, and our values matter to us abroad . . . We're going to continue to press these things; we would not be America if we did not."[40] Yet the three-year period after 9/11 offers up some contradictory evidence. Internationally, the U.S. government has compromised its human rights promotion agenda in its search for military bases, intelligence co-operation, and political support in the war against terrorism. In Pakistan, Uzbekistan, and Indonesia, for example, the Bush administration has moved closer to governments with dubious human rights records, or has modified policies that had been introduced in order to signal disapproval of those countries' human rights provisions.[41] More troubling, it has shown a willingness to contravene international humanitarian law in its treatment of al-Qaeda and Taliban suspects at Guantanamo Bay— a move that has brought condemnation from its own Supreme Court. On the domestic front, these moves have been matched by the swift enactment of the Patriot Act, which contains measures that seriously curtail the civil liberties of those living in the United States by giving bold new powers to law enforcement and intelligence agencies. The most dramatic changes are in the area of enhanced surveillance procedures, which now permit roving wiretaps (when it is not practical to name one particular individual or communications device to monitor), and sneak-and-peek searches, which allow the government to delay notice of the issuance or execution of a warrant. In addition, the Patriot Act widens the definition of terrorism to include political activism, thereby dramatically expanding the targets of these surveillance mechanisms.

Canada has also passed legislation since 9/11 to address the new threat posed by terrorism. While our Anti-Terrorism Act (Bill C-46) took longer to pass through Parliament (and was therefore subject to more reasoned debate), it also contains controversial provisions in the areas of preventative arrest and the definition of terrorism. In fact, Bill C-46 defines terrorism more broadly than either the U.S. or the U.K. anti-terrorism acts. Furthermore, the new law threatens to normalize the exception. It risks turning powers designed for a state of emergency into permanent features of our Criminal Code. The argument in favour of these enhanced powers is that traditional law enforcement tools are inadequate for the novel kind of terrorism we face: if the direct targeting of civilians is now the preferred way of operating and the death of the terrorist is part of the objective, how can traditional notions of deterrence through punishment prevent the crime?

Policy-makers will have an opportunity to debate C-46 again in 2006, when its provisions expire. In preparation, Canadians must engage in a thorough debate about the strength of the arguments of the new powers and assess the impact of the legislation on civil liberties. We must also consider the effects of the past three years of anti-terrorism policy on minority groups in Canada, and whether enough has been done to work constructively with such groups in forging the right balance between security and civil liberties. After all, while individuals or organizations from ethnic communities may be part of the problem, in the vast majority of cases such communities can be part of the solution, by helping to discredit extremist views and to provide information and advice to security officials.[42] In the end, discriminatory measures against particular diasporas in Canada could prove counterproductive, by aggravating the sense of alienation and frustration upon which extremist groups prey.

My vision of Canada as Model Citizen also requires us to be uncompromising about human rights on the international stage, even in the hard cases. Otherwise, the value of our model will depreciate. Again, lest anyone think this is a "soft" agenda, think back to the NATO action in Kosovo in 1999. Here, NATO allies (including Canada) engaged in a military campaign, as a last resort, to deter Slobodan Milosevic in his scheme for ethnic cleansing and to facilitate the return of refugees to their homes. On this dimension, Lloyd Axworthy is absolutely right: the ultimate test of a human security policy is the willingness to use force to uphold the principles of protection.[43] But being a watchdog for human rights also entails other "robust" measures: a willingness to make membership in international bodies (including the UN) conditional on conformity with basic human rights principles; the courage to cut off diplomatic and economic ties with particular states (such as Saudi Arabia) when our citizens or their citizens are being oppressed; and the confidence to meet with controversial figures like the Dalai Lama, despite the protestations of powerful states. There is no doubt that such measures have the potential to affect Canada's economic and trade relationships. But this possibility must be balanced against the crucial symbolic value of these policies—a value that is experienced most deeply by those living inside the borders of states whose governments curtail basic civil and political rights. Sometimes, Model Citizens must be willing to stick their necks out.

ENSURING FAIRNESS

Prime Minister Martin claims that Canadians are motivated by the "moral imperative of fairness." In the domestic context, this has been reflected in the nature of our social security system and in the redistribution of wealth among Canadian provinces. The notion of equality of opportunity has not just been empty moralizing. "Real moral content," Martin says, "backed up by a commitment to results, is the hallmark of Canada at its finest."[44]

But what about fairness in the global community? Here the fundamental aim is more modest: not redistributing wealth at the levels we see domestically, but alleviating the crippling poverty that grips so many societies around the globe. It is no secret that Canada's foreign aid giving has been on the decline—from 0.54 per cent of GNI in the 1970s to 0.24 per cent in 2003. Our new fiscal situation allows us to do much more and the International Policy Statement calls for an increase of 8 per cent per year in official development assistance between 2005 and 2010. But the last three decades have also taught us that money alone is not enough. Model Citizens also need to roll up their sleeves and assist the developing world with the transforma- 219 tional policies needed to bring them into the Information Age.

The good news is that we already have a clear set of benchmarks to measure success and guide our policy. We can no longer hide behind the excuse that, given the magnitude of the problem, we don't know where to start. At the UN Millennium Summit in 2000, world leaders adopted eight "millennium development goals" (MDGs), with clear targets: to reduce poverty, hunger, disease, illiteracy, environmental degradation, and discrimination against women by 2015. These targets have been supported by a global campaign to mobilize political support for implementation, and a monitoring process that reports on both developed and developing countries' progress in meeting their commitments.[45]

The bad news is that the world's governments are falling well short on their own targets. Currently, over one billion of the world's people still live on less than US$1 a day, and poverty is on the rise in countries in Latin America, South Asia, and Africa. Whatever report you choose to consult, whether that of the World Wildlife Fund or the pro-business World Economic Forum (WEF), the global community is receiving a grade of F for "failure." The WEF's April 2004 report claimed the world is making only about a third of the effort required to achieve the MDGs, and called on all sectors of society (including business and civil society) to address the "egregious gap between aspiration and action."[46]

While Canada cannot hope to address this failure on its own, we should focus on three main activities. First, we must increase our financial commitment by setting out a timetable for meeting the 0.7 per cent target and improve the way the funds are dispersed. Second, drawing on our own competitive advantage, we should assist developing countries in building social infrastructure (education, public health, and a strong legal framework). And finally, we must act as a catalyst for other states and non-governmental actors—even if it means shaming them. The Liberal government's decision in the autumn of 2003 to make generic drugs available to the developing world is precisely the kind of behaviour a Model Citizen should exhibit.

Our new prime minister has captured the challenge we face: "A century from now, historians will ask: at what moment did the sovereign nations of the world begin to put in place the structures to shape the forces of globalization for the benefit of all?"[47] Canada can and must be one of the countries that leads the building of these new and more secure foundations.

PRESERVING OUR DISTINCTIVENESS

The final item on the Model Citizen agenda takes us back to that sore spot: improving our relationship with the United States. While I disagree with those who argue that Canadian foreign policy is essentially all about Canada-U.S. relations, I do accept that our relationship with the U.S. is the most significant of our foreign relationships. Given geographic realities, economic linkages, the configuration of power in the international system, and the values and interests we share with the U.S., working constructively with our neighbour to the south should be a focal point for our foreign policy.

It is also true that our influence with Washington is less than it could be. Susan Rice, who served on the National Security Council of President Bill Clinton and acted as assistant secretary of state for Africa between 1997 and 2001, compares Canada to a shy, admiring boy who "gets all spiffed up to win the heart of his dreamboat, while she [the United States] doesn't even know he exists." Beyond trade issues, Rice claims that Canada figures on the U.S. foreign policy agenda only in rare cases, such as when we chair the G8 or hold a non-permanent seat on the Security Council. Nor, she argues, do U.S. officials take much heed of Canadian views. In her capacity as the official responsible for U.S. policy toward the UN, peacekeeping, and Africa, Rice was not expected to consult regularly with Canadian officials. "By contrast," she writes, "I would have been deemed derelict had I not scheduled regular, lengthy discussions with my British, French and EU counterparts. In fact, I had more frequent interactions with my Japanese, Italian, South African and Egyptian counterparts than I did with Canadians."[48]

But how does one have influence in Washington? This seems to be the question that is occupying the brains of foreign policy officials all around the world, from London to Brussels to Moscow. Canadians are not alone in facing this dilemma.

A variety of answers have been put forward. For former ambassadors like Allan Gotlieb, it's all about personal relationships. While previous prime ministers have enjoyed strong ties with U.S. presidents or secretaries of state, Chrétien's notoriously frosty relationship with Bush, according to Gotlieb, took the Canada-U.S. relationship down to a level not seen in several decades. For Gotlieb, good chemistry brings access, and access brings influence.

This is why so many believed the Canada–U.S. relationship would improve under a new prime minister. The very act of changing the guard, it was hoped, would bring about the potential for other kinds of collaboration. Moreover, Paul Martin has repeatedly stressed that Canada's relationship with the U.S. is a key priority of his new government and that he would like to engage with Washington in a more "sophisticated" way. While these moves are important—and welcome—they have not proven to be enough to achieve a breakthrough in our trade disputes or in opening the U.S. border to Canadian beef. Personalities are crucial in politics, but they reach their limit if there is nothing concrete to put on the table. Prime Minister Martin will need more than goodwill to be heard by the White House.

Alternatively, there are those like former defence minister David Pratt who believe the path to better relations with Washington is through a stronger Canadian military. As chairman of the House of Commons Committee on National Defence, Pratt was a persistent critic of the reductions in spending on Canada's military. "If we want to affect U.S. foreign policy," he contends, "we have to almost earn the right to be able to criticize them, which means pulling our weight."[49] This kind of reasoning is dangerous, and potentially counterproductive—dangerous because it will lull us into believing we have a magic solution to the problem of how to win friends in Washington, and counterproductive because we can never hope to rebuild our military in the way that the United States would find most useful (and nor should we). Therefore, we run the risk of bringing on further recriminations from the U.S. Defense Department.

A more sustainable approach to gaining access to U.S. decision makers is to create permanent mechanisms for consultation between our two countries. As Susan Rice explains, while other countries have regular, institutionalized opportunities to meet with the White House on matters of joint concern, Canada lacks this kind of access. For example, the U.S. president currently meets two times each year with the rotating presidency of the European Union. Even though some of these meetings produce few dramatic policy statements, they are preceded by significant preparation by civil servants and extensive negotiation over the text of joint communiqués. Such mechanisms don't automatically yield agreement, nor should the two sides feel compelled to reach a consensus if there are irreconcilable differences. But they are valuable precisely because they force consultation and actively seek out areas for co-operation.

So how could Canada open the door to these high-level consultations? Susan Rice believes Canada needs to play much "tougher" with its U.S. neighbour and emphasize the degree to which the two countries now rely on each other for security. In other words, she argues, we should start to turn proximity into power. As a new prime minister, Paul Martin has an unique opportunity to explain to his American counterpart that Canada too has changed in important ways since September 11, 2001. He can emphasize that while Canada has been willing to collaborate with the U.S. in strengthening the defence of North America, it is no longer acceptable to Canadians to be excluded from formulating and implementing the foreign policies that directly affect our security. In Rice's formulation, Canada should no longer be included just in the defensive huddle: it also needs to part of the offensive huddle.[30]

Another way that Canada could enjoy greater influence in the United States is simply by being a Model Citizen. If we get on with our agenda and begin to develop innovative solutions to the most pressing problems faced by the world community, our experience and ideas will be in greater demand. But getting Washington's ear should not be our purpose—just a welcome side-benefit. Ultimately, the goal is to demonstrate to the United States the *value* of our distinctiveness, in terms of both how we organize ourselves domestically and how we pursue our values and interests abroad. After all, it was precisely this distinctiveness that allowed us to be a safe haven for people and aircraft on September 11.

Finally, we need to put the Ottawa-Washington relationship into the broader framework of Canadian-American relations. Much of what constitutes the relationship between our two communities today is occurring below and beyond official state-to-state channels. Premiers and senators, as well as prime ministers and presidents, play crucial roles in solving day-to-day problems. But so too do "ordinary" Canadians and Americans, in their professional and private capacities. So when we talk about influence, let's think not just about our leaders, but also about ourselves.

Pulling Our Weight

For some of you, the key question about my Model Citizen concept ultimately comes down to this: what does it mean for our military? The 2004 crisis in Haiti highlighted the conflict between Canada's aspirations for its global role and its actual military capabilities. Existing commitments in Bosnia and Afghanistan made it impossible to allocate troops to a country that occupies an important place in Canada's strategic and political calculations.

In my vision, Model Citizens *pull their weight*. But for Canada to do so, we need to re-examine why we have a military and what we want to use it for.

In this context, it is worth understanding one aspect of Norway's foreign policy: its focus on niche military capabilities. Norwegian policymakers have understood that while during the Cold War, when huge militaries were pitted against each other, the potential contribution from smaller nations was minimal, the nature of global threats today is very different. These threats are not always presented in military uniform and are not always carried out by states. In a world where traditional defence is insufficient to protect against such threats, a country that invests in special capabilities or skills can bring something valuable to the table. As American journalist Matthew Brzezinski puts it: "The evolving nature of conflict presents opportunities for Davids to fight alongside Goliaths, if they bring the right slingshot."[51]

There are constituencies within DFAIT and DND that sniff at the Canada-Norway comparison. At roughly 4.5 million people, Norway is thought of as a small country. With only half the number of active members of the armed forces that Canada has[52] and with military expenditures of roughly US$3.5 billion,[53] the Norwegian military is hardly a major force to be reckoned with. Canada, by contrast, is a member of the G8. It has global interests and broad requirements for domestic security, and therefore requires the maintenance of multi-faceted capabilities. This mentality permeates much of the defence establishment, where there is aversion to any talk of niches or overreliance on only one of the three parts of our military.[54] As one DND official put it to me, "If we get too specialized, we may never be called upon. We need to deploy capabilities if we are going to be valuable to anyone."

Norway has understood, quicker than Canada, that focus is the only sustainable strategy in a post-9/11 world for countries that cannot aspire to the status of superpower. In addition, it has moved away from traditional strategies to protect Norwegian territory toward an anti-terrorism agenda that includes a capacity to participate in military missions abroad. Under the leadership of Defence Minister Kristin Krohn Devold, the Norwegian military was radically restructured to focus on a couple of specialized capabilities, based on Norway's traditional strengths and technical expertise: mine-clearing and mountain reconnaissance. In order to finance this shift, Devold didn't bang the cabinet table and demand large increases in her budget. Instead, she closed a third of Norway's bases and cut military personnel by a fifth. In aggregate terms, military spending has increased by only 8 per cent.

Some have argued that Norway's new strategy is designed solely to court favour in Washington. If so, there are limits to the value of their approach for Canada. We should focus and retool our military for *ourselves*—not because we want to be noticed by the Bush administration, but because it is the only way that we can pursue our interests, project our values, and contribute to the resolution of global problems.

What, then, should Canada's specialized capabilities be? Upon assuming the leadership of the Liberal Party, Paul Martin announced a spending increase of $4 billion for military equipment, including new search-and-rescue aircraft (predominantly for use at home), marine helicopters, three naval supply ships that can be used to transport heavy equipment, and new lighter-weight armoured vehicles for use in overseas

missions. The 2005 budget earmarked additional spending for the Canadian Forces, and the International Policy Statement sets a new strategic
course for our military. This new defence policy is long overdue. Many of
the ideas presented have been brewing inside government, academia,
and public policy circles for some time. While there are clearly differences of emphasis, most are agreed that there are two major priorities:
building up Canada's commitment to the defence of North America,
and helping to stabilize "unruly" parts of the world—whether through
combat troops, peacekeeping forces, or civilian peace-builders. Canada's
role will primarily be a value-added as opposed to an independent one:
contributing more strength to create a critical mass or to fill out a mission.

To give concrete meaning to these recommendations, consider two
specific policy dilemmas that have dominated the agenda of Canada's
defence minister over the past three years: whether to participate in
the U.S. scheme for ballistic missile defence, and whether to invest in
upgrading our strategic lift capability.

The first issue is hardly new. Ever since the devastating V2 attacks on
London during the Second World War, the United States has been interested in the concept of missile defence: intercepting a bomb—and its
delivery vehicle, the missile—before it hits the desired target. As we
moved into the Cold War era, and with the new dynamic created by
nuclear weapons, the issue received even greater attention. In the United
States, there was a pressing desire to turn back the clock to the pre-nuclear
era of "perfect" security. In Canada, there was concern about the potential
for Soviet missiles, intended for U.S. targets, to fall on Canadian soil.

In the late 1960s, Canada and the United States engaged in discussions about the possibility of an anti-ballistic missile system being
stationed in Grand Forks, North Dakota. The prevailing view at this
time was that missile defence would be detrimental to world stability,
as it would contradict the logic of "mutually assured destruction."
This doctrine—central to deterrence theory—claimed that as long as
one superpower could survive a nuclear attack by the other and launch

a retaliatory strike, there would be no incentive for either the U.S. or Soviet Union to use their nuclear weapons. The certainty of nuclear destruction, on both sides, was enough to keep the peace. A missile defence scheme, it was thought, would undermine the doctrine by making it possible for one state to survive a nuclear attack and therefore to contemplate first use of nuclear weapons. It was this belief in the destabilizing effects of missile defence that led the Canadian government, in 1968, to ask for an additional clause to be added to the NORAD framework exempting Canada from any participation in an anti-ballistic missile system.[55] When the United States and the Soviet Union signed an Anti-Ballistic Missile Treaty in 1972, research on missile defence was stalled and the issue lost some of its relevance. But it resurfaced as a point of tension between the U.S. and Canadian governments with Ronald Reagan's ambitious scheme for a space-based missile defence shield—known more commonly as Star Wars.

Though Reagan's vision ultimately proved unworkable, a more modest version of missile defence, based on land- and sea-based interceptors and sophisticated radar systems, has become a major priority for the Bush administration. Since 2001, the U.S. has lobbied its allies to join the program to create a network of satellite-tracking stations around the world. To date, Britain, Denmark, and Australia have announced their intention to join the scheme. Other allies, such as Japan and South Korea, are engaged in active discussions with the White House about a regional variation on the U.S. plan. Even the old enemy of the United States, Russia, announced in January 2003 that it would co-operate with the Bush administration in the field of ballistic missile defence, with a set of conditions designed to protect Russian technology and intellectual property. In the end, President Putin calculated that Russia's biggest concern—unbridled U.S. unilateralism—would be best addressed through co-operation with Washington rather than condemnation.

There is still great uncertainty as to whether ballistic missile defence could ever become workable. The effectiveness of what is known as "terminal" and "mid-course" missile defence has come into question, leading the Bush administration to invest in "boost" capabilities that would take out enemies' missiles sooner after their launch. Even if these were to become operational (and the string of failed tests have not been encouraging), there is no guarantee that they would work in every instance. As a result, the United States may be embarking down a road that will bring little concrete benefit and that will potentially incur great costs to its own security. Critics of the plan to intercept ballistic missiles fear that it could create a false sense of security—a "Maginot-line" mentality—that would blind the U.S. government to the other possible ways that its opponents might use weapons of mass destruction against American towns and cities. At the end of the day, ballistic missile defence could not have protected the United States from the attacks of September 11. If terrorism is now the biggest threat to U.S. security, why build an expensive system designed to counteract something else?

These concerns are valid. But they didn't really help our government with the decision facing it in 2003–04. The Bush administration is embarking on the missile defence course anyway, believing that a project of research and development will at the very least strengthen the deterrent against attacks from so-called rogue states and serve as a valuable test facility. The research and development budget for 2004 alone was roughly US$9 billion. Construction is nearing completion on the first six missile defence sites at Fort Greely in Alaska, to be followed by four more at Vandenberg Air Force Base in California. In light of these moves, the Canadian government announced in May 2003 that it would begin talks with the U.S. to explore its future participation in a missile defence arrangement. In February 2005, under pressure from opposition parties and public opinion, Foreign Affairs Minister Pierre Pettigrew announced that Canada would refuse a further role in Washington's scheme.[56]

The decision about participation in a ballistic missile defence scheme illustrates powerfully the difficult balancing of values and interests that confronts Canadian foreign policy-makers. On the one hand, those such as Lloyd Axworthy argue that joining any kind of scheme for missile defence would jeopardize Canada's position as an advocate of arms-control agreements. "Joining in missile defence," Axworthy laments, "would take us dramatically away from a course chartered by generations of Canadian governments—a foreign policy based on the belief that a predictable rule of law, and not the arbitrary rule of men, is the best way of ensuring both national and global security."⁵⁷ A crucial feature of this historical pedigree is Canada's commitment to preventing the weaponization of space. In addition to compromising the value of non-proliferation, opponents such as Axworthy contend, co-operating with the U.S. on missile defence would compromise Canadian sovereignty, by limiting our ability to make independent choices about the deployment and activities of our troops.

On the other hand, using the language of national interest, it can be argued that missile defence would provide a degree of protection for Canadian cities in the case of a ballistic missile attack against North America. Such a position, by the way, also contains a strong element of morality—based on the notion that the highest duty of a state leader is to ensure the protection of his or her citizens. The degree to which you believe that the threat to our citizens is real will determine the weight that you give to this argument. My view is that while Canada is much less likely than the United States to be chosen as a ballistic missile target, it remains an ally of the U.S. and is viewed as such in other parts of the world. (Note that I said "ally" of the U.S., not "slave" or "poodle.") More significant is our close geographic proximity; any engagement between incoming missiles and a missile defence scheme could very well take place in Canadian airspace. That means the probability of an attack on our soil is greater than zero, and therefore demands consideration by policy-makers. Finally, our past policy choices have created a situation in which we treat our defence as largely synonymous with the defence of the United States *within North America*. This is Axworthy's "course chartered by generations of Canadian governments." Some, like Axworthy, may wish it were otherwise. But such is the historical context in which we must make our decision about missile defence.

There is an additional case for joining a ballistic missile defence scheme: its potential to further the Canadian goal of non-proliferation. This statement may seem surprising, but consider this logic. *If* missile defence can be made effective (and this is still a big "if") and is applied to the whole of North America, it could help to create a disincentive for states—particularly those states with limited resources—to acquire ballistic missiles. In order to break through such a shield (which could never hope to be 100 per cent foolproof), these states would need to develop and deploy hundreds, if not thousands, of weapons—and therefore incur prohibitive costs.[58] Of course, this argument works only if the states desiring ballistic missiles wish to use them on North America; if their enemies do not enjoy a missile defence system, then the rationale for proliferation (and use) of nuclear weapons would still exist.

The final argument in favour of participating in talks on ballistic missile defence is the one that motivated Canada's involvement in the creation of NORAD in the 1950s: a desire to have a seat at the table on policy decisions that affect the defence of North America. While Canada's position in NORAD is not entirely optimal, there is a high degree of equality between the two member states that few Canadians appreciate. NORAD involves the *joint* provision and management of air-defence warning, surveillance, and interception. Under the NORAD treaty, Canada supplies the deputy commander and senior Canadian officers share control of day-to-day operations at NORAD headquarters in Colorado. Remarkably, on September 11, it was a Canadian, rather than an American, who sat in the general's chair directing North American air defence.

Given the already existing warning systems that NORAD provides—and that Canadians help to operate—the U.S. has sought, as its first preference, to put a missile defence scheme under NORAD control.[59] Canada took one step towards this in the summer of 2004, when the government agreed to amend the NORAD treaty to allow the transmission of satellite and radar data about incoming missiles to the U.S. Northern Command. However, our decision not to participate raises questions as to where the U.S. will now locate the decision-making apparatus to *respond* to any incoming missiles. In the view of military historian J.L. Granatstein, Canadian abstention from missile defence will give the Americans an incentive to either shut NORAD down entirely or rip the guts out of it—and, along with it, destroy any existing Canadian influence on continental air defence.[60] Far from forfeiting our sovereignty, participation in ballistic missile defence would exemplify the *exercise* of sovereignty. It wouldn't give us the right of veto over all decisions, but it would give us the opportunity to take part in decision-making. It would open up, rather than close down, options.

After a careful consideration of our values and interests, I came down on the side of our government's pursuing missile defence talks with the United States. In my view, the opportunity for some influence ranked ahead of the opportunity for none—especially when Washington's decisions could have a very real effect on Canadians. I did not, however, support negotiations on missile defence as a way of improving Canadian-American relations. Critics of missile defence were right to be suspicious: coming on the heels of our decision not to participate in the war against Iraq, our government appeared to be atoning for the sin of disagreeing with Washington. The process of argumentation I have outlined represents the kind of reasoning that must guide Canadian decision makers in this new century. Knee-jerk pro-Americanism or anti-Americanism is an avoidance of responsibility and a betrayal of the Canadian public. Unfortunately, our final decision—coming on the heels of mixed messages about whether we would participate—made the relationship with Washington more strained than it needed to be.

A decision to co-operate with the U.S. on missile defence could have, as the Russian example shows, contained caveats. Early on in the bilateral talks, the Liberal government (rightly) maintained that Canadian collaboration would be contingent upon the U.S. refraining from any plans to weaponize outer space. While members of the Bush administration have expressed their desire to see missile defence include space-based components,[61] it is important to recall that the plans of the Clinton administration had expressly ruled this out. In other words, there are constituencies within the U.S. that are open to a constructive debate on what missile defence should and should not aim to achieve. We could have supported these moderate voices.

Finally, in choosing to engage in talks with the U.S. on missile defence, we were not closing off other avenues for defence and security policy. Opponents such as Axworthy seem to suggest that once we start the discussion, we automatically commit ourselves "to a self-perpetuating cycle of threats, armed responses and dramatically increased defence budgets."[62] But this logic simply doesn't hold. Can't we walk and chew gum at the same time? I see no reason why Canada could not continue to work toward a multilateral treaty banning weapons in outer space, or participate in discussions with other members of the UN about how to address new threats to international peace and security (including weapons of mass destruction). Similarly, Canada could still work collaboratively with others on all of the issues dear to Axworthy's heart: international crime, pandemic disease, egregious human rights violations, and environmental degradation. Our former foreign minister believes that Canada's reputation would have been irrevocably tarnished by co-operating with Washington on missile defence, thereby ruling us out as a credible multilateral player. According to this line of thinking, Britain, Denmark, Japan, Australia, Russia, and South Korea would also be prevented from playing a constructive role in multilateral forums. The number of potential discussion partners is starting to look smaller and smaller.

The argument about sacrificing multilateralism on the altar of missile defence doesn't hold water. Reputations are made of much more than this. Moreover, other states might have welcomed Canada's involvement in thinking about how to secure the defence of North America, as a potentially calming influence on White House policy. As partners in these discussions, Canadian officials, for example, might have reminded the United States that even a working missile defence shield will not guarantee a perfect state of invulnerability. In fact, many Americans themselves—including a number of retired generals—have encouraged President Bush to postpone deployment of the shield and invest the billions of dollars saved in keeping nuclear weapons out of the hands of terrorists. Or, U.S. administrations could have been encouraged to explore other means of dealing with potential threats from those who possess weapons of mass destruction. In the final analysis, a major component of the problem posed by "rogue states" is *political*, and must be addressed with non-military strategies.[63]

A second example of the tough choices facing Canadian policy-makers is the question of strategic lift capability. One of the key factors supporting Britain's recent successes in international rescue and peacekeeping efforts is its capacity for rapid deployment of troops. After 9/11, the British Ministry of Defence invested in airlift capability by taking on four Boeing C-17 transport planes, which have much greater range and ability than the C-130 Hercules planes that Canada currently operates. When faced with difficult choices about how to allocate resources, our own defence minister, John McCallum, made a different calculation. His priority was to invest in modernizing equipment for ground troops—including new armoured combat vehicles and high-tech communications equipment[64]—rather than spending $3 billion on jumbo cargo planes. It was a difficult judgment call, but one that supported his desire to give greater short-term attention to the needs of the army (as opposed to equal treatment of the three pillars of our military: the army, air force, and navy). As an alternative, McCallum indicated that he would support a NATO plan to buy a number of the valuable C-17s and share them. In the meantime, Canada will continue to rent cargo planes or borrow them from other countries.

Once again, the decision provoked a storm of criticism from opposition parties—this time Stephen Harper and his (former) Canadian Alliance colleagues, supported by members of the defence establishment. Some of the opponents, particularly those representing defence lobby groups, can hardly be called objective. But the disquiet spread to non-military circles, and was heard in the voices of those who lamented Canada's inability to live up to its Pearsonian heritage. But given the constraints facing the defence minister at the time, I would have made the same decision. With an annual increase in the defence budget of $800 million and a capital account in desperate need of replenishing, the minister had to put the immediate needs of soldiers first on the shopping list. For the government of Paul Martin, however, reliable access to strategic lift capacity will be essential to realizing the vision of a transformed and streamlined Canadian military. If, as I have outlined above, we wish to contribute small combat and peacekeeping units to assist in stabilizing missions in troubled regions of the world, we must have an ability to get our units into the field as quickly as possible. This priority, I would argue, is greater than the need to upgrade our submarines or to invest in the latest fighter aircraft. Our stronger NATO allies will increasingly provide the high-tech airpower for overseas missions, but they will still require the kind of well-trained troops and special units that Canada can contribute.

This emphasis on contribution leads me to the last point to make about the Model Citizen agenda: it isn't necessarily a unique identity. Others can play this role as well, and we should enthusiastically welcome them. The goal is not to make Canada the only Model Citizen for the twenty-first century, but rather to help propagate this model so as to create more dynamic and constructive partners for the resolution of the tough global problems we now face. We might encourage others to select different focal points for their activism, so as to avoid duplication and to fill capability gaps, but we shouldn't try to monopolize the Model Citizen path. Multiple Model Citizens will help to make our world community stronger, healthier, and more prosperous.

Conclusion

Y FIRST experience as a warrior for Canada occurred on a warm October weekend in 1995. In a hotel in downtown Montreal, in the midst of the referendum on Quebec's future, I addressed a crowd of young francophones committed to the Canadian cause. The event was sponsored by Le Groupe des Cents, an organization of one hundred young Québécois from all political persuasions and all sectors of society who were campaigning against Quebec independence. It was not only the first time I had participated in a political rally, but also the first time I had spoken publicly in French. I was nervous and uncomfortable, but absolutely determined to raise my voice.

My message, as a Canadian living outside Quebec, was that the Canadian experiment *mattered*. Days before, in drafting my speech with the executive of Le Groupe des Cents, I had been tempted to withdraw my name from the program. The rally's organizers had originally wanted me to speak about Canada's "two founding nations," and the importance of an English-French partnership in forging our country's future. But as a Métis Canadian, I could not deliver on their expectations. For me, the story of the "two founding nations" is exactly that— a cozy but inaccurate tale about our country's origins. If sustaining such a myth was necessary to winning the referendum, then I wanted no part of it. To my surprise, these young francophones were persuaded by my edited version of the story. And so my contribution to the event was a mixture of support for the federalist cause, a demonstration that

235

the "rest of Canada" cared, and a short history lesson about the role of our First Nations, Inuit, and Métis in building Canada.

Ten days later, on the night of the referendum, I sat side by side with members of Le Groupe des Cents as they watched the television coverage of the vote. It was an agonizing experience, as the results for the "yes" side climbed over the 50 per cent hurdle one minute and dipped below it the next. The mood in the room was sombre: we all knew what was at stake. And then, as the "no" side finally squeaked ahead, we all rushed out the door and made our way to the Metropolitan—the Montreal venue for the "no" side's celebrations. As I stood among the jubilant crowd of federalist supporters, tears of relief rolled down my face. But I also realized that while we had faced down the separatists, the real journey was only beginning. Throughout the referendum campaign, the message of Le Groupe des Cents was that young Canadians, from both inside and outside Quebec, could build a better country *together*. If Quebeckers dared to vote no, an alternative future was possible.

Almost ten years on, I am still driven by that promise. Domestically, we are on a promising track. The deficit has been brought under control. The economy is growing. And we are modernizing our public services. Internationally, however, we are still living in the world of 1995. Many observers, both inside and outside of Canada, are speculating about our demise as a relevant actor on the global stage.

I have argued in this book that Canada is at a crossroads. Our history and our reputation have given us much, but they can no longer sustain us. While the threat to national unity has largely subsided, we face a new crisis of identity about our place in the global community. Canada's new leaders must redefine the global role we will play in the twenty-first century and ensure that we make the necessary investments to carry it out. As Chris Alexander puts it, "Canada has traditionally only fully understood its dependence on the world beyond North America in wartime. Our generation has the tools to show it today."

That role has two dimensions. On the one hand, we have a regional destiny. The events of September 11 have created new imperatives for Canada, Mexico, and the United States—not only in the economic realm, which is already well established, but also in terms of defence and security. In this domain, Canada must resist calls for continentalism and carve out a distinct position as a partner in sharing the North American continent. On the other hand, Canada has a global destiny. Our geography, history, and identity demand engagement with the wider world. By blending our values and interests, we can chart a course as a Model Citizen in the community of states in the new millennium. That course must be grounded in a commitment to global governance, human rights, and fairness, but it must also be backed up by new investments in the armed forces and development assistance. Above all, it must strive for a more productive and mature relationship with the United States.

A New Kind of Foreign Policy

The role I've outlined for Canada is a more focused one, designed to contribute with others to the resolution of global problems and to take the lead where initiative is lacking or where the issues that concern us most are at stake. The changes I've suggested are critical not just to reviving a sagging international reputation. They are also necessary to ensure that our government can advance the values and interests of the more than 30 million people that make up our country. But in and of themselves, they are not enough. By way of conclusion, I want to encourage Canada, and Canadians, to think about foreign policy differently in our new century. This involves two changes in mindset.

First, we must move beyond the bureaucratic straitjackets reflected in the organization of government departments. Foreign policy is not the preserve of the departments of Foreign Affairs, International Trade, or National Defence. Due to the changing nature of their policy agendas and to advances in technology, other ministries (such as the Ministry of the Environment and the Ministry of Agriculture) have established their own capacity to transact international business. Similarly, the government resources dedicated to pursuing Canada's interests abroad are not limited to the $1.7 billion spent by Foreign Affairs, $168 million spent by International Trade, and $13.3 billion spent by National Defense.* In today's interdependent world, where countries' fortunes are linked together in a multitude of ways, almost all government departments are, in a sense, involved in foreign policy-making. In fact, it has become harder and harder to separate foreign and domestic issues.[1] Let's consider some of the policy areas that have experienced the greatest shakeup since 9/11: financial regulation, immigration, police powers, and transportation infrastructure. These are issues formerly thought of as within the *domestic* policy sphere; yet it is clear that they cannot be managed exclusively within Canada and that the policies designed around them are often targeted at *international* problems.

Second, and more importantly, we need to rethink the very nature of diplomacy, and diplomats, in the twenty-first century. Professional diplomacy—the institution that once acted as the valued intermediary for states and societies separated by law, culture, and language—now competes with a host of other organizations and individuals that must, and can, interact on the global stage without such intermediation. Ironically, it is Western governments themselves that were the architects of their own decline. Globalization isn't something that happened to us as a result of changes in the world. Rather, as Deputy Minister of Foreign Affairs Peter Harder explains, it is "something we did to ourselves, as a matter of explicit national policy."[2] And so today, when we speak of Canada's relationship with other countries, especially

---

* These are the budget estimates for these three departments for 2004–2005.

the U.S., we are using a convenient form of shorthand. The vast major-ity of the transactions that make up those relationships occur with no reference to government at all.

In other words, we need to conceive of our country not just as Canada with a capital C—the corporate entity represented by the flag or by government officials—but also as *Canadians*. It may be true, as Andrew Cohen has argued, that Canada's influence in the world is declining, but only if we use a state-to-state framework and measure influence in terms of the traditional categories of federal spending on defence, diplomacy, and development. Cohen tells us that our retreat from the world stage is a "flight from responsibility" and has "dimin-ished us as a people."[3] The image this conveys is of a population hap-pily asleep on lawn chairs next to Lake Muskoka. A Canada that is staying at home.

But is this reality? Or is it only part of the picture, seen through twentieth-century glasses? Canadians are doing fantastic things in the world. Many of us are aware of the more high-profile examples of Model Citizens. But younger Canadians, from all sectors, are building upon the Canadian legacy for global engagement and taking it even one step further. They are, like John Hancock, advising the director-general of the World Trade Organization. Or, like Joanna Kerr and Parker Mitchell, they are running non-governmental organizations. All of these roles are part of *what Canada does in the world.*

Some lament this as "brain drain." How do we get these talented Canadians back home? But they are missing the point. In a globalized world, with mobile citizens and problems and opportunities that transcend frontiers, this isn't brain drain. Rather, as the organization Canada 25 has argued, it is more like "brain circulation."

I'm not trying to throw a lifeline to our government—or to give it another excuse for not investing in the traditional tools of foreign policy. New investments to retool our armed forces, to develop a robust intelligence capability, and to promote a good-governance

239

agenda remain crucial pieces of the puzzle. What I am suggesting is that foreign policy is not something others do "out there." It is the responsibility of all of us, as part of the global commons. And it is something many of us, in our day-to-day activities, are already actively engaged in, if only we would reorient our minds to recognize it. In the twenty-first century, it is *real* intelligence—not just the random and raw data that spits out of a computer—that will allow individuals, organizations, and countries to thrive. Developing real intelligence requires moving beyond the information collected at the government-to-government level and digging deeper to gather knowledge about how other societies actually work.

As connected and globally engaged citizens, Canadians are contributing to this intelligence gathering in a myriad of ways. We are— already—at home in the world. Let's acknowledge and build upon that reality.

Afterword

THERE HAS BEEN a series of events and developments, both globally and within Canada, since the first publication of *At Home in the World*. Internationally, we have seen the re-election of George W. Bush as president of the United States, the tragedy of the tsunami in Asia, the formation of an interim government in post-Saddam Iraq, the release of Kofi Annan's agenda for reform of the United Nations, the Orange Revolution in Ukraine, and the French and Dutch rejection of the draft treaty for a European constitution. Domestically, the minority government of Paul Martin has entered into a new security and prosperity partnership with Mexico and the United States, earmarked new spending for Canada's military and for overseas development assistance, announced its decision not to participate in the U.S. ballistic missile defence scheme, and issued the long-awaited review of Canadian foreign policy.

Some things, of course, have not changed. Massive violations of human rights continue in the Darfur region of Sudan. Efforts to forge a common global strategy on climate change remain stalled. Terrorists continue to exploit vulnerabilities in free societies, as seen in the co-ordinated attacks on London's transportation system during the 2005 G8 Summit. A resolution to the softwood lumber dispute between Canada and the U.S. is still elusive—despite rulings from both the World Trade Organization and NAFTA.

These examples of continuity and change do not challenge the central premise of the book. Instead, they give it added energy and meaning. Canada, as one of the world's most successful liberal democracies, must craft a new and more strategic role for itself on the global stage. While managing the Canada-U.S. relationship will be a key part of that new agenda, Canada's national interests, combined with its responsibilities as a member of the international community, demand a foreign policy that is global in its reach and aspiration. To choose between the United States and the rest of the world would be to deny the kind of country that Canada has become.

In setting forth a vision for Canadian foreign policy in the twenty-first century, my book has engendered some lively debate. In these pages, I'd like to pick out the most significant challenges that I have encountered, and rearticulate the case for Canada as Model Citizen.

Let's Face Reality

A common criticism of *At Home in the World* is that it is Utopian. Canadian foreign policy, so the argument goes, has been dogged by a tendency to avoid reality: what we need is a return to the good old-fashioned pursuit of the national interest. Two very distinguished Canadian diplomats, who have represented our country in Washington, have recently made a strong case for this revival of "realism." Allan Gotlieb, in his riveting historical overview of Canadian foreign policy since 1945, decries the tendency of Canadian foreign policy to oscillate between realism and romanticism. In Gotlieb's view, Canadian policy makers must break away from the romantic Utopianism that puts the United Nations, rule-making, and the promotion of the country's values at the top of the foreign policy agenda. In today's world of uncertainty and turmoil, he argues, "Canada must adopt a reality-based foreign policy by responding to the imperatives of geography, history and economics."[1] Derek Burney, in his 2005 Simon Reisman Lecture, warns that if we indulge fancifully about bringing our values to the world, Canada will be "confined more permanently to the periphery as a dilettante, not to be taken seriously."[2] Canadians must deal with the world as it is, he opines, not as we may wish it to be.

The reality card is a powerful one to play. But it is also a very old game. The interventions of commentators such as Gotlieb and Burney are in many ways reminiscent of the 1920s, when the discipline of international relations itself developed. At that time, the "realist school" of international relations appeared—largely in contrast to the "idealists," such as Woodrow Wilson, who dared to believe that the world needed more law and institutions if it was to avoid the kind of carnage wreaked upon Europe between 1914 and 1918. E.H. Carr, the most eloquent of the opponents of Wilsonianism, penned a masterly critique of that age's illusions in his book *The Twenty Years' Crisis.* However, he also wisely reminded us to be wary of so-called realism. "In politics," he wrote, "the belief that certain facts are unalterable or certain trends irresistible commonly reflects a lack of desire or lack of interest to change or resist them ...."[3]

It's hard to disagree with the central thesis: a reality-based foreign policy would be a good thing for Canada. But is the "realist" version of reality irrefutable? While there are certain unalterable facts out there, we live in a *social* world, where interpretation and persuasion also figure prominently. In my tutorials, I encourage my undergraduate students to consider how each theory or approach to international relations depicts the world from 50,000 feet, as if we were flying in an airplane. Traditional realists, as we know, see power—and more precisely, the balance of power. Liberals see something different: in addition to power, they see rules and institutions. Some of them also divide the world not into sovereign states, but into a "zone of democracies" (a world of peace) and a "zone of non-democracies" (a world of turmoil). Marxists and neo-Marxists see something different again: a world economy that has a strong and expanding core, and a weak and underdeveloped periphery.

What global reality do I see?

There is first, and foremost, the reality of power. Call the United

243

States whatever you like—a hyperpower, a hegemon, an empire—but there is little doubt that we are living in a unipolar world, particularly when measured in military terms. Yet, it is also clear that there are other emerging powers, such as China, India, and Brazil, who are already exerting their influence in ways that affect Canadians. This, too, is *reality*. Countries like China and India aren't just markets to tap into; they are the potential leaders of a future multilateral system. If we see them as such, we have an interest in ensuring that in the decades ahead, they become embedded into a global governance structure that continues to reflect Canadian interests and values.

In addition, there are significant limits to American power. Financially, the size of the U.S. economy still allows it to dominate global investment flows and to sustain a large current account deficit. But the degree of freedom the United States has enjoyed is shrinking, thanks to its excessive spending. Each day, the U.S. needs to attract approximately $US 2 billion in capital to finance its current account deficit; its sources are private investors and foreign governments. It is the decisions of key central bankers in Japan, China, Taiwan, South Korea, Hong Kong, and India about their U.S. reserve holdings—perhaps even more than the statements of Mr. Greenspan—that have the greatest effect on U.S. interest rates. In November of 2004, when the Federal Reserve chairman intimated that the U.S. trade deficit was looking "increasingly less tenable," the Dow Jones fell 115 points and the dollar lost 0.4 percent of its value against the Euro. In February 2005, when a Bank of Korea spokesman hinted that his country might want to diversify its exchange reserves away from dollars, the effect on markets was much more dramatic: a 174-point plunge for the Dow and a 1.4 percent decrease in the dollar's value against the Euro. This vividly illustrates how the balance of power in the global economy has shifted.[4]

Politically, the same point can be made. The 9/11 attacks were swiftly followed by an awesome display of American military power against the Taliban regime in Afghanistan. But did this application of military prowess translate into a political solution that the U.S. preferred? According to the first finance minister of post-Taliban Afghanistan, Ashraf Ghani, U.S. power proved necessary but insufficient. A much more intangible phenomenon, legitimacy, was needed to bring about a political settlement. It was only the United Nations, in the form of the secretary-general's special representative, that could create the conditions for a political stability. This, too, is *reality*.

Even in the realm where the U.S. seems unrivalled, military power, there is cause for concern. As of April 2005, the U.S. had approximately 135,000 troops in Iraq, but almost half of these were drawn from the reserves or National Guard. As the historian Niall Ferguson has argued, today the United States "suffers from a personnel deficit": the 500,000 troops that it can deploy overseas are not enough to win all of the conflicts the U.S. has to, or might in future have to, fight.[5] More significantly, its military resources cannot be used in a vacuum: they often require the support, or at least tacit consent, of others. During the recent military action against Iraq, the Turkish parliament's refusal to allow transport of U.S. ground troops across its soil, and Saudi Arabia's reluctance to give Washington permission to use its air bases, greatly affected the conduct and cost of the war to the United States. This is an interesting example of where "soft balancing can have real effects on hard power."[6]

The second "reality" to explore is the U.S.-Canada relationship. The proponents of realism, such as Gotlieb and Burney, believe that Canada must put the United States front and centre in its foreign policy. According to these authors, Canada's best foreign policy years were those in which our officials enjoyed a close relationship with government officials in Washington. Yet what is the state of that relationship today? Looking at the facts, it's hard to argue for a special relationship in which Canada has privileged access to U.S. decision-making on foreign policy, and vice versa.

It is also debatable whether Canada could assume (or restore to itself) the role of bridge between the United States and the rest of the world. This is a vocation British Prime Minister Tony Blair tried to appropriate, with limited success, during the first term of George W. Bush's presidency. But the competition for the part of bridge-builder goes even further. In this first decade of the twenty-first century, when the U.S. stands as the world's only superpower, countries *everywhere* are scrambling to understand and influence what is happening in Wash ington. One need only consider the foreign coverage of the 2004 U.S.

presidential election: foreign journalists travelled to every nook and cranny of the American heartland. Such an important task—under-standing the United States—cannot be left to an interlocutor like Canada. Other governments are intent upon establishing their own channels of knowledge and influence.

I'm not denying the facts: Canada and the United States have a deep partnership, built on more than two centuries of close economic, political, and personal ties. Canadians and Americans intermingle constantly, both professionally and personally, and we have built a regional economy that has outstripped all expectations in terms of trade expansion and economic growth. This is a substantial achieve-ment, and something Canadians can take great pride in. Yet, does any of this mean that Canada and the United States have a special relation-ship, or that Canada is America's *best* friend? I argue in chapter 1 of this book that it does not. This isn't intended as a normative state-ment; it says nothing about what kind of relationship Canada might *want* to have with its southern neighbour. I'm only questioning whether "best friend" is the phrase that Americans would use to describe Canada (and Canadians) today, whether we think of officials in the Bush administration, or the broader U.S. public.

Thirdly, I see different ways of affecting change, and spreading democracy, in contemporary international relations. The U.S. is demonstrating one very bold strategy. But the European Union has shown us another. I would argue that Europe's greatest foreign policy success (despite the challenges of referring to a coherent "European" policy) is EU enlargement. The success began with Spain and Portugal, and it has continued with the latest round of new EU member states. Europe has engaged in peaceful and progressive democratization through the shrewd use of diplomacy and accession criteria. This, too, is *reality*. Before we accept the all-too-easy generalizations about Europe, let's look more carefully at the "zone of peace" which European states have maintained, and extended, on a continent that only sixty years ago was wracked by a conflict that took the lives of so many young men, including Canadians. The process may even end up with Turkey as part of the EU—which would mean that Europe would border Iraq.

247

So let me come back to Carr. Despite his blistering attack on the Utopians, he also drew our attention to the values perpetrated by so-called realists—whether explicitly, or implicitly. Realism, he argued, turns out in practice to be just as much influenced by particular views and biases as any other mode of thought. And so I encourage you to look at the world from 50,000 feet, and to ask yourself what you see. You may see what I see; you may not. But neither one of us can claim the monopoly on a "reality-based foreign policy."

That "Vision Thing"

A second major point of debate is whether Canada needs a vision to drive its foreign policy. Many of my critics have contended that foreign policy should avoid broad, visionary objectives that inevitably bring with them inconsistency and poor implementation. How can a country as diverse as Canada come together around a common purpose with respect to its international role? The goal, according to this logic, should be much more modest: "good policy on a case-by-case basis."[7]

Good policy is most certainly the goal. The question is whether reactive and incremental decision-making is the way to achieve it.

Witness the United States and the European Union in the wake of 9/11: both engaged in a process of analysis and priority-setting which resulted in a strategic vision for responding to a changed global landscape.[8] I hasten to add that I am not advocating that Canada adopt the substance of either the U.S. or EU strategic document—only the discipline of identifying challenges and opportunities, assessing our strengths, and elevating a particular set of objectives.

Here, my experience in the private sector has influenced my thinking. Good strategies emerge from a hard-headed diagnosis of the context within which an organization, or a country, is operating. There will always be a need to respond to unforeseen developments (who, for example, could have predicted a tsunami?); yet, there also remains a sphere of activity that can be driven by conscious and long-term planning. Without an overarching objective, and a set of specific priorities to support it, policy-making becomes fragmented and ineffective. Indeed, this has been Canada's problem.

Take one example: Canadian development policy. Canada's current bilateral development programs are more widely dispersed around the world than those of any other donor. Of the 155 countries that currently receive development assistance from Canada, only 18 receive assistance valued at more than $10 million annually and 54 receive *less than* $1 million annually. Is this a recipe for impact? The wide dispersion of Canada's aid program makes it more difficult to develop the local knowledge and contacts that can ensure that our dollars are used effectively. In addition, the proliferation of small-scale programming on the part of donors such as the Canadian government puts a greater co-ordination and cost burden on those we are trying to help—recipient countries. Finally, and most obviously, the fragmentation of the aid programs increases the management and costs for the government of Canada itself.

To achieve greater impact, Canada must set priorities and make tough choices. In other words, it must be more strategic. By refocusing

Canada's strategy for bilateral assistance, and moving away from a thin but global presence, our financial commitment could make a much greater difference—even if in fewer places. What, in this instance, would be the strategic vision driving Canadian policy? The same objective I set out in chapter 6: bringing a core set of development partners up to the health and education targets set out in the millennium development goals (MDGs). The targets have already been identified and have garnered a high degree of consensus in both the developed and developing world.[9] The question now is whether donor countries such as Canada can assist developing countries as they seek to implement their own national strategies for poverty reduction and economic growth. To be sure, there remain significant obstacles to success. There is a long and checkered history of failed attempts to use foreign aid dollars to bring about progress in the developing world. It is also true that non-aid policies, such as further trade liberalization and debt relief, have an equally important part to play (some would say the greater part) in improving developing countries' prospects. But the fact remains that a more strategic approach to Canadian development assistance is both possible and necessary.

A strategic vision serves many purposes. It provides direction to a disparate set of actors, giving them a sense of what matters most. It also informs the choice of specific spending priorities. Taking the development example again, I would argue that "country concentration" (to use the current buzzwords) is only the first step to greater impact for Canadian development policy. Where more focus needs to occur, and where the potential for greater payoff lies, is in the particular sectors that Canada chooses to support. As set out in the 2005 *International Policy Statement*, sector focus should be informed by an assessment of three factors: what our development partners tell us they need most; which sectors are likely to facilitate achievement of the largest number of MDGs; and what Canada is best placed to provide (drawing on its skills and expertise).[10]

Finally, a strategic vision provides a touchstone for Canadians. It helps them to interpret the global changes occurring around them. It is also a statement of where their government intends to lead them, and how it intends to spend their tax dollars. Since the end of the Cold War, Canada has spent over $240 billion on diplomacy, defence, and development. This alone requires a rationale, and a statement of what kind of impact our resources are seeking to make. Above all, a strategic vision for Canada's role in the world can serve as a reference point for Canadian citizens as they engage in their own day-to-day lives— which, as I show in the book, have a significant global component.

250

Where's the Hard Power?

A third critique of *At Home in the World* is that it doesn't support strengthening the Canadian military. At a time when analysts and think-tanks everywhere are wringing their hands about the state of the armed forces, some ask, why is Welsh chiming on about global citizenship?

This charge misses the mark. At several points in the book, I discuss why and how Canada's military must be reconfigured to meet twenty-first century challenges. For example, I take a strong line on the need for Canada to secure strategic lift capacity if it wants to assist in the rebuilding of failed and failing states. I also argue that a foreign policy based on soft power alone is unsustainable. What I don't do is accept—uncritically—some of the more ambitious estimates for increases in military spending. There are two reasons for this.

First, while new funding for the Canadian Forces is unquestionably needed (both to replenish aging equipment and to finance an increased "operational tempo"), money is only part of the equation. In chapter 6, I highlight Norway as a country which has reconfigured and modernized its military without substantially increasing the percentage of its budget devoted to defence. Ah, but the critics will say: "Norway is a small country, with nowhere near the defence needs or responsibilities of Canada."

Let's accept that point, for argument's sake. What about Australia? Several columns in our national newspapers have been devoted to wondering how John Howard got his invitation to the Bush ranch in Texas. According to some, the key to Australia's special relationship with the U.S. is its investment in, and deployment of, hard power. But consider the figures a bit more closely: prior to the recent budget increases announced by the Liberal government, the absolute figures for military spending for Canada and Australia were not all that different ($US 7.5 billion and $US 7.7 billion respectively).[11] What has Australia been able to achieve with this budget? A successful military intervention in East Timor in 1999 (which was UN-authorized but Australian-led) and a significant contribution to the war in Iraq. Moreover, compared with Canada, Australia resides in a much more unstable and unpredictable "neighbourhood" of the world.

It is true that Australia's military spending is higher than Canada's, when considered as a percentage of GDP (2 percent vs. 1.1 percent using 2002 figures). It is also true that Australia spends more per capita on defence than Canada. But even these figures don't argue for a radical increase in defence spending. What they do argue for is the need to spend *smarter* and to make clear choices about the kinds of threats our military is designed to respond to. Our current chief of defence staff, Rick Hillier, has already begun to do both.

This leads me to my second point: the Canadian military is a *means* by which we fulfill our foreign policy priorities. In other words, we should focus on articulating what we want to be and do in the world, and retool our military as one (very important) way of supporting those objectives. To make military spending *itself* a priority of foreign policy is, from a strategic perspective, the wrong way of thinking about it. In the context of a new century, where challenges to security are multi-faceted, the ways in which the traditional assets of the Canadian military are deployed are changing. To illustrate, let me return to the words of Ashraf Ghani, a man who has worked extensively with the Canadian Forces in the stabilization and rebuilding of Afghanistan. "The most effective development organization I have ever worked with," Ghani said in a recent meeting in Ottawa, "is the Canadian military." For some within the defence community, who want the Canadian Forces to focus only on fighting and winning wars, these words might appear to signal a diversion away from the "core business" of the military. But this is the kind of impact our men and women in uniform are having. I, for one, am proud of them.

252

We Aren't Perfect

The final and strongest criticism I face when speaking about At Home in the World is that it is too optimistic. Canada, I've heard repeatedly from readers, is far from perfect. So how can we claim to have anything to say to the rest of the world? This objection to the book can be unpacked into two distinct issues: one is about Canada's success as a country, and the other about Canadians' reluctance to spread their values.

The Canadian record is not unblemished. Our country is a work-in-progress, and much wrong still needs to be righted. Take just one measure: the much-touted United Nations ranking of countries according to the human development index. In April 2005, the UN Human Rights Commission reported that Canada's ranking (7th place in the most recent scale) would fall dramatically, to 48th out of 174, if the country were judged solely on the economic and social well-being of our First Nations people. The statistics make for grim reading: on poverty, unemployment, infant mortality, suicide, criminal detention, violence against women, child prostitution, and susceptibility to disease, Aboriginal Canadians fare much worse than any other sector of

Canadian society. This track record is not one that I, or any other Canadian, I suspect, would like to share with the wider world.

But it is also true that when I travel the globe, I frequently encounter admiration for the "Canadian way." In fact, whether we like it or not, there is more interest in the kind of country we have built than in the kind of foreign policy we have pursued. In the words of the 2005 *International Policy Statement:*

> Canada's continued success depends on the joint pursuit of democracy, human rights, and the rule of law. Though many countries share these values, we have moulded them into a particular constellation that reflects our historical experience and our current aspirations. Our overarching vision is an inclusive society, where the will of the majority is balanced by a commitment to minority rights. That vision unifies Canadians but also celebrates difference manifest in our official policy of bilingualism, our two legal systems, and our open immigration and refugee policy. Above all, it is a distinctly federal model, incorporating vast differences in size, population and resources between our provinces and territories. . . . This experience also underpins Canada's economic model. By wedding free market principles to a commitment to shared risk and equality of opportunity, we have produced both prosperity and equity.[12]

253

While managing the partnership that is Canada has been a complex task, it has also developed the country's capacity to accommodate power and inequality—the very realities that we confront in today's international system. The features of the Canadian liberal democratic experiment help, as well, to determine our objectives with respect to the promotion of global prosperity and security.

This is where a second category of readers starts to get nervous. This is starting to sound awfully "American." What about our commitment to pluralism? Should Canada be in the business of exporting its model? The short answer is: we already are. Our foreign policy is shaped, in part, by a particular view on what makes for a stable and prosperous world. So, for example, when Canadian programs seek to promote governance, it is not just any kind of governance. If you read the fine print, you'll find a commitment to representative government, an independent judiciary, respect for minority rights, gender equality, civil and political rights, strong public health infrastructure, and a thriving private sector. Canada certainly doesn't have *the* answer to building these components of a healthy society (I'm not sure I would export our raucous first minister conferences anywhere!). But it does have some answers, and some experience.

This leads me to a concluding point: modelling isn't a one-way process of imposition, but a two-way process of exchange. Canadians have much to gain from their interactions with other societies around the globe. That is the magic of global citizenship. By sharing our experience, we make a small contribution to a better future for others and learn valuable lessons about how to improve our own model for ourselves.

Notes

PREFACE

1 *The Works of the Right Honourable Edmund Burke*, ed. Henry Bohn (London, 1854–89), 10:96–97.
2 Mary Weekes, *The Last Buffalo Hunter*, 2nd ed. (Saskatoon: Fifth House, 1994). This story, told to Weekes by my great-grandfather Norbert Welsh, is one of the few surviving oral accounts of the old Northwest during the late nineteenth century.
3 Sylvia Van Kirk, *Many Tender Ties: Women in Fur-Trade Society, 1670–1870* (Winnipeg: Watson and Dwyer, 1980).
4 Christine Welsh, "Women in the Shadows: Reclaiming a Métis Heritage," in L. Pietropaolo and A. Testaferri, eds., *Feminism in the Cinema* (Bloomington: Indiana University Press, 1995), 34–35.
5 Lawrence J. Barkwell, Leah Dorion, and Darren R. Prefontaine, *Métis Legacy: A Métis Historiography and Annotated Bibliography* (Winnipeg: Pemican Publications, 2001).
6 Van Kirk, *Many Tender Ties*, 9.

INTRODUCTION

1 For a detailed account of the arrival of the planes at Gander Airport, see Jim Defede, *The Day the World Came to Town: 9/11 in Gander, Newfoundland* (New York: HarperCollins, 2003).
2 Report by the Office of Critical Infrastructure Protection and Emergency Planning (OCIPEP), cited in the *Globe and Mail*, April 19, 2003.
3 See Darrell Bricker, "War if necessary . . . but not necessarily war," *Globe and Mail*, September 25, 2001.
4 Cited in Rob Granatstein, "Thanks Canada," *Toronto Sun*, September 22, 2001.
5 *Toronto Sun*, September 21, 2001.
6 Christie Blatchford, "Canada does not rate a mention," *National Post*, September 21, 2001.
7 *The Pew Global Attitudes Project* (Washington, DC: The Pew Research Center, March 2004).

8   Jeffrey Simpson, "Why we ended up dead," *Globe and Mail*, April 20, 2002.
9   "Canada opts for combat role," *Globe and Mail*, January 8, 2002.
10 "U.S. says it welcomes deployment of Canadian troops," CBC News, January 8, 2002, http://cbc.ca/news/2002/01/08/cdntroops/020108.
11 Michael Byers, "Agreeing to Disagree: Security Council Resolution 1441 and Intentional Ambiguities," *Global Governance*, 10, 2 (2004).
12 "Canadians oppose war in Iraq without UN," *Globe and Mail*, January 18, 2003.
13 "PM scolds McCallum on Canada's role in Iraq," *Globe and Mail*, January 16, 2003.
14 Cited in "Bush scorns Canadian proposal," *Globe and Mail*, February 27, 2003.
15 "Canada, two-faced? It all depends," *Globe and Mail*, March 29, 2003.
16 Robert Greenhill, Making a Difference? *External Views on Canada's International Impact* (Toronto: Canadian Institute fr International Affairs, 2005), 17.
17 Paul Martin, "Making History: The Politics of Achievement," speech to the National Liberal Convention, Toronto, November 15, 2003.
18 Andrew Cohen, *While Canada Slept: How We Lost Our Place in the World* (Toronto: McClelland & Stewart, 2003).
19 Michael Bliss, "Is Canada a country in decline?" *National Post*, November 30, 2001.
20 This is the theme developed by Anne-Marie Slaughter, dean of the Woodrow Wilson School of Public and International Affairs at Princeton University. See *A New World Order* (Princeton: Princeton University Press, 2004).

CHAPTER I

1   Defede, *The Day the World Came to Town*, 7.
2   "Gambo's Accidental Tourists," http://airtravel.about.com/cs/remembering911/.
3   Merchandise exports to the U.S. are even higher as a percentage of the total, at 87 per cent.
4   All statistics come from *NAFTA @ 10: A Preliminary Report* (Ottawa: Department of Foreign Affairs and International Trade, 2003) and *Performance and Potential 2002–3* (Ottawa: The Conference Board of Canada, 2003).
5   Jean Chrétien, address to the Council on Foreign Relations, Chicago, February 13, 2003.
6   Seymour Martin Lipset, *Continental Divide: The Values and Institutions of the United States and Canada* (New York: Routledge, 1991).
7   For a review of this research, see Matthew Mendelsohn, "Canada's Social Contract: Evidence from Public Opinion," Canadian Policy Research Networks, discussion paper P/01 (November 2002).
8   Environics, Focus Canada, 1995.
9   Environics, Focus Canada–CRIC, 2002.
10 Michael Adams, *Fire and Ice: The United States, Canada and the Myth of Converging Values* (Toronto: Penguin, 2003).
11 Allan R. Gregg, "Scary New World," *Maclean's*, December 31, 2001.
12 "Canadians 'have moved on' since Sept. 11: Pollster," CBC News, September 9, 2002, http://cbc.ca/cgi-bin/templates/2002/09/09/cdn_poll020909.

13 Office of the President, *National Security Strategy of the United States of America* (Washington, DC: September 2002), http://www.whitehouse.gov/nsc/nss/pdf. See also David Carment, Fen Osler Hampson, and Norman Hillmer, "Is Canada Now Irrelevant?" *Canada among Nations 2003: Coping with the American Colossus*, ed. David Carment, Fen Osler Hampson, and Norman Hillmer (Toronto: Oxford University Press, 2003).

14 Margaret Atwood, "A Letter to America," *Globe and Mail*, March 28, 2003.

15 Chrétien, Address to the Council on Foreign Relations, Chicago, February 13, 2003.

16 Kim Nossal, "Trends in Canadian Foreign Policy: Past, Present and Future," Address to the 75th Anniversary Conference of the Canadian Institute for International Affairs, Toronto, March 29, 2003.

17 Jeffrey Simpson, "Here's my two cents' worth," *Globe and Mail*, April 5, 2003.

18 "Ambassador's comments fuel political storm," CBC News, March 26, 2003, http://www.cbc.ca/cgi-bin/templates/2003/03/26/libscelluccio30326.

19 Lawrence Martin, "Just who is insulting whom?" *Globe and Mail*, March 29, 2003.

20 "Australia knew 'right from wrong': Bush," CBC News, May 3, 2003, http://www.cbc.ca/cgi-bin/templates/2003/05/09/bush_australia30503

21 Barrie McKenna, "Toeing U.S. line won't guarantee economic payoffs," *Globe and Mail*, March 28, 2003.

22 Quoted in Michael Den Tandt, "Energy-hogging U.S. can't stay sore at us forever," *Globe and Mail*, April 3, 2003.

23 See, for example, John Ibbitson, "Canada has become the black sheep of the White House family," *Globe and Mail*, March 26, 2003.

24 "Warm welcome cheers CEOs," *Globe and Mail*, April 8, 2003.

25 Quoted in "Rift over Iraq expected to heal," *Globe and Mail*, April 7, 2003.

26 Cited in the *Ottawa Citizen*, June 4, 2003. The Pew project surveyed 16,000 people in twenty countries around the world.

27 Timothy Appleby, "U.S. still upset with Canada: Rice," *Globe and Mail*, May 31, 2003.

28 Allan Gotlieb, "No access, no influence," *National Post*, December 3, 2002.

29 Stephen Handelman, "The Rise of North America Inc.," *Isuma* 1, no. 1 (Spring 2000): 17–23.

30 Quoted in the *National Post*, February 8, 2003.

31 See, for example, Richard Gwyn, "Our foreign policy is making us invisible," *Toronto Star*, February 23, 2003.

32 Donald McKenzie, "U.S. our best friend, says poll, but feeling not mutual," *Vancouver Sun*, March 15, 2004.

33 Donald Rumsfeld, remarks on *Face the Nation*, CBS, September 23, 2001.

34 Quoted in the *National Post*, February 8, 2003.

35 *The Pew Global Attitudes Project* (Washington, DC: The Pew Research Center, June 2003).

36 Doug Saunders, "Why Canadians are the new Americans," *Globe and Mail*, January 3, 2004.

37 These terms are borrowed from columnist Jeffrey Simpson. See "Choose your side: Puerile or servile?" *Globe and Mail*, April 4, 2003.

38 Mel Hurtig, *The Vanishing Country: Is It Too Late to Save Canada?* (Toronto: McClelland & Stewart, 2002).
39 Susan Mitchell, *Generation X: The Young Adult Market* (Ithaca, NY: New Strategist Publications, 1997), 164.
40 G. John Ikenberry, "The End of the Neo-Conservative Moment," *Survival* 46, no. 1 (Spring 2004): 7–22.

CHAPTER 2

1 Peter Andreas, "A Tale of Two Borders: The U.S.-Canada and U.S.-Mexico Lines after 9-11," in Peter Andreas and Thomas J. Biersteker, eds., *The Rebordering of North America: Integration and Exclusion in a New Security Context* (London: Routledge, 2003), 1–3.
2 "Toward a Partnership for Prosperity: The Guanajuato Proposal, Joint Communique," February 16, 2001, http://www.presidencia.gob.mx.
3 See Robert A. Pastor, *Toward a North American Community: Lessons from the Old World for the New* (Washington, DC: Institute for International Economics, 2001).
4 The detailed proposals can be found in Pastor, *Toward a North American Community*, chapters 5 and 6.
5 Stephen G. Brooks and William C. Wohlforth, "American Primacy in Perspective," *Foreign Affairs* 81, no. 4 (July/August 2002): 20–33.
6 Jennifer M. Welsh, "A Peoples' Europe? European Citizenship and European Identity," European University Institute Working Paper ECS No. 93/2 (1993).
7 Robert O. Keohane and Joseph S. Nye, Jr., *Power and Interdependence*, 3rd ed. (New York: Longman, 2001).
8 The task force is due to release its full report in the spring of 2005. The interim Chairman's Statement can be found on the website of the Canadian Council of Chief Executives. See http://www.ceocouncil.ca.
9 *Rethinking North American Integration*, Report from the PPF/EKOS Conference, Toronto, June 18, 2002.
10 Stephen Randall and Herman W. Konrad, eds., *NAFTA in Transition* (Calgary: University of Calgary Press, 1995), 37–46.
11 Lloyd Axworthy, *Navigating a New World: Canada's Global Future* (Toronto: Knopf, 2003), 106.
12 Ibid., 119.
13 Darrell Bricker and Edward Greenspon, *Searching for Certainty: Inside the New Canadian Mindset* (Toronto: Doubleday, 2001), 313.
14 For 1981 and 1990, World Values Survey; for 1998 and 2002, Ekos.
15 I have argued this point more fully elsewhere. See "Is a North American Generation Emerging?" *Isuma* 1, no. 1 (Spring 2000): 86–92.
16 *NAFTA @ 10*, 48.
17 Ekos, 2002. In fact, while in 2001 45 per cent of Canadians believed that it was likely that Canada would become part of a North American Union, this number had dropped to 31 percent by February/March 2002.
18 Ekos, 2002.

19   Robert Wolfe, "See You in Washington? A Pluralist Perspective on North
     American Institutions," IRPP, *Choices* 9, no. 4 (April 2003): 7.

20   Isabel Studer Noguez, "A Mexican Perspective," paper presented to the Institute
     for Research and Public Policy Conference, "Thinking North America: Prospects
     and Pathways," Montebello, Quebec, October 17–19, 2003.

21   For an overview of the key policy-related developments in Canada-U.S. relations,
     see Stephen J. Randall, "Integrating Canada and the US: The Historical
     Framework," *Isuma* 1, no. 1 (Spring 2000): 32–38.

22   James Laxer, *The Border: Canada, the U.S., and Dispatches from the 49th Parallel*
     (Toronto: Doubleday, 2003), 29.

23   Randall and Konrad, *NAFTA in Transition*, 37.

24   This was known as the Rush-Bagot Accord.

25   J.L. Granatstein, "A Friendly Agreement in Advance," C.D. Howe Institute,
     Commentary, no. 166 (June 2002): 3.

26   Ibid., 4–5. As Granatstein notes, if Japan had been invaded by the U.S. in 1945,
     a Canadian infantry division (armed and trained with U.S. weapons) was ready to
     serve under General MacArthur.

27   For a listing, see "Treaties and Agreements in Force between Canada and the
     United States," http://www.can-am.gc.ca/menu.

28   Denis Stairs, "Liberalism and the Triumph of Efficiency in Canada-US
     Relations," *Isuma* 1, no. 1 (Spring 2000): 11–16.

29   Allan Gotlieb, "A grand bargain with the U.S.," *National Post*, March 5, 2003.

30   Wendy Dobson, "Shaping the Future of the North American Economic Space,"
     C.D. Howe Institute, *Commentary*, no. 162 (April 2002).

31   *Security and Prosperity: Toward a New Canada–United States Partnership in North
     America (NASPI)* (Canadian Council of Chief Executives, January 2003).

32   Robert Wolfe, "Where's the Beef? A Pluralistic Approach to North American
     Integration," paper presented to the Institute for Research on Public Policy
     Conference, Montebello, Quebec, October 17–19, 2003.

33   Drew Fagan, "The vibes were very, very good," *Globe and Mail*, January 14, 2004.

34   Adams, *Fire and Ice*, 6.

35   Fagan, "Canada to boost presence in the U.S. with addition of seven consulates,"
     Globe and Mail, September 15, 2003.

36   Allan Gotlieb, "The paramountcy of Canada-U.S. relations," *National Post*,
     May 22, 2003.

37   Paul Martin, "Canada's Role in a Complex World," speech to the Canadian
     Newspaper Association, Toronto, April 30, 2003.

38   David M. Malone, "A Question of Style," *Literary Review of Canada* (March
     2004): 3–5.

39   See Loukas Tsoukalis, *The New European Economy Revisited* (Oxford: Oxford
     University Press, 1997), and Alan S. Milward, *The European Rescue of the Nation-
     State* (London: Routledge, 1993).

40   Andrew Moravcsik, *The Choice for Europe: Social Purpose and State Power from
     Messina to Maastricht* (Ithaca, NY: Cornell University Press, 1998).

41   I am grateful to Robert Wolfe for raising this question.

CHAPTER 3

1 Paul M. Tellier, "The dollar question," *National Post*, December 19, 2001.

2 Matthew Mendelsohn, "Canada's Social Contract: Evidence from Public Opinion," Canadian Policy Research Networks, discussion paper P/01 (November 2002), 6.

3 Matthew Mendelsohn and Robert Wolfe, "Probing the Aftermyth of Seattle: Canadian Public Opinion on International Trade," *International Journal* 56, no. 2 (June 2001):234–60.

4 Gilbert R. Winham and Sylvia Ostry, "The second trade crisis," *Globe and Mail*, June 17, 2003.

5 Madelaine Drohan, "We're no. 2—and falling," *Globe and Mail*, December 15, 2003.

6 Mendelsohn, "Canada's Social Contract."

7 John Helliwell, *Globalization and Well-Being* (Vancouver: University of British Columbia Press, 2002), 85.

8 An OECD report released in June 2002 showed that government subsidies represented 17 per cent of the total value of Canadian farm output in 2001, compared with 21 percent in the United States.

9 Michael Hart, "Lessons from Canada's History as a Trading Nation," *International Journal* 57, no. 1 (Winter 2002–3): 25–42.

10 Gotlieb, "Why not a grand bargain with the U.S.?"

11 Conference Board of Canada, *Performance and Potential 2002–3*, 114.

12 Wolfe, "See You in Washington," 10.

13 The idea of using joint commissions is explored by the Canadian Council of Chief Executives in *Security and Prosperity*.

14 John Greenwood, "Canada urged to hang tough on softwood," *Financial Post*, January 14, 2004.

15 Wolfe, "See you in Washington," 8.

16 Conference Board of Canada, "Renewing the Relationship: Canada and the United States in the 21st Century," *Briefing* (February 2003).

17 "The North American Linkages Project: Focusing the Research Agenda," *Horizons* 6, no. 2 (Ottawa: Policy Research Initiative, 2003).

18 Quoted in Steven Chase, "Canada, U.S., Mexico reject customs union as next step," *Globe and Mail*, October 8, 2003.

19 The butterfly metaphor was developed by meteorologist Edward Lorenz. For more on complexity and chaos, see Thomas Homer-Dixon, *The Ingenuity Gap* (Toronto: Knopf, 2000), chapters 4 and 5.

20 This assessment of the blackout was produced by Cambridge Energy Research Associates. See "Experts retrace a string of mishaps before the blackout," *New York Times*, August 23, 2003.

21 Thomas S. Axworthy, "Emergency planning too thin—throwing off too much spin," *National Post*, August 18, 2003.

22 EIA/Petroleum Supply Monthly (November 2002); Cambridge Energy Research Associates.

23 Manik Talwani, "Will Calgary be the next Kuwait?" *New York Times*, August 14, 2003.

24 Brent Jang, "Canada seen as top oil-growth region," *Globe and Mail*, February 23, 2004.

25 Timothy E. Wirth, C. Boyden Gray, and John D. Podesta, "The Future of Energy Policy," *Foreign Affairs* 82, no. 4 (July/August 2003): 132–55.

26 Gary Park, "Canadian pipeline group wants red tape untangled," *Petroleum News* 9, no. 4 (January 2004).

27 "Tax U.S.-bound energy, Layton advises," *Globe and Mail*, February 12, 2004.

28 Bruce Little, "Weak loonie seen as boon to firms," *Globe and Mail*, April 18, 2002.

29 Don McIver, "Can You Spare a Buck?: The Case for and against a Single North American Currency," *Viewpoint* (Conference Board of Canada, 2001) 1–4.

30 Herbert Grubel, "The Case for the Amero: The Economics and Politics of a North American Monetary Union," *Critical Issues Bulletin* (Fraser Institute, September 1999).

31 William B.P. Robson and David Laidler, "No Small Change," C.D. Howe Institute, *Commentary*, no. 167 (July 2002) 2.

32 Anne Golden, "In loonies, we should trust," *Globe and Mail*, November 29, 2001.

33 Robson and Laidler, "No Small Change," 10.

34 Stephen S. Roach, "The productivity paradox," *New York Times*, November 30, 2003.

35 Henry Mintzberg, "Productivity is a time bomb," *Globe and Mail*, June 13, 2002.

36 Heather Scoffield, "Canada has less to recover than U.S.," *Globe and Mail*, May 15, 2002.

37 Michael R. Sesit, "Some analysts suggest era of strong U.S. dollar is over," *Wall Street Journal*, May 14, 2002. In fact, this is a view that U.S. treasury secretary John Snow has encouraged.

38 Robson and Laidler, "No Small Change," 7.

39 Ibid.

40 Ekos, 2001.

41 Alanna Mitchell, "Canadians support closer ties with U.S," *Globe and Mail*, April 29, 2002.

42 "Americans Say No to Sharing Currency with Canada: Survey" (Toronto: NFO CFgroup, June 2002).

43 Robson and Laidler, "No Small Change," 25.

44 *The Human Development Report* (United Nations Development Programme, 2004).

45 *Performance and Potential* (Ottawa: Conference Board of Canada, 2001).

46 See, for example, the findings and recommendations of the U.S. Commission on National Security in the 21st Century, in a report entitled *New World Coming: Major Transformations and Implications: The Phase 1 Report on the Emerging Global Security Environment for the First Quarter of the 21st Century* (September 15, 1999).

47 According to the Conference Board of Canada, approximately $1.3 billion of goods cross the Canada-U.S. border every day. See *Border Choice* (Ottawa: Conference Board of Canada, October 2001).

48 For details, see "Action Plan for Creating a Secure and Smart Border" (December 12, 2001), http://www.can-am.gc.ca.

49 *Securing an Open Society: Canada's National Security Policy*, http://www.pco-bcp.qc.ca/docs/Publications/NatSecurnat/natsecurnat_e.pdf.

50 Stephen Clarkson and Maria Banda, "Congruence, Conflict and Continental Governance: Canada's and Mexico's Responses to Paradigm Shift in the United States" (2002), unpublished paper on file with author.

51 Ward Elcock, speech to the Vancouver Board of Trade, November 7, 2002.

52 This is one of the key recommendations of the blue-ribbon task force on the future of North America. See Paul Kovina, "Task force urges joint security perimeter," *Globe and Mail*, March 14, 2005.

53 "Dismantle the border, CEOs say," *National Post*, January 18, 2003.

54 "Renewing the Relationship: Canada and the United States in the 21st Century," Conference Board of Canada, *Briefing* (February 2003).

55 John Manley, "Canada's Policy Choices: Managing Our Border with the United States," address to the Public Policy Forum, Toronto, November 28 and 29, 2001.

56 "U.S. report faults the roundup of illegal immigrants after 9/11," *New York Times*, June 3, 2003. The report found, for example, that 84 inmates held in Brooklyn in terrorism investigations were subjected to a highly restrictive, twenty-three-hour "lockdown." They were limited to one phone call a week and were put in leg irons and heavy chains any time they moved outside of the cell. Of the 762 illegal immigrants jailed after 9/11, most have not been deported and none have been charged as terrorists.

57 Daniel Stoffman, *Who Gets In: What's Wrong with Canada's Immigration Program — and How to Fix It* (Toronto: Macfarlane Walter & Ross, 2002).

58 Niall Ferguson, *The Cash Nexus: Money and Power in the Modern World 1700–2000* (London: Allen Lane, 2001): 309–12.

59 Andrew F. Cooper, "Canadian Foreign Policy after September 11th: A Preliminary Analysis," paper presented to the Annual Conference of the Canadian Political Science Association, Toronto, May 31, 2002.

CHAPTER 4

1 For more on the challenge of defining middle powers, see Denis Stairs, "Of Medium Powers and Middling Roles," in Ken Booth, ed., *Statecraft and Security: The Cold War and Beyond* (Cambridge: Cambridge University Press, 1998), 270–86.

2 Adam Chapnik, "The Canadian Middle Power Myth," *International Journal*, 55, no. 2 (Spring 2000): 188–206.

3 Cohen, *While Canada Slept*, 128.

4 Ibid., 11.

5 The earliest reference I found to "middle powers" is in the works of the Renaissance writer Giovanni Botero. See *The Reason of State*, transl. by D.P. Waley (London: Routledge and Kegan Paul, 1956), book I, section 6.

6 The full report can be found at http://www.dfait-maeci.gc.ca/foreign-policy/cnd-world.

7 *Financial Times*, February 4, 1998, cited in Ferguson, *The Cash Nexus*, 279.

8 See Ronald Deibert and Janice Gross Stein, "Hacking Networks of Terror," *International Organization Dialogue* 10 (February 2002): 1–16.
9 Charles Krauthammer, "The Unipolar Moment," First Annual Henry M. Jackson Memorial Lecture, September 18, 1990, reprinted in *Foreign Affairs* (Winter 1990–91): 23–33.
10 Charles Krauthammer, "The Unipolar Moment Revisited," *The National Interest* (Winter 2002/3): 5–17.
11 These two alternatives—assertive superpower and multilateral leader—are explored by Carment, Hampson, and Hillmer in "Is Canada Now Irrelevant?"
12 Joseph S. Nye, *The Paradox of American Power: Why the World's Only Superpower Can't Go It Alone* (Oxford: Oxford University Press, 2002).
13 "A famous victory and a tough sequel," *Financial Times*, April 10, 2003.
14 See Robert Dahl's classic discussion of behavioural power in *Who Governs? Democracy and Power in an American City* (New Haven, CT: Yale University Press, 1961).
15 This is the central thesis of Nye's latest book, *Soft Power: The Means to Success in World Politics* (New York: Public Affairs, 2004).
16 John Toye, "Order and Justice in the International Trade System," in Rosemary Foot, John Lewis Gaddis, and Andrew Hurrell, eds., *Order and Justice in International Relations* (Oxford: Oxford University Press, 2003), 103–24.
17 Inis L. Claude, Jr., "Collective Legitimization as a Political Function of the United Nations," *International Organization* 20, no. 3 (Summer 1966): 367–79.
18 John Ruggie, "Measuring the legitimacy of UN vote," *Financial Times*, March 14, 2003.
19 Krauthammer, "The Unipolar Moment."
20 Andrew Coyne, "For a 'Council of Free Nations,'" *National Post*, April 14, 2003.
21 "A Year after Iraq War," Pew Research Center for the People and the Press, March 16, 2004, http://people-press.org/.
22 Timothy Garton Ash, "Anti-Europeanism in America," *New York Review of Books*, February 13, 2003.
23 Robert Kagan, *Of Paradise and Power* (New York: Knopf, 2003), 23, 36.
24 Michael Ignatieff, "Why Are We in Iraq? (And Liberia? And Afghanistan?)," *New York Times Magazine*, September 7, 2003.
25 Chris Patten, "'The End of History': The Sequel," the 2003 Cyril Foster Lecture, Oxford, January 30, 2003.
26 For example, following the Iraq war, research shows that Turks and Eastern Europeans ranked Europe ahead of the United States in playing a positive role on issues ranging from fighting terrorism to reducing poverty. See the European Commission's *Eurobarometer*, Candidate Countries Eurobarometer, Spring 2003.
27 "Europe favoured over U.S. poll says," *Toronto Star*, October 6, 2003.
28 Denis Stairs, David J. Bercuson, Mark Entwistle, J.L. Granatstein, Kim Richard Nossal, and Gordon S. Smith, "In the National Interest: Canadian Foreign Policy in an Insecure World," paper prepared for the Canadian Defence and Foreign Affairs Institute, October 30, 2003.

29 Nye, *Soft Power*, 81. It is particularly noteworthy that Europeans currently provide 70 per cent of overseas development assistance to poor countries—four times more than the United States.

30 Statistics Canada, "Canada's Ethnocultural Portrait: The Changing Mosaic," 2, http://www12.statcan.ca/english/census01/. Prior to 1960, 90 per cent of all immigrants to Canada came from Europe and only 3 per cent were born in Asia. Today, 58 per cent of our immigrants come from Asia and the Middle East, and only 20 per cent come from Europe.

31 Quoted in William Drozdiak, "Bush plan worries Europeans; Removing US troops from Balkans is seen as divisive," *Washington Post*, October 24, 2000.

32 George W. Bush, remarks by President Bush and Prime Minister Koizumi of Japan in photo opportunity (September 25, 2001), http://www.whitehouse.gov/news/releases/2001/09/20010925-1.html.

33 For more on the evolution of U.S. war aims in Afghanistan, see Simon Chesterman, "Humanitarian Intervention and Afghanistan," in Jennifer M. Welsh, ed., *Humanitarian Intervention and International Relations* (Oxford: Oxford University Press, 2004), chapter 9.

34 Michael Ignatieff, *Empire Lite: Nation-Building in Bosnia, Kosovo and Afghanistan* (London: Vintage, 2003), 17.

35 For an assessment of past international administrations and the lessons learned from them, see Simon Chesterman, *You, the People: The United Nations, Transitional Administration, and State-Building* (Oxford: Oxford University Press, 2004).

36 Andrew Cohen, "Time to Wake Up," *Time* (Canadian edition), May 26, 2003, 21.

37 Robert Wolfe, moderator, "Most Safely on the Fence? A Roundtable on the Possibility of a 'Canadian' Foreign Policy after 9/11," *Canadian Foreign Policy* 11, no. 1 (Fall 2004), 97–118.

38 Andrew F. Cooper, Richard A. Higgott, and Kim Richard Nossal, *Relocating Middle Powers: Australia and Canada in a Changing World Order* (Vancouver: UBC Press, 1993), 5.

39 One of the most significant contributions to this debate was Paul Kennedy's *The Rise and Fall of the Great Powers: Economic Change and Military Conflict from 1500 to 2000* (New York: Random House, 1988).

40 David R. Black and Heather A. Smith, "Notable Exceptions? New and Arrested Directions in Canadian Foreign Policy Literature," *Canadian Journal of Political Science* 26, no. 4 (December 1993): 745–75. A notable exception to the overly systemic approach is Robert Cox, "Middlepowermanship, Japan, and Future World Order," *International Journal* 44 (1989): 823–62.

41 Stairs, "Of Medium Powers," 279.

42 Andrew Medd, "We're young and we're ready. So listen up," *Globe and Mail*, June 27, 2003. Medd is executive director of Canada 25.

43 Anthony DePalma, *Here: A Biography of the New American Continent* (New York: Public Affairs, 2001).

44 I am grateful to André Beaulieu, an executive member of the Banff Forum, for coining this phrase.

45 Denis Stairs, "Canada in the New International Environment," presentation to

the Inaugural Meeting of the Canadian Consortium on Asia Pacific Security, York University, Toronto, December 3–4, 1993.

CHAPTER 5

1 *The World Factbook 2003*, www.cia.gov/cia/publications/factbook/index.html.
2 Ibid.
3 "Canada and the United States: An Evolving Partnership," *The CRIC Papers* (Montreal: Centre for Research and Information on Canada, 2003), 17–19.
4 Gotlieb, "The paramountcy of Canada-U.S. relations."
5 Allan Gotlieb, "No access, no influence," *National Post*, December 3, 2003.
6 Anthony Giddens, *The Third Way and Its Critics* (Cambridge: Polity Press, 2000), 2.
7 The full text of the letter can be found at http://news.bbc.co.uk/1/hi/uk_politics/3660837.stm.
8 For an account of the relationship between Blair and Bush during the build-up to war, see Bob Woodward, *Plan of Attack* (New York: Simon and Schuster, 2004).
9 Jeremy Greenstock, "Iraq and the Polarization of World Politics," lecture at the University of Oxford, May 11, 2004. Greenstock was the U.K.'s Representative to the United Nations from 1998–2003 and served as Prime Minister Blair's Special Representative to Iraq from September 2003 to March 2004.
10 Hart, "Lessons from Canada's History."
11 Ibid., 39.
12 Quoted in Hart, "Lessons," 37–38.
13 Paul Heinbecker, "Canada got it right on Iraq," *Globe and Mail*, March 19, 2004.
14 Steven Frank, "Where Has Canada Gone?" *Time* (Canadian edition), May 26, 2003.
15 J.L. Granatstein, *Who Killed the Canadian Military?* (Toronto: HarperCollins, 2004), 3.
16 "Canada no longer a tower of peace," *Globe and Mail*, December 22, 2001.
17 Mike Harris, "You call this a foreign policy?" *Globe and Mail*, April 2, 2003.
18 See, for example, the Ipsos-Reid poll from December 2001, in which 66 per cent of Canadians agreed that the federal government has not done enough "to make sure that Canada's military is properly equipped to do their job."
19 Douglas L. Bland, ed., *Canada without Armed Forces?* (Queen's University, November 2003), xii.
20 For an overview of the new strategy, see http://www.cds.forces.gc.ca.
21 Doug Saunders, "Canadians split over future role of military," *Globe and Mail*, November 11, 2002.
22 Martin Wolf, "The limits of America's military power," *Financial Times*, July 8, 2003.
23 Air Marshal Sir Timothy Garden, "After Iraq: The Fallout," presentation to the International Institute of Strategic Studies, London, November 18, 2003.
24 See the discussion in Cohen, *While Canada Slept*, 26–27.
25 Joseph S. Nye, Jr., *Bound to Lead: The Changing Nature of American Power* (New York: Basic Books, 1990).
26 Nye, introduction to *Soft Power*.
27 Axworthy, *Navigating a New World*, 74–75.

28 The International Commission on Intervention and State Sovereignty released its report, *The Responsibility to Protect*, after Axworthy had left office (Ottawa: International Development Research Centre, 2001).

29 Nye, *The Paradox of American Power*, 10.

30 S. Neil MacFarlane, "The Soft Power Question in Canadian Foreign Policy," presentation to the Commonwealth Studies Institute, London, February 7, 2002.

31 One of his earlier formulations can be found in Lloyd Axworthy, "Human Security and Global Governance: Putting People First," *Global Governance* 7, no. 1 (January–March 2000): 19–23.

32 Emma Rothschild, "What Is Security?" *Daedalus* 124, no. 3 (Summer 1995): 53–98.

33 Yuen Foong Khong, "Human Security: A Shotgun Approach to Alleviating Human Misery?" *Global Governance* 7 (2001): 233.

34 I have addressed this theme in greater detail elsewhere. See Jennifer M. Welsh, *Humanitarian Intervention and International Relations* (Oxford: Oxford University Press, 2004).

35 Axworthy, *Navigating a New World*, 165–68.

36 Rothschild, "What Is Security?" 71.

37 Tzvetan Todorov, "Right to Intervene or Duty to Assist?," *Human Rights, Human Wrongs: The Oxford Amnesty Lectures 2001*, ed. Nicholas Owen (Oxford: Oxford University Press, 2002), 33.

38 Axworthy, *Navigating a New World*, 409.

39 Rothschild, "What Is Security?" 61.

40 Todorov, "Right to Intervene," 33.

CHAPTER 6

1 T.H. Marshall, "Citizenship and Social Class," in *Class, Citizenship and Social Development: Essays by T.H. Marshall* (London: University of Chicago Press, 1964), 92.

2 See Will Kymlicka, *Multicultural Citizenship* (Oxford: Clarendon, 1995), 175.

3 "Plan for Canada's missing," *The Guardian*, May 13, 2004.

4 President George W. Bush, Remarks on the 20th Anniversary of the National Endowment for Democracy, November 6, 2003, http://www.nytimes.com/2003/11/06/politics/06TEXT-BUSH.html.

5 Joseph Heath, "Why Have a Constitution at All?" *Policy Options* 24, no. 9 (October 2003): 42.

6 Ibid.

7 Jeremy Waldron, "Democracy, Human Rights and the Rule of Law: Constellation or Unified Ideal?" (2003), unpublished paper on file with author.

8 See Janet L. Hiebert, "From Equality Rights to Same-Sex Marriage—Parliament and the Courts in the Age of the Charter," *Policy Options* 24, no. 9 (October 2003): 10–16.

9 Centre for Research and Information on Canada (CRIC), February 2002. This poll found that 66 per cent of Canadians trust judges to do the right thing either all or most of the time, while only 22 per cent of Canadians trust politicians to do the right thing either all or most of the time.

10 Fareed Zakaria, *The Future of Freedom: Illiberal Democracy at Home and Abroad* (New York: Norton, 2003).

11 Michael Ignatieff, *Human Rights as Politics and Idolatry* (Princeton, NJ: Princeton University Press, 2001).

12 Waldron, "Democracy, Human Rights, and the Rule of Law," 26.

13 George W. Bush, Remarks on the 20th Anniversary of the National Endowment for Democracy.

14 Fareed Zakaria, "Iraq is not ready for democracy," *The Guardian*, November 12, 2003.

15 John Stuart Mill, "A Few Words on Non-intervention," in *Dissertations and Discussions*, 2nd ed., vol. 3 (London, 1875), 153–78.

16 UNSC Resolution 1511 called on the U.S.-backed Iraqi Governing Council to announce a timetable by December 15, 2003, for elections and the drafting of a new constitution. It also stated that "the day when Iraqis govern themselves must come quickly."

17 Drew Fagan, "Canada tiptoes into Mideast politics," *Globe and Mail*, March 3, 2004.

18 Quoted in Cohen, *While Canada Slept*, 158.

19 Thomas S. Axworthy, "On Being an Ally: Why Virtue Is Not Reward Enough," address to the Institute for Research on Public Policy Conference on North American Integration, Ottawa, April 1, 2004.

20 "First wave of troops leaves for Kabul," CBC News, July 19, 2003, http://www.cbc.ca/cgi-bin/templates/2003/07/19.

21 J.L. Granatstein, 'The Importance of Being Less Earnest: Promoting Canada's National Interests through Tighter Ties with the US," C.D. Howe Institute Benefactors Lecture, Toronto, October 21, 2003, 26, 19.

22 I am grateful to the great historian of U.S. foreign policy Melvyn Leffler for pointing this out to me.

23 For more on the false dichotomy between values and interests, see David Malone's review of Granatstein, "A Question of Style," *Literary Review of Canada* (March 2004), 4–5.

24 Prime Minister Tony Blair, speech to the Labour Party Conference, *The Guardian*, October 3, 2001.

25 In May 2005, the government announced the deployment of another 1,000 combat troops to Southern Afghanistan and a provincial reconstruction team made up of 250 personnel.

26 Hugh Segal, "Tough Choices in Canadian Foreign Policy," presentation to the Annual Conference of the Canadian Institute for International Affairs, Toronto, March 30, 2003.

27 For an overview, see http://www.dfait-maeci.gc.ca/cip-pic/ips/ips-en.asp

28 Ramesh Thakkur, "A doubly damaged UN needs to change," *International Herald Tribune*, September 26, 2003.

29 Matthew Mendelsohn, "Canada and the U.S.: Growing Up but Never Leaving Home," presentation to the Banff Forum, Second Edition, October 10, 2003.

30 See *Views of a Changing World 2003*, (Washington, DC: Pew Research Centre for People and the Press, June 2003).

267

31 Richard Price, "The League of Nations Redux?" in Richard Price and Mark Zacher, eds., *The United Nations and Global Security* (New York: Palgrave, 2004), 264–72.

32 Axworthy, *Navigating a New World*, 235.

33 Steven Edwards, "UN will urge Ottawa to pull its weight," *National Post*, March 6, 2004.

34 Quoted in Felicity Barringer, "UN senses it must change, fast," *New York Times*, September 19, 2003.

35 Price,"The League of Nations Redux?" 265.

36 I have elaborated on these problems elsewhere. See "Authorizing Humanitarian Intervention," in Price and Zacher, *The United Nations and Global Security*, 177–90.

37 Secretary-General Kofi Annan, address to the UN General Assembly, New York, September 23, 2003. The Panel Report can be found at http://www.un.org.secureworld.

38 Drew Fagan, "PM's plan pushes UN to sidelines." *Globe and Mail*, April 30, 2004.

39 For a fuller discussion of the dilemmas facing liberal democracies after 9/11, see Michael Ignatieff, *The Lesser Evil: Political Ethics in an Age of Terror* (Princeton: Princeton University Press, 2004).

40 Quoted in Lorne W. Craner, "Balancing Military Assistance and Support for Human Rights in Asia," testimony before the Senate Foreign Relations Committee, Washington, DC, June 27, 2002: U.S. Department of State press release. (Craner is the assistant secretary of state for democracy, human rights and labor.)

41 Rosemary Foot, *Human Rights and Counter-terrorism in America's Asia Policy*, Adelphi Paper 363, International Institute for Strategic Studies (Oxford: Oxford University Press, 2004).

42 Margaret Purdy, "Targeting Diasporas: The Canadian Counter-terrorism Experience," paper presented to the Conference on Curbing Human Rights Violations by Non-State Armed Groups, Centre for International Relations, University of British Columbia, Vancouver, November 13–15, 2003.

43 Axworthy, *Navigating a New World*, 186.

44 Paul Martin, "The Politics of Achievement."

45 A progress report was tabled by the economist Jeffrey Sachs, and his team, early in 2005. See "Investing in Development: A Practical Plan to Achieve the Millennium Development Goals," available at http://www.unmillenniumproject.org.

46 See World Economic Forum, *The Global Governance Initiative: Annual Report 2004* (Geneva: World Economic Forum, April 2004). The report provided rankings on a scale of 0 to 10 in seven areas related to the MDGs. In no area did the world receive more than a grade of 4. Available at http:// www.weforum.org/globalgovernance.

47 Paul Martin, "The Politics of Achievement."

48 Susan E. Rice, "Canada's Relationship with the U.S.: Turning Proximity into Power—An American Perspective," in Graham F. Walker, ed., *Independence in An Age of Empire: Assessing Unilateralism and Multilateralism* (Halifax: The Centre for Foreign Policy Studies, 2004), 124, 125.

49 Quoted in Sheldon Alberts, "Riding on America's shoulders," *National Post*, January 28, 2003.

50 Rice, "Canada's Relationship with the U.S."
51 Matthew Brzezinski, "Who's afraid of Norway?" *New York Times*, August 24, 2003.
52 International Institute for Strategic Studies, *The Military Balance: 2003–2004* (London: Oxford University Press, 2003).
53 Centre for Defence Information, March 2003.
54 Douglas Bland, ed., *Canada without Armed Forces?*
55 See Ann Denholm Crosby, *Dilemmas in Defence Decision-Making: Constructing Canada's Role in NORAD, 1958–1996* (London: Macmillan, 1998).
56 See Oliver Moore, "Canada refuses further role in missile defence," *Globe and Mail*, February 24, 2005.
57 Lloyd Axworthy and Michael Byers, "Say no to missile defence," *Globe and Mail*, April 29, 2003.
58 I am indebted to James Fergusson, of the University of Manitoba, for articulating this argument.
59 J.L. Granatstein, "A Friendly Agreement in Advance," C.D. Howe Institute, *Commentary*, no. 166 (June 2002), 10.
60 J.L. Granatstein, "A Friendly Agreement in Advance."
61 See, for example, the 2001 report of the Commission to Assess U.S. National Security, Space Management and Organization, which was chaired by Donald Rumsfeld before he became secretary of defence.
62 Axworthy and Byers, "Say no to missile defence."
63 David Rudd, "The myths of missile defence," *Globe and Mail*, May 8, 2003. Rudd is the president of the Canadian Institute of Strategic Studies.
64 Early on in his tenure as defence minister, McCallum approved $700 million in spending over a ten-year period on state-of-the-art communications equipment (known as ISTAR) to facilitate real-time information- and intelligence-sharing between troops on the ground and commanding officers. While the army will be given this equipment first, it will eventually be placed on ships and planes as well.

CONCLUSION

1 Janice Gross Stein, "The Emergent Security Architecture: Will Canada's Security Be 'National'?" (2002), unpublished paper on file with author.
2 Peter Harder, luncheon address to Retired Heads of Missions Association (RHOMA), Ottawa, March 17, 2004.
3 Cohen, *While Canada Slept*, 195.

AFTERWORD

1 CD Howe Lecture, "Realism and Romanticism in Canadian Foreign Policy," 2004.
2 Derek H. Burney, "Foreign Policy: More Coherence, Less Pretence," The Simon Reisman Lecture in International Trade Policy, Ottawa, March 14, 2005, p. 5.

3 E.H. Carr, *The Twenty Years' Crisis: 1919–1939*, 2nd ed. (London: Macmillan, 1984), 89.

4 See Chris Giles, "Why George Bush should heed Asia's central bankers," *Financial Times*, February, 26–27, 2005.

5 Niall Ferguson, "Sinking Globalization," *Foreign Affairs* 84 no. 2. (March/April 2005): 73.

6 Joseph S. Nye, Jr., "Soft Power: The Means to Success in World Politics," *Public Affairs* 10 (May 2004): 1–16.

7 Reed Scowen, "Re-inventing Foreign Policy: A 'Model Citizen' concept for Canada may not work." *Literary Review of Canada*, 12, no. 10 (December 2004), 23.

8 See "The National Security Strategy of the United States of America" (Washington, September 2002), available at http://www.whitehouse.gov/nsc/nss.pdf; and "A Secure Europe in a Better World: European Security Strategy" (Brussels, December 2003), available at http://www.iss-eu.org/solana/solanae.pdf.

9 "Investing in Development: A Practical Plan to Achieve the Millennium Development Goals," *The Millennium Project Report to the UN Secretary-General* (New York: UNDP, 2005).

10 "A Role of Pride and Influence in the World," *Canada's International Policy Statement: Overview* (Ottawa: Department of Foreign Affairs, 2005), 24. Also available at http://www.international.gc.ca.

11 I am grateful to Kim Richard Nossal for drawing my attention to these figures and for helping me to develop my argument.

12 "A Role of Pride and Influence in the World," *Canada's International Policy Statement: Overview*, 4.

Acknowledgements

I BEGIN by thanking those who assisted me in the painful but illuminating task of naming this book. Two lively dinner parties on different sides of the Atlantic were crucial to the process. The first was in Oxford, at the home of Lois McNay and Murray Hunt, where my grandiose ideas about Canada were tempered with a healthy dose of British skepticism and understatement. The second was in Montreal, at the home of two great Canadians, Pearl Eliadis and Rob Yalden, who—along with Robert Greenhill and Michael McAdoo—encouraged me to "think big" about Canada and infused me with some New World optimism. I hope the result of this transatlantic exchange, *At Home in the World*, has something for everyone.

Several people read, contributed to, and commented on various chapters of the book. My sister, Christine Welsh, filled in important blanks about the Welsh family history and the nature of fur-trade life in Canada. Graham Flack, John Hancock, and Matthew Mendelsohn refined my ideas about Canada's regional destiny and relationship to the United States. My Oxford colleagues Andrew Hurrell and Neil MacFarlane shared their perspectives about how Canada relates to other actors and forces on the international stage, and Kalypso Nicolaidis helped me to develop a vision for Canada that is distinct from but complementary to Europe.

My work was informed and enhanced by two cheerful and efficient research assistants, Julie Dzerowicz and Rachel Ziemba. In addition to keeping me up to date on things Canadian, they taught me a great deal about their own areas of expertise. Ailish Johnson, from International

Trade Canada, responded to my last-minute pleas with precise data on tariffs and budgets.

I also benefited from several discussions with Andrew Cohen, whose wisdom, experience, and jokes (usually about my frequent flyer status!) I have come to cherish. Andrew and I have spoken together on several panels over the past two years, and my views have been shaped and improved through this interaction. I hope the conversations continue.

I would also like to thank those who organize and participate in the annual Banff Forum—a new and exciting institution in Canada that I am proud to be part of. It was at the First Edition of the forum in 2002 that I summoned the courage to write a book about Canada and the challenges it faces in a post–9/11 world. Thank you for the inspiration.

Margaret Hancock, the warden of Hart House, gave me an opportunity to experiment with the idea of the "Model Citizen." I thank her and the energetic team of organizers of the 2004 Hart House Lecture for their hospitality.

My agent, Beverley Slopen, is largely responsible for this book's evolution from a vague idea in my mind to words on a printed page. Since 1998, Beverley has been my conscience and my cheerleader, encouraging me to speak out and reassuring me that I am saying something worthwhile. Her charm, quick wit, and general life advice have sustained me through the writing process. I only hope that the finished product lives up to her expectations.

I express deep gratitude to the troops at HarperCollins for their professionalism and creativity. (Somehow, the fit between us is just right: their style and energy bring out the best in me.) I thank, in particular, Iris Tupholme for having confidence in me and my editor, Chris Bucci, for being a true discussion partner.

Lisa Zaritzky—the woman with the best eye for handbags in Canada—is a superb publicist. The whirlwind publicity tour she organized across Canada has left me even more inspired by my country and its people.

I wrote the conclusion to this book on a Friday evening in late April, when spring finally came to England. From my office window, I could see the soft spring light reflecting off the red-brick walls of the library and showering the tulips in the quadrangle. Carefree undergraduates were playing Frisbee on the lawn and strumming their guitars. The scene reminded me that no amount of money can buy academic freedom or a true intellectual community. And so I thank the principal (Dame Fiona Caldicott), fellows, and students of Somerville College for giving me "a room of my own" and the space to think and grow.

To my partner, Frank, I want to apologize for all the days and nights I have spent on the other side of the world. But introducing him to my homeland—the first time in the tranquility and beauty of Algonquin Park—has been one of the greatest pleasures of the past year.

Finally, *At Home in the World* would never have seen the light without the support and love of that "little platoon," the Welsh family. To Christine, Jane, Brenda, Laura, Paul, and Mom and Dad, I thank you. You are, and will remain, my Canada.

JMW
July 2005
Oxford, U.K.

277